Corporation Man

Antony Jay

CORPORATION MAN

Jonathan Cape Thirty Bedford Square London

FIRST PUBLISHED IN GREAT BRITAIN 1972
© 1971 BY ANTONY JAY
THIS EDITION © 1972 BY ANTONY JAY

JONATHAN CAPE LTD, 30 BEDFORD SQUARE, LONDON WC I

ISBN 0 224 00678 9

PRINTED IN GREAT BRITAIN
BY EBENEZER BAYLIS AND SON LTD
THE TRINITY PRESS, WORCESTER, AND LONDON
ON PAPER MADE BY JOHN DICKINSON AND CO. LTD
BOUND BY G. AND J. KITCAT LTD, LONDON

Contents

Who sees the variety
and not the unity,
wanders on from death
to death.

KATHA UPANISHAD

Preface

ANYONE who tries to force a crystal to yield up the innermost secrets of its structure encounters an intriguing problem: the only available method is X-ray diffraction, but it provides two-dimensional photographs, whereas the atoms are arranged three-dimensionally in the crystal. From one single picture you cannot possibly tell how the individual atoms are arranged: you have to take more and more, until finally you are able to deduce the shape of reality from the shadowy images. Eight atoms arranged in a simple cube may surrender their secret after three or four diffraction photographs; the double helix of the DNA molecule took years of work by some of the world's leading scientists.

I use this parallel because this book is an attempt to explain the central reality of the modern corporation, and yet I always mistrust those writers who claim to have done so. Each seems to come up with a new complete explanation. The corporation is an economic unit. The corporation is a complex of personal relationships. The corporation is an organization chart. The corporation is a concept, a pyramid, a state, a monster, a game, a jungle, a battlefield, a way of life. How can all these truths be true, and what on earth is the point of my adding another unsubstantiated assertion to a list that is too long already?

That is why I started with crystallography. The point is that none of these generalizations can be the whole truth because the complexity of the corporation, as of the crystal, is three dimensional; but any or all of them can be valuable two-dimensional diffraction photographs which help us to build up more and more understanding of the elements that compose the complex three-dimensional whole and of their relationship to each other. Some of these photographs are so close in angle to previous ones that they tell us hardly anything we did not know already. Others, by taking an unfamiliar or unexpected angle, can be a revelation. For me the original idea of *Management and Machiavelli*, the concept of business corporations being the same as political states, came like a diffraction photograph from a new angle, exposing all sorts of new elements and relationships which had been concealed in all the other plates I had looked at. Nevertheless, when I had finished the book I had a feeling that there was still something lurking inside that corporate crystal, some even more revealing picture to be taken, if only I could find the angle to look from.

I believe that I have now found the angle, and this book is the picture which it has revealed. It makes sense—at least for me—of a great many elements of the modern corporation that did not previously fit together. But I want to emphasize that this book is not the full and sole truth about the nature of the corporation, which has somehow been concealed from all previous writers. It is just one more photograph, even if it is taken from a new angle, and it does not make sense unless it is looked at in conjunction with the other familiar pictures which we have all been looking at for some time. The most I would claim is that none of the others makes sense either, unless looked at in conjunction with this one.

A.R.J.

1 The Evolution of Corporation Man

ONE OF the most important discoveries of my working life was made between 8.30 a.m. and 6.00 p.m. on Thursday, April 9th, 1964.

On Wednesday, April 8th, I had left the Corporation, the B.B.C., which I had joined more or less straight from university and National Service nine years earlier. I had been a trainee, a production assistant, a producer, a programme editor, a head of department. But at 8.30 a.m. on April 9th I was just me, sitting at my desk at home with a number of writing assignments which I had prudently contracted before giving in my notice. The discovery I had made by 6.00 p.m., to express it the way it appeared at the time, was the enormous amount of work that could be done in a day. Nine years in a great corporation had obliterated the memory of how much time there was if you had no telephone calls, correspondence, minutes, routine meetings, departmental meetings, budget reviews, requests for authorization, annual interviews, policy documents, appointments with visitors, and all the rest of that endless succession of events and non-events that compose the manager's day, and his year, and his life.

But the discovery can be expressed in the opposite way: that the corporation day is absurdly, ludicrously short. Only a week before I left I had spent a whole morning at a meeting with the head of my group, my three fellow departmental heads, and the group administrative officer. Our problem had what the Caliph in *Hassan* called 'the monstrous beauty of the hindquarters of an Elephant'. It was this. In the past year we had recruited a large number of trainee producers to prepare for the opening of the B.B.C.'s second channel. In a few more months, when we thought they were ready, we would be inviting them to make formal applications for permanent posts in our group. But—horror!—the head of a rival B.B.C. group was advertising his vacancies already, and the trainees in our group wanted to apply for them. What could we do? There was a B.B.C.

staff agreement saying that every employee must be free to apply for any advertised vacancy. Did this mean we had to stand by and watch our rival cream off all our best trainees, the young men and women we had spent a year selecting and training to work on our own programmes? Should we privately warn them that applications would bring our displeasure? Should we put up a case to the head of personnel to suspend the normal ruling? Should we put up a case to the director of programmes to impose simultaneity on all groups' advertisements? There were many possibilities, and six of us to discuss them, so it is not surprising that the meeting lasted nearly three hours.

The important point about the problem was that the Corporation itself had created it. It had nothing to do with producing good programmes or controlling their costs or developing new people or ideas. It was entirely concerned with, and consequent upon, the Corporation's internal organization, and yet it took half a day—10 per cent of a week—of the time of six senior managers to resolve it.

The next morning I had one of my producers on the phone in a panic. The planning department wanted to take away his staff film editor and get him to put his work out to a freelance. For several reasons this was impossible, but the planners did not seem to understand why. I spent most of that day in a telephone battle, arguing with planning, appealing to the head of programmes, going back to the producer for more ammunition, drafting powerful memos, consulting the film department, proposing alternatives. By the end of the day I had won. The planning department had seen reason, they had withdrawn the proposal, and my producer and his programme were safe. But what had I actually achieved in positive terms? I had merely stopped a silly mistake from being made.

It is pointless (though it would be easy) to multiply these instances. Everyone who has ever worked in or with large corporations has his own parallel experiences. I wish I had spent a week noting how much of my time was spent doing my real job—the job determined by the needs of our market, the television audience—and how much in administrative machine maintenance, stopping the Corporation from grinding to a halt. The ratio would have been impressive.

But it is not only time that evaporates in large corporations.

Money evaporates as well. Just before I left, I went into a stationery shop to buy typing paper, carbons, paperclips and so on. I actually paid money over the counter for them. Real money, the sort that gets you into theatres and out of restaurants, and buys groceries and furniture and presents for the children. Previously, all stationery was bought for me with Corporation money, which bore no relation to human money. It was a purely notional currency that appeared on forms and memos, but never passed through pockets or wallets. Indeed the budget for a single edition of a weekly programme might be more than the producer's annual salary, which meant he would be spending some quarter of a million pounds a year. Dealing with such large sums, it was only worth a very limited effort to save £100 of Corporation money on a £10,000 programme budget, even if there were any incentive to do so. By contrast, £100 of human money could take a year's hard and conscious saving to accumulate. Equally, you could save 10s. by shooting 12 seconds less film, and 10s. was the difference between a glass of beer and a bottle of wine for supper. But it was impossible to make the connection: Corporation money, like Corporation time, was simply something that was there. It had to be used up somehow, and each of us was allocated separate quantities of it to achieve various objectives. There was a certain professional pride about keeping to your own budget, but a great deal of Corporation money was not on your own budget; carpets, curtains, offices, and any number of other central facilities. These we wheedled and cajoled and argued and fought for without any compunction at all, and if we finished up with more research assistants or film units or studio time than we needed we would not have dreamt of handing any back; we could always use them somehow.

An illuminating manifestation of this attitude to money appeared when I was discussing with a top executive a proposal which might earn a considerable profit. He was not very interested (it would have meant more work for him) and more or less terminated the discussion by saying, 'You realize that even if it made £500,000 a year, that's still only 1 per cent of our gross revenue?' So it was; it was also £500,000, which, if offered to him privately, in human money instead of Corporation money, would have been worth almost any effort or sacrifice. But for all the relationship he felt between it and the money in his wallet, he might as well have been playing Monopoly. The classic case was the £100 that the B.B.C. advanced to Frank Muir and Denis Norden for a programme that was ultimately cancelled. Some time later they received a request from the B.B.C. to send it back, and they replied, 'We regret we have no machinery for returning money.' This apparently was a completely satisfactory answer, and they never heard about the £100 again. No individual human would accept such a reason for surrendering £100 of his own money—but obviously the rules for corporation money are totally different.

Even while I was a member of the B.B.C. I wondered if this attitude to time and money was unique or unusual among corporations. After leaving, I worked with quite a number of big organizations, and realized that in fact the B.B.C. was rather good. I ought in fairness to point out that the present B.B.C., after an almost complete change of top management and a going-over from McKinsey's, bears little relationship to the Corporation I knew; but even the old B.B.C. would have shuddered at some of the examples of corporate behaviour I have since collected. My favourite instance happened to a friend who was also a freelance writer. He had worked out a series of comedy commercials for a detergent firm, and the agency were so delighted they fixed up a whole-day conference with him and the clients at a London hotel. A dozen of them met in a room; pads and pencils and blotters were set at each place on the table; and around the walls were waiters and waitresses manning three sideboards, one with urns full of coffee and milk, another groaning under bottles of every conceivable drink, the third piled high with plates of cold ham and chicken and tongue, salads, trifles and gateaux ready for the marathon session. The clients opened the proceedings by saying they thought comedy diminished the dignity of cleanliness. The agency men turned and stared at my friend. He agreed that it might well be so—he was a writer, not a market researcher. They thereupon agreed it was better not to risk it, and the meeting was over. They all trooped out into the London street, but my friend is convinced that he was the only one who was haunted for the rest of the day by the thought of the empty room, spread with a vast banquet which no one was going to eat. But then I suppose it was corporation food.

Outside the B.B.C. I found that the corporations' incredible unreality about time and money also extended to people. Time and time again the best and most logical person for a job was passed over in favour of some unlikely and unsuitable candidate from outside, who proceeded to make a mess of it. Often the passed-over manager would leave and discover to his astonishment that he could quadruple his income and devote to his new enterprise ten times more energy and productivity than the corporation was ever able to release or harness. I found horrifying schemes for reporting on staff that tried to turn every manager into a cross between God and a consultant psychiatrist. I found people treated with an indulgent softness that in ordinary life no one would show to a plumber or car mechanic who had fallen down on the job a quarter as badly, or with an inhuman callousness that the same people would privately not inflict on a stray dog.

But even more remarkable is the absence of a sense of belonging to the corporation. This has become such a normal feature of many large corporations that they accept it as inevitable, and yet by the simple standards of an ordinary human community it is quite extraordinary. Of course in all corporations there are some people who feel they belong, and in some corporations almost everyone feels part of it. They are the ones who say 'we' when talking about what the corporation makes or sells or plans to do. But 'they' seems to be the more common expression, and as mergers and takeovers create fewer, larger units, the 'they' to 'we' ratio increases. And yet the individual members of the corporations nearly all like to belong to some organization, to feel part of it, to be proud when it succeeds or depressed when it is going through a bad patch. It may be a football team, a golf club or a rose-growing association, but it is not the corporation which occupies by far the largest part of their waking life.

Of course the corporations are aware that something is wrong: over the years this awareness shifts from one symptom to another, and each shift calls into being a new branch of management consultancy and stimulates scores of postgraduate theses in management or social studies. If money-wasting is the focus, there is cost accountancy, management accountancy and all manner of stock and budgetary control procedures. If it is the use of time, the organization and methods and operational research men are standing by to help. If it is the misuse or alienation of people, there are shelves full of books on personnel recruitment and motivation, bonus schemes, personality tests and management development programmes. What they all have in common is that they do not go to the heart of the problem: they are like ointment for spots, fine if you have one or two spots, but if you have chicken-pox you will not cure it by putting ointment on every spot; the disease has to be attacked at the root. The most recent corporate anxiety focus is 'communication', and no doubt we shall soon be seeing a troop of communication consultants come galloping over the horizon, blowing their bugles and brandishing a score of lengthy comparative studies of vertical and lateral communications in General Motors, I.B.M. and Du Pont. They will serve up the usual compound of common sense, jargon and waffle in the name of Claude Lévi-Strauss or Marshall McLuhan or that professor from Harvard Business School or M.I.T. whose name I didn't quite catch, and the corporations will set up internal communications programmes and send managers off to communications courses, and one more spot will be covered with ointment. But the disease will not be cured.*

Perhaps the most significant objective finding about large corporations was published a year or two ago in *Economica*.[1] It showed how the average profitability of companies increased up to one or two million pounds employed capital, and then descended steadily as the amount of capital employed rose higher and higher. And yet the tendency of all industrial countries is towards larger and larger industrial units.

Of course it is this very largeness that is at the root of all the other problems: small private companies of twenty or thirty people, even companies of a few hundred, do not spend ages sorting out their own managerial muddles; they do not spend money as if it were a centrally provided facility; they do not tolerate continuing incompetence or behave with impersonal cruelty; and the people who work there usually feel they belong. When Lotus were flooded out, the 600 employees heard about it on television and came in late that night to help mop up. That sort of loyalty at Ford or British Leyland would make headline news across the nation.

Does it have to be so? Do we have to accept that this is more and more the nature of the industrial world in which we shall spend the rest of the century? I am convinced we do not, and there are enough

* General source references will be found at the end of the text, pp. 259–61.

corporate exceptions to the rule to show that large does not have to mean impersonal, inefficient and inhuman. And what is more, the exceptional few have not found corporate success by accident; there is a factor at work which can be isolated and used to help us improve the vast, clumsy modern corporation not only as a place for humans to work in but also as a profit-making industrial unit. The fact is that all these problems spring from a single root, and that root is deep in our own natures. The truth about how a great corporation should be organized is a personal truth which each of us can recognize in himself. But the scientific knowledge which enables us to relate our personal experience to scientifically authenticated fact has been published only in the last decade. It has already caused a revolution in science, and it is hard to see how it can avoid causing a revolution in the corporation.

The name of the revolution is the New Biology. Its findings and theories are scattered over thousands of papers, books, theses and learned articles published over the past twenty years and more, and most of them concern particular discoveries and observations, and experiments with individual species of animal. But it is in the past decade that a handful of writers have begun to arrange all these separate mosaic pieces into a new picture of the origins and nature of man. The best known are Konrad Lorenz,[2] Desmond Morris[3] and Robert Ardrey; and it was above all Ardrey's three books, *African Genesis*, *The Territorial Imperative* and *The Social Contract*,[4] which started off the various trains of thought that have come together in this book. The New Biology is still very new, but before it is much older it will bring as profound a change in our thinking as Freud and his successors brought a century ago. Indeed there is a sense in which the New Biology, although it compels the most profound revision of Freud's theories, is nevertheless the completion of his work. Hard though many of Freud's explanations were to accept, there was one element in them that struck a sympathetic chord in the minds of most of his readers, and that was his assertion that the spring of human action was not the controlled logical working of the reason, but the uncontrollable surge of much deeper subconscious or unconscious emotional drives. There is nothing in the New Biology to conflict with that insight, though there is a great deal to modify our views on what those drives are, and where they come from.

2

The basis of the New Biology is evolution. Ever since Darwin we have understood the operation of evolution and natural selection on physical characteristics: we know that giraffes have long necks because somewhere back in time there was not enough food on the lower branches of trees, with the result that the longer-necked of each generation survived to breed, and the shorter-necked died without issue; we know that tigers are striped because the unstriped varieties stood out from the dappled shadows, with the result that their breakfast saw them in time and escaped, while their better camouflaged brothers and sisters ate and survived. But the New Biology takes Darwin a whole stage further: it shows animal behaviour, and human behaviour, as the consequence of the same evolutionary pressures that produced claws and teeth, feathers and fur, or hooves and horns. Status-seeking emerges not as an unworthy failing of jealous executives, but as an immutable ingredient in man's make-up—an ingredient he shares with many other species including the jackdaw, the baboon and the domestic hen. The same is true of exploring, and aggressive behaviour, and defence of territory, and protection of young: they are deep in our nature because the apes and hominids who lacked these qualities died out, while those who had them survived to become our ancestors.

The trouble with Darwinism, of course, is that it explains too much. The Darwinian principle, coupled with an intoxicating absence of concrete evidence, can be used to prove almost any theory you choose. And so its importance to this book is not for the new ideas it provides, but for the unity it gives to a whole range of ideas, discoveries and observations recorded by many people over many years. Its particular importance to me is for the sense it makes of my own personal experience of the corporation, reinforced by many years of obsessive discussion with friends and colleagues. I feel as if I have spent the past ten years working at a jigsaw puzzle. The pieces have been assembled from my own experience and memory, from observation and consultancy, from discussion and interview, from books and articles, from history, politics, management, behavioural science and a number of related subjects. The New Biology has not provided any more pieces: what it has done is to reveal the picture on the front of the box.

The subject took off only when scientists realized that observations of animal behaviour, and especially primate behaviour, ultimately depended on observations made in the wild. And so for the past thirty years or more they have tramped over mountains and through jungles, across swamp and savannah, and lurked inconspicuously in silent discomfort to try and observe the natural behaviour of their quarry. My own fieldwork may have been less systematic but it has been a good deal more comfortable, since the species I have been studying—*Homo sapiens corporalis*, Corporation Man—flourishes in a much more accessible and agreeable habitat. I have also had the advantage that, in contrast with other species, this one has been abundantly observed and recorded; accounts of its behaviour have come in from every country in the world and stretch back over thousands of years.

There is one other unique factor which has operated in my favour. I have been able to do something which is impossible with any other species in the animal kingdom, namely to be accepted so completely by the objects of my study that my presence in no way inhibited or modified their behaviour. Indeed there were times when I could honestly say that I felt I was one of them myself.

2   The Picture on the Box

IN ONE sense it is almost impossible to date my first observations of Corporation Man: it could have been when I joined the B.B.C., when I was called up for National Service, or even my first day at school. But in that sense, all of us have any amount of evidence as to how the species behaves in its natural state. There is, however, another way of looking at it; I have also observed the natural behaviour of cats and dogs, wasps and spiders, flies and birds and bees, all my life, but I still have little more than a jumble of impressions of what they are doing and why. The reason is that I have never watched them with clear questions in my mind, with something precise that I was trying to establish. A scientist on the other hand, although he may see no more than I do, will understand what they are doing in a way that I never shall; the actions which to me look haphazard and arbitrary are to him part of a pattern, a pattern formed by the imperatives of survival in a hostile world. He looks at them to verify theories, explain anomalies, and provoke new questions, so that the pattern may become even clearer. I cannot claim scientific methods or scientific standards, but as an enthusiastic amateur I have begun to see patterns in the behaviour of men in large organizations just as zoologists observe patterns in flocks of starlings or colonies of ants. Until I encountered the New Biology it never occurred to me that there might be ancient survival imperatives at the root of them, but already several years ago a part of the pattern, a corner of the jigsaw, was beginning to fit together. And in that sense I can put a fairly accurate date to the time when my observations began.

It was the late summer of 1962. For the past five years I had been working on *Tonight*, a television magazine programme on current affairs that went out five nights a week, forty minutes a night, at the start of the peak evening viewing period. The starting of the programme in 1957 by its founder-editor Donald Baverstock had been one of the success stories of the B.B.C. in its competition with commercial television: 20 per cent of the nation watched it every night, it had a high reputation for its treatment of current affairs, it regularly beat the commercial opposition for audiences, critics hailed it as irreverent, provocative and original, and it was produced remarkably cheaply. I had worked very happily on the programme from the start, but in 1961 Donald Baverstock was promoted, the next year his successor Alasdair Milne followed him into the higher reaches of management, and the editorship fell on me. It was then that I realized that, as far as I was concerned, the party was over.

Some of the reasons for this lay in my own shortcomings and unfitness for the job, and there was nothing I could do about them: had they been the only ones, I might in time have overcome them. But in addition, I found myself up against what I came to think of as 'the third factor'. Previously, as a director, producer and writer, I had been aware of only two factors that limited what we could do on the programme: on the one hand the equipment, resources, money, techniques and skills at our disposal, and on the other the interest, comprehension and tastes of the audience. Part of the fascination of the job lay in exploring and extending those frontiers. Now, as editor, I came up for the first time against the third limiting factor: the Corporation itself.

Of course I had been aware of the Corporation before, of its various divisions and departments and levels of hierarchy, but I had just accepted them as permanent and unalterable features of the corporate landscape. Now I found it a frontier that had to be explored and attacked like the other two. At first I simply accepted its restrictions: if I wanted more studio rehearsal, I had to ask planning; if I wanted vision lines to Paris I had to ask engineering allocations; if I wanted three film units one week and one the next, instead of two each week, I had to ask the film department; if I wanted to fill a vacancy for a production assistant, it had to be done through the appointments department; if I wanted to pay a researcher more money, the establishment department had to agree: and so on. There were at least twelve separate authorities who restricted my freedom, and if I wanted to challenge any of them I had to do it through the head of my department, who would then have to go up to controllers and directors until the lines of authority finally met in a single man. All too often it was the Director General, who frequently had more important things to worry about than an extra five pounds a week for my research assistant. And in the intervals between meetings and memos and all the laborious paraphernalia of case-making, I had a forty-minute programme to get on the air every night.

It did not occur to me in those days to read books on management, or to study organization theory; life was too short, and my time was oversubscribed by several hours a day. But it was abundantly clear that something was wildly and hopelessly wrong. It might have been the people, but I had to admit that most of them, when not refusing me resources I needed, were quite sensible and able. And so I was forced to the conclusion that it was something to do with the way they were organized.

In my early days as a television producer I used to find bad programmes much more instructive than good ones. A good programme you simply enjoyed and admired; a bad one made you work out why it was bad, what principles it violated, and this in turn made you work out what the principles were. So I now started to think in the same way about corporations and organization: clearly the B.B.C. was violating some of the principles of organizing television — very probably all of them; so what were those principles?

I had not the remotest idea what they were, or even where to look for them. But it was clear that, whatever they might be, their broad purpose must be to stimulate and facilitate the production of the highest quality programmes at the lowest possible price while remaining within the terms of the B.B.C.'s charter. And so, in the absence of any other guidance, the best course seemed to be to look around the television service and find out what actually worked in practice. And that was extremely interesting.

Television programmes in the B.B.C. had been built up around the individual producer and the department he worked in. The departments were drama, light entertainment, documentary/current affairs, children's and so on: within them, the producers were given budgets and resources for each programme or series they produced. But already a new, unofficial organization was growing up inside the official one. Not surprisingly, some of the programmes or series had been better than others. More were wanted, and the producer was allowed an assistant producer or two, to enable him to produce thirteen a year instead of six. Out of these programmes, some would be wanted for even longer, in effect as permanent fixtures; the producer would then have quite a large production team on what was, for practical purposes, a permanent basis. Moreover, instead of being given the precise resources and budget for each programme, he would be given staff, studios, cameras, design effort, cutting rooms, viewing-theatre time and budget for the whole year.

This system had grown up spontaneously in all the departments. *Tonight* was only one example of it: there was also *Panorama*, *Monitor*, *Sportsview*, *Maigret*, *This Is Your Life* — and these 'production team' programmes were by far the most successful, the shock troops of the B.B.C.'s effective counter-attack on the commercial opposition. And when you examined them you discovered why. It was because they united in a triumphant way the two forces which many people thought were doomed to irreconcilable conflict: administrative logic and creative logic.

The administrative logic was fairly obvious. Production teams responsible for output right through the year meant that studios, film crews, design effort, staff and money could be blocked out for twelve months ahead, instead of being endlessly juggled around for hundreds of separate programmes, and projections could be made for even longer periods. It meant that the illness of a single producer did not throw everything back in the melting-pot. It meant that an evening's viewing could be planned with some knowledge of what the programmes would be like, instead of the sty full of pigs in pokes of the earlier days. It meant that orders and contracts could be placed for twelve months, with the consequent advantages of price to the B.B.C. and security to suppliers, writers, and performers. And the relationship between the production team's budget and the audience research figures gave a quick and easy measure of cost-effectiveness.

More interesting, at least to me, was the creative logic. It was also more surprising. The accepted stereotype of the creative artist is as a solitary — the painter alone in his studio, the composer alone at his piano, the poet alone in his garret. When working on *Tonight* I came to believe that this was a lot of romantic nonsense: the act of creating a work of art has to be solitary, but the artist does not have to be a solitary. The busy Florentine studio-workshops that produced Leonardo and Michelangelo and Raphael, the German Court choirs and orchestras where Bach and Haydn learnt their art, the companies of English players that Marlowe and Shakespeare wrote for — these groups formed the creative surroundings and attracted the patrons, the admirers and the customers that the artist depended on.

It was on *Tonight* that I learned the creative logic of a production team, and although we produced no Raphael or Bach or Shakespeare I am privately quite sure that the same logic operated for them as for us. The basic requirement is a demand for something you can supply, which of course also operates for the solitary. But the team is much better equipped to supply it, for a number of reasons. We found, to start with, that, although an idea can only originate in one person's mind, it often emerges in a half-formed state; it can be greatly improved if six or seven people question it and add to it and elaborate it and refine it. In the same way, after the programme was over, six or seven people were much better than one at evaluating it, drawing conclusions, seeing new possibilities to exploit or errors to be corrected. A solitary producer was too prone to elation or depression, his own ego was too intimately bound up with every decision, to be able to achieve the objectivity of a production team.

We also found that an idea tends to be limited by the originator's executive ability and production capacity. A composer writes music for the sort of choir and orchestra that he can get to perform it, an author writes his play for the cast and theatre he is likely to get; indeed the closer the writer–actors–theatre or composer–orchestra–choir relationship, the more fruitful the result is likely to be. As they become more skilful and the author's (or composer's) confidence in them grows, so he attempts more original, varied and demanding works. In the same way, a solitary producer's ideas are only for programmes he can carry out on his own, they are limited by the skill, experience, judgment and inclinations of one man; but a production team can initiate ideas that use a far wider range — a good example was *That Was The Week*, which united musicians, singers, actors, political comment, studio audiences, comedy writers, news film, documentary film, studio cameras, benchwork and other techniques demanding a range of experience and expertise that no single producer could possibly command.

There is also something you might call collective wisdom. Of course a single producer adds to his personal skill and experience with each programme, but his programmes are infrequent, and at the end he alone possesses the wisdom, which dies with him, so to speak. This wisdom is a compound of knowledge of the audience and understanding of the medium, the residuum of many lessons painfully or excitingly learnt about what the audience can and cannot take in or enjoy, and what cameras, microphones, interviewers and writers can and cannot achieve. A production team, with its greater frequency of output, learns much more much faster, and shares that experience among the whole team. It becomes a body of knowledge which remains even if some of the team depart, and for the higher management it is a much more significant and enduring guarantee of programme quality than the talent of a single producer. And just as it is refreshed by new people who join the team, so it is available to them as a guide and teaching aid: it makes a production team the best place for any novice to learn the craft. And it does more than give him access to this body of accumulated folk-wisdom: it also offers him a variety of different roles—writer, film director, researcher, studio director, interview producer—with a correspondingly better chance of finding a suitable niche than he would have if apprenticed to a single producer.

Yet another advantage is flexibility. A solitary producer might be allocated a week's filming, a week's editing, and two days in the studio. If he later wants to postpone the filming, that is too bad—the next week is allocated to someone else. Anyway, it is then too late for the editor, who has to move on to another programme. He cannot even trade two of his filming days for an extra day in the studio, for the same reason. But a production team with permanent facilities all through the year can do any amount of internal juggling so long as it comes out right in the end. It also gives that bit of elasticity that makes private experiment possible—the sort of experiment for which a single producer has to put up a case for special budget and resources. A production team can just try it out with a spare hour or two in the studio or a half day with the film unit, and if it does not work no one need ever know. This makes it much easier to keep up with changing tastes and techniques, and to stop the programme from solidifying or getting into a rut.

It did not occur to me at this stage that I had stumbled on to something with a relevance beyond television. All I knew then was that the production team worked in a way that neither the solitary producer outside it nor the cumbersome structure above it could ever work. It had formed itself naturally, spontaneously, and almost in spite of the existing formal structure, and it was carrying the television service. All the same, isolating the successful element did not solve the problem. How should production teams relate to the rest of the B.B.C., the institution entrusted by Parliament with the provision of the television service?

The answer came quite suddenly, and it came in the form of another question. Suppose *Tonight*, and all the other production team programmes, were completely outside the B.B.C. organization? Suppose they simply contracted with the B.B.C. to produce a certain number of programmes each year at a certain price? The prospect was Elysian, not just for the money I could save if it were my own, but for the simplicity it would bring to my life, the problems it would take out of the job, the freedom I would have to think about the programme. Instead of the endless internal negotiations, the cajolery and threats and memos and proposals and meetings, I would use a very simple device called money. It would buy carpets and film and scenery and stationery, it would pay staff and performers and insurance and rent, and I could at any time apply it where it was needed and withdraw it where it was unnecessary.

There were several reasons—quite sound ones—why complete independence was not possible: for instance, the B.B.C. had to answer to Parliament for its programme content, and it also had a huge investment in studios and equipment as a result of starting up television in Britain and being the sole producer for many years. But there was no reason why the B.B.C. should not simulate the system in organizational terms: it could give me a total annual budget, lay down its rules on political balance and financial procedures and staff policy, and leave me to get on with it. I could hire the B.B.C.'s studios and other facilities or buy them outside as I chose. I need never ask for authorizations from the film department or engineering allocations or the accommodation unit or the establishment department or programme contracts or any of the other little power enclaves; I would simply report to the Controller of Programmes or one of his team, and if he was satisfied, that was that. If he was dissatisfied he could reduce the budget, curtail the programme, or remove me. Too easy.

It was all so beautifully obvious that I wrote a brief paper to my superiors proposing it, and, although it rather spoils the story, they in fact took it seriously and made a number of changes along the lines I suggested. Not enough, I felt, and not all for the better, but at least it showed they were aware of the problem and wanted to do something about it. In time I might have had another go at it; but by now the idea of working outside large corporations was becoming more and more attractive; and so I resigned, and started to make the discoveries listed in Chapter 1. I also met Doug Hughes.

Doug is a production engineer with International Computers, and we met because part of my freelance work involved making documentary films. He wanted a film made about the computer and the numerically controlled machine-tool. At the outset I thought it sounded like a piece of straightforward technical exposition, but as soon as I met Doug I realized that it went right to the heart of how you organize an engineering business. He felt about the engineering industry much as I felt about the B.B.C., and at first that was the only connection that I could see. However, as he led me further and further into the dark recesses of the average engineering factory, lightening my path with dazzling flashes of sarcasm fuelled by his rich sense of the absurd, it all began to look unbelievably familiar.

To Doug, the average engineering factory was chaos. Metal came into it in a few basic shapes—casting and sheet, billet and strip and bar—and then went through thirty or forty processes before the finished machined part went off to assembly: heat treatment, milling, drilling, grinding, reaming, then more of the same, with each process under a different manager's control. Away in one building were designers stipulating tolerances that could not be achieved, and in another were estimators playing happy games with fairy-tale figures that bore no relation to the nasty realities of the factory. If any part had to be scrapped, it was never anyone's fault—the milling foreman and drilling foreman each blamed the other, and the works manager's office turned into a law court. The system worked by a sort of selective panic called 'expediting', which meant that urgent parts were rushed through at the expense of logic, order, economy and efficiency. Machine operators alternated between waiting for parts and being submerged in a flood. Once when we drove past a strange engineering factory, Doug said to me, 'Know how many parts they make?' Of course I didn't know. 'Nor do I,' he said, 'but I can tell you one thing: 50 per cent of them are overstocked and 50 per cent are in deficiency.' The

B.B.C., in retrospect, started to look like a model of smooth management.

Doug had been in engineering factories all his life, but he hadn't been able to change anything until one day he was given the design of a card punch so complex that he knew it could not be manufactured by the normal methods. There was only one way: and with a remorseless logic which I now recognize, a production team took shape. A small group of men were put together in a separate shop with the necessary machines, and took the card punch through from raw metal to finished machine. The production volume, the degree of precision and the delivery date were all met.

That could have been that. But Doug realized that in a situation almost totally wrong, he had stumbled on something right. And he began to see an engineering factory exactly as I had begun to see the B.B.C.—as a collection of independent workshops with a boss in charge of each who was responsible not for a process but for a complete part or a complete product. He also saw that once these discrete groups were formed, with their known output of parts and hourly cost in men and machines, their production could be controlled by a computer in a way that was impossible for every single man and machine.

The film we made about all this was called *The Future Came Yesterday*, and among the first people to see it were two of Doug's colleagues. Both of them had separately come to conclusions very like Doug's, and had already begun to put them into practice in their factory in Belfast. It wasn't quick, and it wasn't easy, chiefly because of the novelty of the ideas, but gradually their managers caught on. First of all they moved in on the pressing shop, and gave it the necessary drills and other equipment to turn out finished pressed parts, as if it were an independent little company. Once the other managers saw it in operation, they were over the hill: there was a hectic period of machine-shifting and they were in business.

It was some time later that I made my first visit to Belfast, and by then I could see that they were getting close to every Corporation Man's ideal—gaining all the advantages of bigness without losing any of the advantages of smallness. Not only were the machines grouped so as to produce complete parts, they actually had white lines painted on the floor round each group. And a few yards from each group's machines, behind glass panels, were its offices; in there were the group boss, his administrative assistant and staff, work study, inspection and production engineering, and his group store next door. For all practical purposes he had his own business. Each day he would tell the computer what had been produced, and the computer would tell him what he still had to produce and by when. But the exact allocation of men and machines, the problems caused by sickness, machine faults, holidays and so on—those were for the boss to sort out for himself.

Strangely enough, it was a strike which showed that the system was working. Always in the past if any of the milling machine operators struck, they all struck. One day after the group system had begun, one of the groups struck, including the milling operators, but the milling operators in the other groups stayed at work. The groups had arrived.

So already, before I encountered the New Biology, I had collected a number of pieces for the jigsaw puzzle, even if I did not see how they fitted together. As I have said, the New Biology did not give me any more pieces: but by revealing to me the picture on the box, it enabled me at last to put the pieces together for myself.

3 The Hunting Band

IN THE front of my house there is a short, semicircular drive which in a more gracious age allowed carriages to drive up to the door, set down the occupants, and continue on into the road again. In those days there were gates at each end, but they proved a nuisance in the age of the motor car, so now there are two open gateways. A few months ago I looked out of the window and saw three strange young men walking along the pavement. As they came level with the house they had the unbelievable audacity to turn off the pavement and in through the gateway, through my garden, past my front door, and back into the road again. The insolence of it! Who did they think ... as I watched them, the whole emotional range of the Enraged Householder syndrome welled up inside me, the same response that I myself used to provoke when as a small boy I climbed over suburban fences to get my ball back. But in this case it was different; I had just finished reading Lorenz's *On Aggression*, and recognized that my instinctive anger was not a private and personal quirk, but an ancient aggressive response to a territorial threat. The knowledge could not subdue my feelings, but at least it restrained my actions and prevented me from trying to pretend to myself that the resentment was an entirely rational and logical consequence of an act which in fact was only the most harmless of adolescent larks.

This is the real fascination of the New Biology; not the data but the programmes, not the new facts it unearths but the new way of looking at the world that it gives you—above all, the new way of looking at yourself and your fellow men. Perhaps the best way to express this is by the phrase 'acceptance of the irrational'. The New Biology shows us how powerfully the irrational operates within us, and how much of our behaviour is not the logical response of the intellect to the facts of the situation, but an emotional reflex set off by some primitive survival mechanism. I felt a surge of aggression towards those three young men because I belong to a species that for millions of years had to defend its territory to survive. Chance no doubt brought into the world many variants who had no urge to defend their children or their cave: they could not continue their line, and they were selected out. I am here because there were some who fought tooth and nail against every intruder to protect their home and their young. It may be that in the orderly western suburbs of London in the 1970s the sharpness of that reaction is no longer necessary. That is not the point: my instincts and emotions are governed not by current social supply and demand, but by age-old genetic history. It is enough that an aggressive response to territorial aggression was a survival necessity once; and who is to say that it will not one day be a survival necessity again?

However, it was not an awareness of territorial aggression that made the pieces of the corporation puzzle come together; it was a sudden revelation about the evolutionary, biological nature of the production team. The New Biology shows beyond all argument that the group, so far from being an accident of corporate organization, is one of the most ancient characteristics of our species. However far back you trace our primate line, you do not encounter any solitaries. You find groups; and not just the family group, but something larger. Moreover, this applies to all species of ape and monkey except the gibbon and the orang-outan. True, the apes are only collateral branches of our evolutionary line; but if you go back seventy million years to a direct ancestral species, the lemur, you still find a larger grouping than the family as the basic unit. This is now so deep in us that we have to accept it as immutable: wherever we live, whatever projects we undertake, whatever dangers we encounter, we will form a group if it is remotely possible.

This simple primate grouping, however, is only half the story, and for the purposes of this book the least important half. It is something we all know instinctively: not just that the solitary hermit in his cave is a rare oddity, but that there is something very strange about the man who never mixes with his fellows at work, or the housewife who never talks to any friend or neighbour, or the family that cuts itself off from all the other families in the district. All this is obvious; it is the other half of the story, the half that makes us different from all the other primates, that has the profound implications for the modern corporation.

Most of the scientists seem to agree that this difference began well over a million years ago — more likely five million, and perhaps as long as fifteen million. Before then we, or rather our ancestors, were vegetarians like the rest of the family. But then, at some point in the Pliocene (or Miocene) era, we turned from vegetarians into carnivores. Perhaps we started by catching or trapping the small mammals, monkeys and rats and rabbits, but as the ages rolled by a new meat supply opened up, meat on the hoof; the great herds of large grazing animals where a single kill could feed a community.

There was, however, a drawback to those large varieties of antelope and waterbuck and oryx; they were too large and too swift for any man or hominid to catch and kill on his own. But they were not too large for a group of them working together. Already we were a social species; we travelled around together, and banded together for defence, even if each one collected his fruit and vegetables for himself. Now we adapted the existing co-operative way of life to a purpose different from that of any other primate: the systematic hunting and killing of game. Begotten by opportunity out of necessity, millions of years ago, the hunting band was born. And it has taken one branch of the primate family down from the trees and up to the moon.

The hunting band—why had I not seen it before? I think perhaps my realization was delayed by thinking of man's early history as a farming history: but it was only ten thousand years ago that we learnt to plant crops, domesticate cows and pigs and sheep, and build ourselves a more comfortable and less precarious way of life. You only have to think about it to realize that ten thousand years of farming cannot possibly dissipate a genetic inheritance built up and handed down over perhaps fifteen million years of hunting. Indeed if we go back a quarter of those ten thousand years we meet Plato and Sophocles and Aristophanes, whose intellects and emotions were so similar to ours today (and that is flattering ourselves) that it is impossible to think that the other three-quarters can have had any noticeable genetic effect at all. The employees and the managers of the modern corporation, in their sprawling factories and towering office blocks, have been formed into what they are, not by three hundred generations down on the farm, but by half a million generations in the hunting band.

I can think of another reason, too, why I had not seen this before. It brings back to mind the answer I was once given by Francis Crick, the DNA Nobel Prize winner, when I asked him what it was that kept one scientist from making a breakthrough which another scientist made. He said that it was very rarely an absence of the necessary facts: you always kicked yourself if you were the one who had missed it, because all the facts were in front of you all the time. There were various obstacles he mentioned—for instance a piece of experimental evidence that was wrong—but the one I chiefly remember was this: an assumption you are not aware you are making. I had unconsciously assumed until a year or two ago that our organizations, if they were to be explained historically, must be explained in terms of *recorded* history. The trouble with that assumption was that it worked—a great many features of the corporation can be found in medieval and Renaissance politics. Indeed, the parallel between the modern corporation and the medieval or Renaissance state, the behaviour of corporate barons and courtiers and princes, was the theme of my book *Management and Machiavelli*.[1] But a demonstration of parallel is not a demonstration of cause and effect; and even before I started to write it, it occurred to me that perhaps somewhere there was a deep unity that I could not see, a hidden root out of which they had both grown. Several people noticed that there was a part of the book, the part dealing with cell structures and creative groups, which owed very little to historical analogy and nothing at all to Machiavelli. I could only admit that this was so, but that I believed it was true and important so I was damned if I was going to leave it out. I certainly did not suspect that it was the part of the book in which I had come closest to stumbling on the answer.

But there was one further reason which delayed my recognition of the hunting band. Just as our farming and manufacturing history is brief compared with our hunting history, so too our hunting history, even if it stretches back for fifteen million years, is not all that long in evolutionary terms. There is certainly time in fifteen million years for a species to develop new instinctive responses, but it is very unlikely that they will have the compelling, over-riding force of the older ones such as hunger or fear of death or reproduction or defence of young. In his book *On Aggression* Konrad Lorenz talks of 'the parliament of instincts' which governs an animal's behaviour, and which debates and divides when, say, fear of a predator suggests one course and defence of young another. In that parliament, the instinct to form hunting bands is a newly elected member whose voice will not be heard when the powerful

3

older representatives hold the floor. It is still there, it is still an important instinct, but it is not an irresistible compulsion. So long as we have the family group and the purely social gathering, we can live happy lives without forming hunting bands, as indeed people can live happy lives without having children. Something may be missing, but it is not something indispensable, and consequently the organization—government department, corporation, small company—does not have to form them, even though they are the best and most natural way to collective success. The tendency and the impulse are there, but these can be resisted: not everywhere, and not all the time, but in particular places and at particular times. Sometimes it seems that such resistance is the objective of the corporation.

And just as the hunting band is a comparatively recent development, so it has never been the sole form of organization for the whole community. The mothers had to stay behind in the camp to rear their slow-maturing young: the hunting band was only for the fit adult males. Lionel Tiger suggests in *Men in Groups*[2] that the reason women cannot throw overarm, in the way men can, is that they never had to—they did not join in the hunt. Perhaps a strong and childless female could occasionally take part, but in principle the hunting band has always been and still is an all-male group, and the urge—perhaps I should say the instinct—to form such groups is almost irresistibly powerful in most men. No reason or objective is necessary, though once the group is formed reasons and objectives will be found easily enough: war has often been the most simple and, to many men, most satisfying objective, but there are many others. The drive is not particularly towards conflict with other hunting bands, nor even (which would be much more explicable) towards the extermination of the larger ungulates. The primary drive is simply towards the formation of the band: all objectives are secondary to that, and in a sense a consequence of it. It is this urge to form all-male hunting bands that has been the great instrument of survival down the millions of years that we have evolved as carnivorous primates: the object of the hunt has been a variable.

It is hard to describe the nature of the bond formed by membership of a modern hunting band, and perhaps impossible to comprehend it unless you have felt the force of it yourself. An interesting sidelight on the all-male nature of the group is the difficulty that many husbands have in explaining its compulsions to their wives. To the wife it is, very reasonably, just 'work', something that has to be done to support the family and keep the home together. 'But we don't *need* the extra money—the children need you at home much more than they need a holiday abroad.' There are of course other compulsions as well, but the pull of the hunting band is the hardest to resist or convey. It recalls Kipling's ancient complaint of the Viking women to their warriors,

> What is woman, that you forsake her
> And your hearth fire, and your home acre,
> To go with the old grey widow-maker?

But it was not the call of the sea they found irresistible—and the complaint is as hard to answer for the modern executive as it was for the Viking warrior.

What makes it so hard is that the bond operates at a depth beyond language. Hunting animals co-operate without need of speech— their co-operative instincts produce what Carveth Read calls 'perceptive and contagious sympathy'.[3] Any member of a successful sporting team knows how powerfully this still operates within us if we allow it to develop. To quote John Spencer, England's Rugby football captain in 1971: 'It's amazing what an understanding you build up. You know when a chap's going to stay outside you, and you know when he's going to come inside. You don't even have to shout.' That sort of unspoken, animal understanding is clearest in sport but common to all hunting bands in a less physical way, and illustrates the primitive nature of the bond that holds the members together.

The strength of the bond is of course increased with time, but it is surprising how strong a bond can be formed in a short time if the conditions are right. The most extreme example is war, and I suppose the trenches in France during the Great War are the outstanding example in living memory. If you read about the conditions men had to endure for those four years it is almost impossible to understand why they did not desert in droves after the first few weeks. Different writers explain it in various ways— they were fighting for freedom and democracy, and for the forces of light against the forces of darkness, or else they knew they would be shot if they ran away, or it was a triumph of army discipline and training; but the men who were there, if they explain it at all, talk in terms of their friends. They could not let them down. The bond formed in the trenches was a true, primitive survival bond: each had been forced to depend on the others not to betray positions, to give covering fire, to warn of attack, to help the wounded, to co-operate day and night on a matter of collective life and death. It was not for themselves nor for their country that they endured so much for so long: it was for the ancient hunting band. As long as those bands remain, the fight goes on: to military historians, an army ceases to exist when those small basic bands are so depleted and dispersed that the bond is dissolved. When that stage is reached, the army becomes a rabble, and the factor which prevents degeneration into rabble is usually called morale: it rests on that basic military unit, the section, the band who risk their lives for each other because an ancient survival instinct demands it.

Just how ancient that instinct may be is illustrated by the South African naturalist Eugène Marais in his book describing the two years he spent in a lonely mountain home next to a baboon colony. The book is called *My Friends the Baboons*,[4] and contains a story about a leopard who appeared on a ledge above the troop. Two of the older male baboons saw him, detached themselves from the others, and crept along a branch overhanging the ledge. Then they dropped; the leopard killed one and wounded the other, but not before his jugular had been fatally severed by the teeth of the baboon who landed on his neck. The older baboons could easily have run away; instead they risked their lives for the survival of the troop. Greater love hath no baboon ... did Christ too lay down his life for his hunting band?

A troop of baboons or the soldiers in the Flanders mud may seem a long way from the office block or the factory floor, and indeed Corporation Man is scarcely ever placed in a situation of such hazard. But corporate survival, the survival of the group within the corporation, the fear of irretrievably lost customers and markets, the fear of cancellations of big contracts, the fear of hostile takeover, of factory closure—these can turn on the heat and apply the pressure powerfully enough for most people. If the extra effort of one man can tip the scales for his group, that effort will be made even at great sacrifice. How many marriages have been sacrificed on the altar of the hunting band? How many warnings of coronaries have been fatally disregarded? But those who have belonged to such a band, especially one that has been heat-welded or pressure-welded in that way, know how great the rewards can be. When they have all had to depend utterly on each other, to trust each other's loyalty completely, and found that trust upheld even under great stress, the strength of the bond thus formed gives a tremendous sense of security through fellowship.

The experience is on an emotional and not an intellectual level, and those who share it are sharing exactly the same emotional bond that united the primitive hunting band. All such groups share a deep reluctance to let the group break up, and when this does happen there is a deep sense of loss. Some people find it hard to understand how anyone could regret the end of a war, but anyone who has worked in a good research group or pit gang or production team knows the sense of loss when a heat-welded group is dissolved. The ex-servicemen's associations which meet year after year are evidence of how long this band can endure: for many of them it is the one function of the year they continue to attend after ill health has forced them to abandon all other excursions.

Large corporations have their less formal counterparts to ex-servicemen's associations, and you often find annual dinners of a quite unofficial nature, instituted to preserve on at least one day of the year the comradeship of a successful group dissolved many years before. There was an interesting article in the *Sunday Times* in the mid-1960s in which an astute gossip columnist discussed what he called 'networks'.[5] A network was a number of individuals who, while they had no formal or operational relationship with each other, had nevertheless such a close understanding and powerful informal relationship that the connection was a force to be reckoned with in the affairs of the country. He was particularly concerned with these networks in the political parties, journalism, banking, broadcasting, and other areas with direct bearing on public life; as far as I could tell from my own knowledge, he was quite correct. But the interesting fact was that all these networks could be traced back to an earlier hunting band, to a political ginger group, or newspaper or periodical or television programme which had brought the members together, worked them extremely hard, brought them success and public notice, and then fizzled out as they dispersed to follow separate paths. Often the political group or journal or programme continued after they had left it, but it was an extinct volcano: the glory was departed, and it never flared into life again. But for the rest of their lives each one knew that if he wanted an urgent meeting with one of the others he would not have to disclose the reason; the urgency and the bond were sufficient to clear a space in the most crowded diary at the shortest notice. In the same way, no one ever really understands the informal power structure and information flow of a corporation unless he can identify its networks, and trace the history of the directors and senior executives back to the hunting band, perhaps twenty years previously, where they first came to prominence. Most of them would also privately admit that whatever subsequent honours and achievements they may have enjoyed, they have never since been as effective separately as they were collectively all those years before.

Some commentators have resisted the idea that these ancient, pre-human emotions can still operate within modern, civilized people, but that is to misunderstand what the New Biologists are trying to say. Of course Corporation Man is a great deal more than a hunter: he can speak and write, he can compose music and poetry, he can learn and reason, he can experiment and invent with an ingenuity and adaptability that are unique in the animal world. But all these are additions to, not subtractions from, the hunting primate. The hunting band is still there, and when we are dealing with the corporation, we are dealing with a very recent adaptation of it. Donald Baverstock with *Tonight*, Doug Hughes with the card punch, the production groups in the Belfast factory, and all the thousands, maybe millions, of successful groups in industry and commerce, banking and government and war, indeed every area of collective human enterprise, have not been forging a new weapon on the anvil of modern industrial civilization: they have picked up an ancient one and used it with only the smallest of modifications.

This book, then, is an examination of the primitive hunting band in the modern corporation. Survival no longer requires the hunting and killing of game, so this particular skill has been allowed to atrophy; it has been replaced by agriculture and mining and manu-facturing, by the skills of devising, making, transporting and selling goods, by thousands of entirely new survival activities. But although the end product may have changed, it has changed very recently: the way we organized the hunting band, its method of operation, its communication system, its survival mechanisms—all these are still there, and we will begin to understand our human organizations in a new way if only we can see them; or rather, if only we can see them for what they are, since they have been staring us in the face all our lives.

There is one other question we must answer before we know what we are looking for in the corporation. How many men are there in a hunting band? Obviously there cannot be just one number which is the only possible one, and for a long time it did not occur to me that the question was worth asking. A group is a group is a group. If it works, then it's the right number. Obviously it must be more than one, but whether it was two or twenty or two hundred did not seem to signify. But of course the moment you start thinking numerically, you realize that you have in your own mind an upper and lower limit, and that they are not all that far apart. A group, a team, in the sense that I mean and operating as I have seen them operate, could not conceivably be two hundred. Nor could it be two, though it could be three: I would therefore put three as the lower limit. What about the upper limit? If it could not be two hundred, could it be twenty? All my experience, and the verdict of the many practising managers I have discussed this with, says no. A group of twenty cannot have the unity of a hunting band, nor can it get down to serious business without subdividing into two or more groups. Parkinson, in one of his celebrated insights, asserts that no board or council or cabinet or committee can ever function when membership rises above twenty.[6] It will of course continue to meet, and membership may be a sought-after honour, but if it is that big a smaller group will have formed which does the real work and makes the real decisions. Parkinson is certainly talking about the right sort of numbers, but I believe that twenty is too many. Six or seven is comfortable, and ten is extremely effective; twelve cannot be ruled out, but fifteen starts to become improbable. I would take a great deal of convincing that twenty could ever operate as a single team: if a meeting of twenty ever works it works because several people are subordinates of others present, or specialists advising on particular topics, and though there are twenty faces round the table, there are only ten voices that matter.

The more I reflected on my own experience and probed other people's, the more convinced I became that there was indeed an optimum size for a group, and that it lay somewhere around ten. At first it was a personal and subjective conviction, and I did not imagine it would ever be anything more. But then I thought about the army. I had spent two years of National Service as recruit, cadet and officer, and although I entered it with no enthusiasm for the military way of life, I emerged with considerable respect for the way it was run. The army is a good place to look: the organization of an army is not a question of having fun with charts, it is a matter of life and death; its structure has been hammered out by the logic of survival over many centuries of bloody experience. With a strong organization you may bring a citizen army together at short notice and win a single victory over another scratch side, but if a regular army is to succeed over a long period of time there is a strong likelihood that it will find the best way. And it was quite clear that in the British Army the basic unit of survival, the group that stood or fell together, was the infantry section. There were platoons, companies, battalions and brigades, but all these were assemblies of smaller units; the section was a band of men, and the section was ten or eleven in number when at full strength. And this applies not only in the British Army: the U.S. Army squad is also ten men; the Roman Army was based on units of ten, the squad who shared a tent; the army of Genghis Khan was based on units of ten; indeed almost every long-standing successful army, whatever larger formations it might adopt for battle, rested for its permanent organization on units of that sort of size. And it is not just the army. When we play games together, the same size keeps cropping up. Almost all team games have teams of between eight and fifteen in number. Juries are twelve. The Jewish minyan is ten. Indeed once you look around at human groups with the hunting band in mind, the number leaps out at you. As I said, every practising manager I have discussed the subject with agrees without question that ten is close to the maximum for a board or project team or work group, and if I had wanted any further corroboration of its application to industry, it was supplied by the paper on productivity bargaining that won the Institute of Management Consultants' Sandford Smith award for 1969. The author, Robert Spillman, says:

Whatever the formal organisation, people develop an informal organisation, which may or may not coincide with the formal

organisation, and within which certain of their needs are satisfied. The basic unit of informal organisation is the work group;
and this may consist of from three to about eighteen persons
carrying out a common task or engaged in linked operations.
Each person in that group reacts or responds to the other persons in that group, and the result is that each group tends to act
as a cell or unit with characteristics and needs of its own.
Members of a social group will tend to subordinate their individual needs to the needs of the group as a whole; but in
return the work group protects and shields its members.[7]

By the time I had got this far, I was convinced. Since no one
could go back to the Pliocene epoch and check up, I was sure that
the only evidence we would ever have about the size of those hunting bands would have to be supplied by projecting back from
Corporation Man or forward from the lemur, and as far as I was
concerned they both pointed in the same direction. But in assuming
that we could find no direct evidence, I underestimated the ingenuity of the palaeozoologists. They approached the question like
this: the hunting band would have to bring its kill back to the camp
with it, because of vultures and other scavengers, and it would
normally have to return before nightfall for collective security
against lions and leopards, and to feed the women and children if
stores were low. From this they plotted the maximum hunting
radius. Meanwhile from other evidence they discovered the density
of game population in that part of Africa at that time. And they
have worked out that within the human or hominid radius there
was about enough food to support a total population of forty, which
would mean a male hunting band of something between nine and
eleven.
This then is the first premise upon which the book rests: that
the tendency to form 'hunting band' groups of about ten people,
nearly always men, is a part of our nature; that these groups have
been the instrument of our survival for up to fifteen million years;
and that any human organization today, however large it grows,
still depends on these groups for its survival. (Of course there is
nothing mystic or magical about the number ten—a group can
function effectively with five or twelve: I am simply taking the ten-
group as the convenient optimum to describe the primitive hunting

band as we encounter it in the modern corporation.) I call it a premise because I cannot prove it; but there is a great deal of evidence to suggest that it is so, and most people who have worked in large organizations will know it in their hearts: they too will have an intuitive knowledge that if you want something done you form a project group, and that somewhere around ten is about the optimum number to start working on it. Indeed the project group is a quite common instrument of management: what the New Biology proves is that it is a great deal more than an instrument of management.

The hunting band, the ten-group, is the foundation of every corporation, the base which supports the whole corporate edifice. No organization theory that does not rest on this base can ever make sense. Already I find myself impatient when I ask the size of a company or division and am given the answer in employed capital or turnover: it is the number of ten-groups that expresses the size of the management task, not the number of pounds or dollars, and it is the morale, effectiveness and output of groups, not of individuals, that is the proper measure of corporate health and strength. Every manager must know cases of men who collect glowing reports in one group and then leave it, perhaps for a solitary job, and dismally fail to live up to their reputation—or who have looked unpromising until they got into the right group and have turned into successes.

I have said that every corporation rests on ten-groups whether it realizes it or not: indeed the tendency to form such groups is so powerful that they sometimes form within but in opposition to the corporation, and there is plenty of evidence of this as well: it will be discussed later in the book. And if groups are going to form anyway, then clearly one of the prime tasks of the corporation is to get the largest possible number of effective groups all pulling in the same direction, all hunting on the corporation's behalf. But how can this be possible when a group has an absolute maximum of about fifteen, while a corporation employs tens or hundreds of thousands? And since ten people arbitrarily put together do not automatically form a band, when is a ten-group not a ten-group? How do ten-groups organize themselves internally? Which conditions make them flourish and which make them wither? All these questions have to be asked if we are to understand corporate organization in the light of this powerful male urge to band together for survival, and the succeeding chapters will attempt to answer them. The answers are a fusion of the knowledge I have acquired from the New Biology and other relevant sources, and the experience I have gained first-hand in large organizations and second-hand from friends and colleagues. The knowledge is still new and some of it is still being challenged by scientists of repute, and the experience is necessarily narrow and limited; the answers must therefore be taken as tentative. And there is a third and totally unscientific ingredient which I might as well admit: my own feelings, emotions, instincts and intuitions, in so far as I have been able to isolate and analyse them, as a group member, and group manager, and in particular when I have seen the same emotional irrational reactions provoked time and again by the same sort of stimuli in other group members. And is it so unscientific? If a member of a baboon troop could tell us how he reacted to different situations, what emotions were stirred up in his breast by the behaviour of enemies, rivals and friends, this would be evidence of a kind; if he could also report on many conversations with members of other troops and pass on to us what seemed to be the common elements of all their experience, we would take this into account as well. Why should not the self-observation of a past, and perhaps future, member of the subspecies *Homo sapiens corporalis* be equally valuable?

4   The Bond

ANYONE who has worked in a large organization knows
that ten people set down round a table do not automatically form a
ten-group; most of us have the scars to prove it. Obviously there are
certain conditions that have to be met before a group of people
turns into a united hunting band; but what are those conditions?
Or to put it another way, what are the chief obstacles by which the
corporation stops ten-groups from forming?

The first and most important of the conditions concerns mutual
dependence. I remember encountering a classic manifestation of
what happens if it is missing when I attended a meeting called by
the chairman of an engineering corporation, to which all the heads of
the operating companies were summoned. It was a natural situation
for a ten-group; there, round the table, were the eight or nine people
who between them carried the top-line authority of the whole group.
And yet nothing could have been further from ten-group behaviour,
though any poker player would have recognized the atmosphere at
once. Cards were being played very close to the chest; remarks
were studiously non-committal, and clearly framed for their effect
on the others, especially the chairman. The only subjects which
relieved the taciturn caution of the meeting were the trivial ones,
when suddenly everyone seemed to have a great deal to contribute
about what business organizations the corporation ought to sub-
scribe to at fifty guineas a year, or what quality of car should be
allocated to assistant works managers. It would all have been very
puzzling to me as an observer, if I had not at other meetings and as
a participant behaved in exactly the same way myself.

My meetings were at a much less exalted level, back in the days
when I was head of a department, but my motives were the same.
I knew that my department's interests and my own ego were better
served by keeping quiet about facts, figures and intentions which
might not meet with approval, or which might provoke the other
departmental heads to outcry or rivalry, or proof of their superior
awareness or achievement. I would happily talk about unimportant
subjects or general principles of policy, but my department's opera-

tions were my own business, and just like the executives of the
engineering company I intended them to stay that way.

Exactly the same thing used to happen (and no doubt still does)
at television programme meetings. The production team, the
behind-the-screens men, form a real ten-group, but it very rarely
includes the performers who appear on the box. The performers
build their own reputations as individuals, and resist suggestions
that might impair the personal image they are cultivating even
though it might be good for the programme as a whole, whereas
the production team is bound together by a collective interest in a
successful programme. Fleet Street magazine editors are in the
same position: their editorial group cannot happily include the
regular, named feature writers who are permanently conscious of
each article not just within the week's issue but for its contribution
to their personal reputations and careers.

All these group-inhibiting situations spring from the same root,
and that root is the root of the ten-group and of the survival of
many other species besides ours. The fact is that by our evolutionary nature we could not survive on our own. The group, in the
end, only survived as a group. We made our kill together, or we
returned home empty-handed; we ate together, or we all went to
bed hungry; we survived together, or we all died. The hunting
band was dominated by the need to survive as a hunting band, it
was composed exclusively of individuals who survived collectively
or not at all. No one could hunt in that band who had a private
meat supply to fall back on if the chase was too tiring, the ground
too rough, or the risks too great. What held it together was the
common objective, which meant survival for all if it was attained and
extinction for all if it was not. No wonder the production meetings
do not work with performers who can succeed while the rest fail,
or the editorial meetings with writers who can improve their reputations with a marvellous article in a disastrous issue. No wonder the
meeting of corporation executives was a failure when any individual
executive could raise his personal standing by producing marvellous
profits for his division while the corporation as a whole was declar-
ing a loss. The meeting, like my departmental meeting, was in fact
a threat to survival rather than an instrument of survival.

The first condition for a ten-group, therefore, is that there must
be a common objective, a single criterion of success by which all

succeed or all fail. If it is possible for one of the group to succeed while the others fail, he does not belong in the group and will impair its effectiveness if he remains in it. And so the ten-group must never be placed in a situation where someone outside distributes praise and blame, rewards and penalties, to the separate individuals who compose the group. The ten-group is rewarded or it is not rewarded: other ten-groups may be rewarded instead. But if it is to be rewarded, it must know from the start that the reward goes to the whole group without distinction—it must not be a prize for which individual members of the ten-group compete against each other. They, and only they, know which individuals really earned it. It does not signify whether the ten-group is composed of miners or salesmen or machine operators, or whether it is a management committee or a football team or a board of directors: if this condition is not met, the group is an assembly of individuals not a ten-group.

It is in fact immediately noticeable in committee meetings how the atmosphere changes when a subject is raised which enlists the co-operative emotions of the members instead of the competitive ones. The meeting I described in Chapter 1, when we discussed our trainees' applications for posts in a rival's group, was extremely united and co-operative despite its fundamental futility. Indeed, that sort of meeting should hardly ever be convened to discuss divisive topics: they can usually be sorted out separately, and the unifying purpose of the meeting is almost always damaged by them. The chairman should go through the draft agenda to see that every topic concerns the whole group collectively, and that they spend the whole meeting discussing the difficulties, dangers and opportunities that beset them all equally. Departmental litigation and treaty bargaining can be dealt with at other meetings for interested parties only—starting at 5.15 p.m.

It is perhaps worth establishing at this stage what an objective is, or rather what it is not. Telling a man to stand in front of a machine and pull and release a handle ten times a minute is not setting him an objective, and telling ten men to do the same at ten machines is not setting them a group objective. But if you tell them to produce a certain result, a certain number of drilled parts or quantity of coal or cars loaded on to the ship, by the end of the day or week or month, then you are setting them an objective, and you leave it to them to work out how to achieve it. In H. Estes's phrase, it is 'the difference between getting a janitor to keep the floors clean, as contrasted with sweeping routinely every half hour with a 20-inch broom, 10 strokes to the minute'.[1] The currently fashionable technique of Management by Objective goes into this question in some detail; and although it is fashionable it is also, if properly understood, very close to the heart of our kind of human organization: more than any other management theory it brings Corporation Man into line with his ancient ancestors.

A common objective does not, of course, entail working shoulder to shoulder; the hunting band was never a football scrum. Certainly they must meet regularly; the meeting when they all talk over the last hunt or plan out the next one is essential to the maintenance of any ten-group—it is the source of all the group's strength and unity. But just how often they come together will depend very much on the nature of the work: for some kinds of task they may have to foregather two or three times a day, while for others a week or more may elapse before they all come together again. Most of the time the members will very likely be working on their own—the solitary salesman on his rounds is the modern descendant of the solitary stalker creeping round up wind to drive the game into the trap— but they are members of the ten-group all the time. Sometimes a man will spend months on end away from the group, perhaps on the other side of the world; but as long as the bond is strong and he is devoting all his efforts to the group's objectives, they will feel he is just as firmly embedded in it as their fellow members in the offices down the corridor. He too, in his distant outpost, will be working not for his pay cheque or bonus or the greater success of the corporation, but for his ten-group back home, and his real reward is his knowledge (and their occasional acknowledgment) that his work is providing a vital element in their collective survival and success.

Once you have been part of a ten-group, there are several signs by which you can identify others when you drop in on them. The first one came to my notice very early in my B.B.C. days, and it was particularly obvious because our part of the television service had overflowed into a number of tall, narrow Victorian houses that stretched down Lime Grove from the studios. There were always builders about the place, trying to adapt parlours and bedrooms and attics to the fluctuating needs of television programmes: moving telephones, putting up shelves, knocking down walls, erecting partitions, taking filing cabinets up and downstairs, and composing an impromptu unfinished symphony of hammers, drills, saws, planes and breaking glass. At first I could see no logic or pattern to their activity, but one day it dawned on me that the successful programmes were always needing walls knocked down, separate rooms joined together, hatches and doorways built, and extra desks in existing offices, while the unsuccessful ones were having doors blocked, partitions put up, and desks moved out. In other words, the successful hunting bands were constantly trying to come together physically, to spend as much time as possible within sight and sound of each other, to share all the information and keep in constant collective touch with every move; while similarly there was a correlation between failure and the break-up of the hunting band into little producer-and-secretary caves where demoralized and fragmented couples lurked in lonely seclusion. Certainly it seems a common characteristic of ten-groups to keep popping into each other's offices, to go off to the club or canteen together, to seek contact and association far more frequently than corporation duties require. This goes with a great deal more laughter, and a great deal less formality; they are the first out of their jackets in the warm weather, they drop the polite corporation prefaces ('Would you mind if I ...', 'Could I just ... ', 'You don't happen to remember if ... ', 'I wonder if I could ... ') in their dealings with each other, their operational conversations are very brief, and after a period of time a number of words acquire special good or bad connotations that are not akcnowledged by the dictionary.

One consequence of this is that the more confident and successful a ten-group becomes, the harder it is for a newcomer to join it. This could be because they have hammered out so many principles and shared assumptions that there is a lot to learn, but usually it is something far deeper. The initiation ceremony is a ritual which crops up all over the world, from the most primitive tribes to the college fraternities (it is discussed at some length by Lionel Tiger in *Men in Groups*), and it surely had a survival value for the hunting band. To admit a newcomer was to take a big risk: if he was to bear his full weight, you would have to trust him with your life; and you do not put your life into another man's hands unless you have proved to yourself that they are strong and true. The risk is not as mortal in the corporation, but it is still big enough; and recruits to existing ten-groups find that it takes a long time to be accepted as a full member. There is no initiation rite, no ceremony of acceptance; but many who have joined could nevertheless put their finger on the action or project or special effort which finally proved to the others that they were fit to be admitted.

This resistance to newcomers looks from the outside like arrogance. Perhaps it is. But if so, it is one of the facets of high morale and as such essential to survival. Morale in corporations is regressive: at its highest, the identification badge of every member is the whole corporation—'I'm with General Motors', 'I work for Marks and Spencer's'. But it gradually works down, so that a British Leyland engineer building Jaguars is more likely to say 'I'm with Jaguars' than 'I'm with British Leyland'. We attach our self-importance to the highest unit we can feel proud of, though that unit can be very small. But however low the morale of the corporation, so long as the ten-groups are intact it can be rebuilt. Even if the maximum claim of an employee is, 'We've got a bloody good little design group, but what's the use if you're working for idiots?', there are still bricks there to start rebuilding with. Once those are gone, nothing is left. The Nazis were so conscious of this force that they constantly shifted the population of prisoners in concentration camps to keep these groups from forming or break them up when they had formed: if they left a prison population undisturbed for too long, groups formed and morale started to rise. There is a strange parallel today in the treatment of mental illness—doctors have found that in many cases a ten-group of patients can be helped collectively much more than by individual treatment.

The current preoccupation of personnel management in the corporations is the motivating and developing of individuals. This is in the best liberal tradition, stemming from the Romantic movement which began two centuries ago, and supported by Freud in his concern with the individual psyche. But perhaps the time is coming when we can forget the Oedipus complex and think of the hunting band; when we can get back beyond the personal self-indulgence and romantic individualism of Byron and Shelley, to the older disciplines of the group whose members depend on each other for survival, as they have for fifteen million years. If that happens, the managers of corporations will come to see the formation, support

4

and development of effective ten-groups as their major task to
ensure the morale and long-term future of their organizations.
It may be a difficult switch, but there is a powerful force operating
on their side: the ten-groups, as we shall see, are trying to form
themselves all the time.

5　The Instrumental Fallacy

FOR a long time I was puzzled by the comparative scarcity of ten-groups in industry and government and other large organizations. If they work so productively and give so much satisfaction, if there is a natural tendency to form these groups, and if all they need is a common objective, then why are they not the normal base of any corporation? And then it occurred to me to put it another way: why had it taken me as an employee and manager so long to cotton on to them? What was my own blockage? And in worrying out the answer to that one I isolated a basic fallacy in myself that for most of my working life had dominated and distorted my view of organization and management, and had dominated it all the more effectively for being one of the assumptions I was not aware I was making. The best name I can think of for it is the instrumental attitude to management, and I suspect that it still underlies the thinking of most managers, and causes more ulcers, unhappiness, disputes, inefficiency and waste than any other single idea.

An examination of this attitude reveals another of the conditions necessary to the formation of a ten-group. Someone who is a victim, or an example, of the instrumental attitude to management sees the people under him as the instruments with which he has to carry out his job, to execute his plans. Every man has a separate role, perhaps a separate skill, and it is his job as manager to use each one, as a good carpenter uses his saw and chisel, his plane and drill, to turn the idea in his head into a final result. In the same way he sees himself as one of the instruments of his superior manager, being used for the larger task as he uses his subordinates for the smaller one. He does not of course carry this sort of image or model consciously in his head, but it nevertheless corresponds quite closely to his attitude. It certainly corresponded to mine for most of my managerial life, and shows up most clearly in the way I set about the most exhausting and nerve-racking job I ever had to discharge in television: the job of directing a topical, last-minute, live sports news programme.

To recall those days in full detail would be an inexcusable exercise in nostalgic masochism and retrospective self-pity. To explain the task simply, I was given a running order by the editor and had two hours to turn it into a television programme. The material would all come in during the last hour, and it would include films, interviews, still photographs, charts, reports from remote studios; they had to be planned within the technical limitations and then carried out by cameramen, studio hands, designer, floor manager, lighting engineer, sound and vision mixer and several other technical staff. The junction point between the editorial conception and the technical execution was me.

I had not the slightest doubt about what I had to do: get hold of the running order at the earliest possible moment, turn it into a camera script, and then brief each of the key figures on what I required of him. I told the sound recordist what the microphone booms had to cover, and what other film or disc sounds would be needed, I briefed the vision controller on film sources and camera positions and movements and cuts, I told the designer where I needed chairs and tables, I explained to the floor manager about setting and striking caption easels and moving people on and off the set, I went through the plot with the lighting engineer. And then, after a sort of dummy rehearsal (if there was time), we went on the air and I directed the programme: I called out cues and cuts, gave standby warnings, passed messages to interviewers, prayed the film would be there in time, tried to reshuffle the order if remote sound lines went down, and emerged at the end of it all more completely drained and mentally exhausted than ever before or since in my life. The others did what I asked them to, looked compassionately on my suffering, and went home relaxed and untroubled.

All this took place before I started working on *Tonight*, and of course I can see now, fourteen years too late, what I should have done. The moment I got the running order I should have sat down not alone but with my five key technicians, and we should have worked it out together. Several times, in fact, the vision controller had suggested after the programme a better or easier way I might have done it: once or twice the floor manager had suggested a camera move that was not strictly his business: once, the sound recordist came up with a suggested line of script which was better than the one we had transmitted; but although I was appropriately commendatory, I never saw the point that was staring me in the face. The point was this: if we had all thought together about the whole programme, letting the designer talk about shots and the floor manager about sound coverage and the vision controller about scenery in a complete free-for-all, it would have done much more than take the tremendous pressure off me: it would have made a far better use of time and skills and facilities, and improved the programme; they would have enjoyed it much more, there would have been six people instead of one to see a crisis looming and work out its implications for each sector, and we would all have learnt much more about the whole business of television. Instead, because of my instrumental attitude, I managed to keep all those things from happening and nearly drive myself into a premature grave.

All this took place before Douglas McGregor described Theory X and Theory Y management in *The Human Side of Enterprise*.[1] But Theory X management—'People don't want to work, they don't want responsibility, they have to be controlled and directed and coerced'—was anathema to me even then. I would have called myself a really advanced and enlightened Theory Y man—'People want to be involved and trusted'; I sought to involve the technicians, told them what I could about the contents of the programme, asked if my camera script set them any difficult problems, congratulated anyone who produced a specially nifty bit of work, and thanked them all at the end. What more could an encouraging, involving, Theory Y manager be expected to do?

There was one other factor which I might plead as an extenuating circumstance: the B.B.C. itself was organized at least partly on instrumental lines. The editorial production team were of course all in the same department, but the technical staff were not; the designer belonged to one department, the floor manager to another, the vision and sound and lighting engineers to a third, and none of them to the same department as me; this was the operational consequence of the power enclaves I described in Chapter 2. As long as the picture and sound quality were good, it did not reflect on the technical staff if the programme as a whole was terrible or marvellous. But I know in my heart that this is only an excuse, though quite a good one; I operated the system in that way not because I was compelled to by the organization, but because I believed in it, just as the B.B.C. believed in it. Had I at that stage really wanted to form a group on an informal, personal and practical level I could have got a great deal closer to doing so without the system ever finding out. I did not do so because the instrumental fallacy was so deep inside me.

And of course it is not only the B.B.C.: indeed the B.B.C. represented the rule rather than the exception. There was a computer firm with three different types of staff who called on customers: the salesmen, to interest them in replacing or extending the configuration; the maintenance engineers, to repair and service the equipment; and the soft-ware representative, to talk about applications. All of them worked independently and came under different divisions, with the consequence that any experienced Corporation Man could foresee without being told: the maintenance man privately told the customer that the equipment was at fault, the salesman mentioned (off the record) that it would have been all right if it had been properly maintained, and the soft-ware representative excused all failures in application by implying that the salesman had claimed a capacity of performance which was beyond the powers of the equipment and programmes. If the three of them had been part of a single ten-group whose collective job was to keep the customer happy, they could have got to the root of the trouble amongst themselves and presented a united front to the customer and a true report to their company, instead of suggesting a state of civil war to the customer and each sending a selection of self-vindicating half-truths to their superiors. But the company embodied the instrumental attitude: they saw management as the business of making individuals responsible for functions, and not of making groups responsible for objectives (in this case keeping the customer happy); and consequently they provoked damaging instrumental behaviour.

Where did the instrumental approach to management originate? Does it go back to the basic division of labour for manufacturing? Did it begin in the craft guilds of the Middle Ages, perpetuated or revived in the craft unions of the last century and this one, where a man's skilled function as mason or carpenter was more important to him than his membership of a group that built houses? Or was it devised by managers early in the Industrial Revolution, who thought the only way to get industrial productivity from farm labourers was to give them a single function to perform and make sure they did it? Perhaps in those days, with an uneducated and industrially unsophisticated labour force and starvation as the alternative to employment, it achieved its limited objective. The basic fears of pain, hunger, thirst and death take precedence over all the other instincts until they are satisfied. But once they are quietened the others begin to clamour, and for many years now the fear of starvation has ceased to haunt the industrial worker, and he is no longer uneducated or industrially unsophisticated. Consequently the system, even if it achieved results then, is almost totally inappropriate now; yet the instrumental fallacy remains.

The reason the origin of the instrumental approach is puzzling and intriguing is not just that it so obviously does not work now, but that it cannot have worked even in early agricultural communities. If the crops were not sown at the right time, the community went hungry: there was no special store of grain for the ploughman who cut such beautifully straight deep furrows and so succeeded where the others failed. No one refused to help with the haymaking because he belonged to the poultry department. Certainly everyone will have had his own special skills — this is how groups work — but equally certainly they must have organized themselves for collective success. The ploughman's reward, like everyone else's, was a good harvest, not a citation for furrow-digging and an empty plate. Everyone knew the final objective and could contribute to the discussion on how to achieve it, even though he would have his own special role in the actual work.

And if it cannot have worked in an agricultural community, how much less can it have worked for the ancient hunting band? Perhaps it is only my deficient imagination, but I simply cannot picture a leader of such a band telling one member that his job was just to throw stones, and so he could shut up and stick to the job he was given, or saying to another that all he had to do was stalk, and he didn't have to worry about what the others were up to or what the actual plan was. I cannot see him assuming that it was his job and his alone to bring the kill back to camp, and that all the rest of the band were instruments provided to help him in his private task. I cannot see it because a band organized with one leader and nine or ten functional automata would be selected out as soon as the leader was killed; none of them would have the experience or the will to take over the planning and directing of the band after years as a functional instrument. I cannot see it because the hunting band apparently formed long before the critical enlargement of the human brain or the development of speech, and a hunt is such a fast-moving and rapidly changing situation that to control it instrumentally instead of by common understanding of the objective is beyond the power of man, let alone hominid or carnivorous ape. And privately I cannot believe it because it corresponds to nothing I have ever seen work in the ten-groups I have belonged to or dealt with. After all, it is known that when a pack of wolves has a large and strong elk or moose at bay, the leaders of the pack all put their noses together and somehow 'decide' whether to risk trying for a kill or to call it a day. It is known that the leaders of baboon troops come together when a difficult choice has to be made, and after their 'conference' they act in unison. How can we imagine a hunting band acting otherwise? It is as easy to picture one of them knocking off halfway through the hunt to attend a trap-building course, or another refusing to kill the prey as it came towards him because it was not his department's responsibility, or another remaining in his ambush long after the herd had disappeared over the horizon, because no one had countermanded his original instructions.

This, then, is as important a condition for forming a ten-group as giving them a group objective: that the whole group should be able to agree on the objective and decide for itself how it is to be achieved. The impulse to be involved in this way is actually a part of man's nature, a genuine instinct, even if it is not one of the more ancient and powerful ones; and to deny it is to deny a man a part of his nature.

The idea that a group should decide on, or at least concur with, its own objective, and then work out for itself how to achieve it, will hardly come as a surprise to anyone who has worked on a management team, or research group, or the board of a company. What is extraordinary is the readiness with which people who understand this principle intuitively in their own work deny it to their employees on the factory floor. But if it is a part of our nature, it applies just as forcefully there. Indeed, when people paint doom-laden pictures of the bleak future for the worker in a technological society, the industrial part never contains teams, only individuals pushing buttons; this prolonged solitude emphasizes what is most unnatural and soul-destroying in industrial work, as it has been for many years. Some psychologists have seen this deadly dull individual functional work as one of the major problems of industry, and have been studying ways of 'enriching' jobs. Some have tried rotating these functional jobs, so that a worker does several in a day, but they have found (not surprisingly) that several boring jobs are still boring. Their problem of course has been the instrumental view of management: as long as a man is seen as an instrument to perform a function, no real solution to the problem of job boredom is possible. The only approach is to take the hunting-band principle down to the factory floor, and give the ten-groups problems to solve and objectives to achieve at the physical manufacturing level, in exactly the same way that management teams approach the problems of planning and organizing and controlling the longer-term operations.

I always dislike Utopian recommendations of that kind when I read them in management books. It makes me long to hear a practical man speak out for the realities of industrial life and blast the theorist back into the study where he belongs. But in fact this is not Utopian or theoretical: it is the common practice in much of Japanese industry. To quote from *Modern Japanese Management*:

> One other feature of Mitsubishi Heavy Industries also typifies an important aspect of Japanese industry—the system of quality control, which centres essentially not on inspectors but on the workers themselves. In almost all Mitsubishi plants workers in each section meet together in their free time, possibly under the chairmanship of the foreman, and at the foreman's house, to discuss the way the job is done and how to do it better. Once this was done entirely without pay for the four to six hours a month that these discussions might take up—now Mitsubishi pays a token two hours pay a month in recognition of these efforts.[2]

If the Japanese have found a way of basing all their heavy industry on committed, participating ten-groups, that would go a long way to explaining their industrial achievement. But it is not only the Japanese. *Time* magazine (November 9th, 1970) reported how Polaroid now involve the workers in deciding which new machinery to buy, and how Donnelly Mirrors of Holland, Michigan, improved their results by turning shop-floor decisions over to employees (and also abolishing time-clocks and putting all workers on a salary). And there are sufficient examples of this approach in Rensis Likert's *New Patterns in Management* to take the concept of self-organizing, factory-floor ten-groups out of the realm of theory and putting it firmly into the world of practical experience.

Since the impulse to form ten-groups is instinctive, it is likely that if it is repressed in one direction it will burst out in another. The enormous burgeoning of social clubs, sports clubs, recreational clubs, residents' groups, amenity societies, professional associations and the like represents, in a large part, the impulse to form ten-groups which is not satisfied at work. Of course the function of these associations is necessary and useful in its own right, but the drive to form a committee, start the thing off, get it moving, plan its activities and keep it running—that is the ten-group impulse releasing itself. It is only a hunch, but I'd be willing to bet that few members of strong and successful corporation ten-groups are prominent members of outside committees.

This activity, of course, is usually harmless and often beneficial. The damage comes when the ten-groups start to form within the organization but in opposition to it. This can easily begin if the ten-groups are there, but are denied any say in what their objectives should be or how they should organize themselves to achieve them. They make an attempt at having some say: for instance the machine operators query the engineer's designs, and are told sharply to mind their own business and do what they are paid to do. Next day they receive a drawing with an obvious mistake in it: with dutiful glee they do exactly what they are paid to do and spend hours and hours machining an unusable part. This increases the mistrust and resentment and they are given even less of a hearing than before. So they meet and start airing grievances over their tea break. Meanwhile other groups are doing the same. Then a big grievance common to the whole factory is fixed on, a busy and energetic ten-group forms itself into a strike committee, and a familiar pattern begins to develop: the ten-groups which were not allowed to form and organize themselves to further the corporation's ends are forced into the next best thing—they form and organize themselves to frustrate the corporation's ends.

There is one particularly ironic consequence of this which instrumental management brings on itself, making the strike even more crippling than it need be: it is a result of the malignant cell.

The term 'cell' or 'cellular organization' is a good one, since it implies that the ten-group, or larger unit, contains the necessary framework of a complete organization in microcosm, as the biological cell contains the framework of the full organism. The Belfast factory groups which we saw in Chapter 2 were healthy cells in that sense. But instrumental management, by putting all the lathes in one place and all the presses in another and all the draughtsmen somewhere else, creates malignant cells instead of healthy ones. And so when the draughtsmen resent their instrumental treatment, they find grievances which unite draughtsmen. These can of course antagonize all the other cells and prevent the draughtsmen from getting the support they might need. However, being a malignant cell they do not need it—they can destroy the organism on their own. If a healthy cell strikes, its own total production is lost but the other cells can often stay at work. If all the draughtsmen strike— just as if all the drilling operators strike—there is precious little that the factory can go on producing.

Of course the strikers will have a sensible-sounding pretext— more money or longer holidays or shorter hours—but the reason for these broad aims is that they serve as a focus for all the resentments of everyone in the group or the factory, for all the smaller and more detailed causes of frustration of natural ten-group activity. The pretext is secondary; it merely sanctifies a much more primitive emotional outburst. And the reason it can become so prolonged and bitter, is that both the strikers and the corporation management find in each other one of the most powerful aids to forming, welding and sustaining a powerful ten-group and encouraging it to expand: they find an aggression focus.

So far we have talked about the ten-group as a form of hunting organization some fifteen million years old. But there is a much older instinct that events can sometimes call up to reinforce it: fear—the fear of a hostile attack by an enemy. And in very many species of living creatures there is a standard response to the threat of an attack: aggression. If a group, as opposed to an individual, is threatened, the response is group aggression which exerts a powerful binding force. Leaders throughout recorded history have known and used this power of threat by finding an aggression focus to bind a large group: the aggression focus can be Catholics, Huguenots, Jews, Blacks, Whites, communists, the management, the workers, or what you will—if people will believe they are a threat to survival, that is usually sufficient.

The classic case, in every sense of the phrase, of the inventing of an aggression focus is Cassius's speech to Brutus in *Julius Caesar* when he is enlisting him as one of the ten-group of conspirators to murder Caesar. He presents Caesar as the threat to everyone's liberty, the man who wants to become king and hold every other citizen in subjection, the object of fear and hatred, and he does it with a sensitive skill that would have made him a masterly shop steward. But nearly all leaders of ten-groups, whether consciously or subconsciously, keep an aggression focus firmly in the group's mind. Usually the aggression focus is harnessed to an abstract principle: not 'the newspaper that is competing for our readers', but 'the newspaper that is debasing the standards of honest journalism'; not 'the store that is trying to lure our customers away', but 'the store that deceives the public with cheap and flashy goods that fall to bits in a week'; not 'our rival car manufacturers', but 'the manufacturers who pay for their glamour gimmicks with the money they save on safety'. About four years ago I lunched with the chairman of a small company that was about to launch an electronic consumer product to compete with a product made by a rival firm, and I decided to test the theory, so I said to him, 'I imagine you tell your staff how disgraceful it is that the public should have this low-quality high-price product foisted on them by an inefficient giant corporation, and how people have a right to high sound quality at a price that makes it available to a much larger number?' I had never actually seen a jaw sag before, though I had read about it. He did not see how I could possibly have known that those were almost exactly the words he used. But in fact it had been clear from what he had said earlier that Phillips was the enemy and price and sound quality were the weapons, and the rest was a lucky guess based on the principle of the manufactured aggression focus.

It is obviously not very difficult to present the corporation to the labour force as a threat to survival. Logic, in a broad and general sense, may say that the corporation is the reverse—that it is the hope and cause of survival. But unemployment is the closest that most workers in industry can come to being in danger of not surviving, and the fear of unemployment can easily turn those who may terminate the employment into the aggression focus, with the attitude of 'Let's get everything out of them while we can.' Instead of being the focus of unity, the corporation becomes, as it were, a dangerous prey that can provide meat but also terminate life. It is not insignificant that the Japanese industrial climate, in which ten-groups of workers can be so closely involved in the success of a giant corporation, is also one in which it is almost unheard of to lay off employees or to sack managers.

The result, therefore, of the instrumental approach to managing large concentrations of men is to force the growth of a natural organization of ten-groups in opposition. The corporation then has two management structures—the official one it draws up and circulates, and the one on the factory floor that controls the work. There were many cases during the Second World War when in the prisoner-of-war camps officers carried no authority and corporals or sergeants emerged as the leaders everyone looked to. It is the same principle that was dramatized by J. M. Barrie in *The Admirable Crichton*, where a wealthy industrialist is wrecked on a desert island with his family and staff, and the butler Crichton emerges as the natural leader of the community. When natural ten-group activity is blocked and defeated by the management as a means of achieving the corporation's objectives, it is inviting the Admirable Crichtons to rise up and frustrate them.

6   The Leader

THE Macavity system of management is not widely discussed, nor is it advocated by any authority on personnel administration—chiefly because I have only just invented the term. It is, however, as common in most large organizations as the instrumental approach, and may perhaps be a consequence of it. I first encountered it in the B.B.C., though I have met it since in any number of corporations and government institutions. One year I was given a bonus in recognition of something or other, and I received (as well as the formal notification) a heart-warming letter from my director explaining why he had singled me out for such an honour. In the course of the next few days several of my superiors expressed their pleasure at the award, and each of them let it slip out that it was in fact owing to his initiative and efforts that I had been enriched by £40 (£24 13s. 8d. after tax). On each occasion I expressed the appropriate degree of gratitude. Then, some time later, I was left out of a general salary raise on the grounds that I had recently been given a special increase. The pretext was so flimsy and specious that I sought out my superior in a fever of righteous fury. He explained that it was not his doing at all. Nor was it his superior's, I discovered. Nor that of the personnel officer who notified me of the decision—he was merely the instrument of a greater (and apparently invisible) power. It was impossible to find anyone who had in fact given this ruling, or indeed whose hands had been soiled by it on its way down to me. Obviously there must have been one Judas Iscariot amongst all the Pontius Pilates, but I never located him—a sharp contrast with the occasion of my bonus when it had transpired that there was a Father Christmas in every office. It was then that I found that couplet of T. S. Eliot's going round and round in my head:

> You may meet him in a by-street, you may see
>   him in the square—
> But when a crime's discovered, then *Macavity's*
>   *not there!*

But the Macavity system is only a symptom of a much deeper reluctance to talk about leadership, or accept it, or admit that it happens. The corporation has fabricated dozens of elegant euphemisms to avoid saying that someone is a leader: management, administration, executive responsibility, line authority, reporting to, immediate superior—all of them are used to hide the unpalatable or shameful fact that there is something called leadership which people, actual named human beings, have to exercise. Why are we so embarrassed about it? Perhaps it is because the army seemed so preoccupied with it, and the present generation is reacting against its prolonged and enforced service in the army. Perhaps it is because the word enshrines an old-fashioned heresy that if a man had character and authority, all the other qualities like intelligence and scientific knowledge and market flair were unimportant. Or perhaps it is another aspect of romantic liberalism, whereby leadership is seen as an oppressive denial of human equality, with all its implications of curbing the will, restricting the freedom and insulting the individuality of other human beings. Whatever the reason, the taboo seems to belong exclusively to the upper reaches of the corporation; lower down there is no such delicacy, and though the term may vary between governor and chief and squire and gaffer and boss, the concept of leadership is clearly understood and unambiguously expressed.

This inhibition is a pity, not only because of the tremendous importance of leadership in all human affairs, but also because of the wide divergence of beliefs about the nature of leadership that open discussion would reveal. The textbooks have many descriptions of management, marketing, profit, and similar corporate abstractions, but descriptions of a leader are hard to come by. It is hardly surprising: any list of qualities that meant anything at all would be bound to exclude someone who had succeeded in leadership and include many who had failed. This complexity came home to me when I was invited to speak at the biographies presentation at the Administrative Staff College at Henley. Each of the six syndicates on the sixteen-week residential course had to study, discuss and write a paper about a famous historical figure, and then each syndicate chairman had to make a speech about him at the presentation. The subjects chosen were Newton, Pepys, Rhodes, Cromwell, Lenin and Marlborough. I looked at the list in dismay.

What on earth could I contribute that would be remotely original or important on such widely known characters, or that had a hope of interesting sixty sharp-minded successful managers in their middle thirties who had been investigating them in detail for weeks? And then it occurred to me that it would be possible to look at them all as if they were candidates for the vacant post of chief executive in a company under my control. As well as giving a different perspective, it would be an interesting study of the nature of the leader. I do not know if the audience profited from the discourse, but I at least found it an intriguing exercise.

Newton was a wash-out from the start. There was no evidence that he had ever led any group of people in a successful enterprise: on the contrary, he was spiky, proud, obstinate and prone to vicious feuds—the kind of researcher who is only really happy in his laboratory but who needs approbation and admiration lavished on him by the chairman to keep him with the corporation. All too many corporations would assume that the only way was to pay him more money, and the system would then force them to take him away from actual research and appoint him head of the research division, which would be a disaster for him, for the corporation, and for science. The wiser ones would leave him at his bench, pay him more than the chairman (and make sure he knew it was more than the chairman) and invite him to lunch regularly in the directors' dining-room. He might be one of the greatest geniuses in history, but as a leader he would not even be short-listed.

It needed only a little more reflection to see that Pepys would not be short-listed either. Although he was a top civil servant, the secretary of the navy, he never seemed to have any urge to seize or shape events. Like so many successful Corporation Men, he was constantly trying to get himself noticed, hoping to get jobs when they became vacant, attaching himself to powerful men and glowing with spaniel-like pleasure when they gave him a pat on the head. Certainly he was likable, and had an eye for essentials and a powerful grasp of administration and its problems, but he was in no sense a leader; he had the mind of a clerk and the soul of a courtier.

It was equally obvious that Rhodes, Cromwell, Lenin and Marlborough would have to be on anybody's short list, and the moment you started to consider them in detail you came up against the difficulties of finding any common thread, of isolating any single quality of which you could say, 'This is the essence of leadership.' Rhodes, for instance, had one characteristic which is the hallmark of a certain kind of leadership: it is sometimes called vision, and in his case it was the specific vision of his own destiny to unite the divided. He started with the uniting of a lot of South Africa's divided diamond companies into De Beers; then, having made his fortune, he turned to the wider task of uniting the separate African territories into a solid hunk of British Empire from Cairo to the Cape. But this kind of vision seems dangerously tied up with the ego of the visionary, and resistance (in this case Kruger's) calls forth intemperate actions in response. It also makes one question whether great size and unity really serve any useful purpose except that of enlarging the ego of the man who creates it. Many corporation mergers have prompted the same question. Hitler and Napoleon had a similar vision, and so did Rockefeller and Carnegie. The great danger comes when the desire to grow at any cost becomes compulsive, when expansion reaches the stage of addiction. My feeling about Rhodes was that he would be marvellous for restructuring a Balkanized industry based on small family businesses, and I would like an equity stake in his operations from the start; but I would not want him in my organization. The risks would be too great, and there would be every chance that the organization would end up as his instead of mine.

And then, for a contrast, look at Cromwell. Whereas you might think there was some quality in Rhodes that you could have picked out from the start—he was busying himself in the diamond fields in his twenties and had made De Beers and his fortune at thirty-five—I do not see how anyone could have spotted the young Cromwell. Without the Civil War he would surely have lived and died an unknown country squire. He did not make any national mark until he was well over forty, and yet within a few years he had risen from a cavalry officer to the absolute head of a powerful nation, and was able to impose his own will on it with a breathtaking power and confidence. On the other hand, he was hopeless at delegating. A wonderful man to take over a vast run-down business, sack the management, restructure the organization, and make it vigorous and profitable again, but not the man to run it once it was on its feet.

5

And what about Lenin? For a revolutionary leader, his behaviour was quite inexplicable. He spent most of his life outside
his country; when the fighting was going on in 1905 and 1917 he was
not in the thick of it but lurking out of sight; he split the Marxist
movement over points of principle: yet he emerged as head of the
government of Russia. It is easy to see the qualities of a leader in
Stalin, or for that matter in Trotsky, but Lenin up to 1917 looks
like a writer, the ideas man of the Revolution. I saw him much
more as a passionate management consultant who had written any
number of papers on corporate restructuring and suddenly found
himself as chairman being told to get on and do it. I might give him
the leadership of a complex project that required energetic dedication, but I would not let him anywhere near the complex realities
of long-term corporate management.

Only one common factor seemed to unite these three disparate
leaders: each one professed to act in the name of an idea greater
than himself. Whether it was the British Empire, the Bible, or
International Communism, it provided a unifying ideal for the
faithful and a means of turning anyone who opposed or resisted
the leader into a collective aggression focus. But as soon as I came
to consider the final candidate, that last thread snapped. I had never
seriously doubted that I was going to give the job to Marlborough.
He was every manager's idea of a leader; he had been in the corporation (the British Army) from the beginning, was tremendously
skilful and made a success of every job he was given, shot up the
management hierarchy on his merits (lieutenant-colonel at twenty-
five, lieutenant-general at thirty-eight), stood up for his English
managers when the new chairman from the Dutch company came
over and started giving executive jobs to his friends, never lost a
battle or failed in a siege, was respected by his officers and loved by
his men, and yet for all his dynamic and thrustful leadership he
worked diplomatically with overseas allies and (up to a point)
tactfully with politicians at home. But so far from being impelled
by a single ideal, he actually switched sides from James II to William
of Orange at the critical moment for the control of the corporation,
and tilted the balance. He had no grand vision of Britain in Europe;
he simply saw a French competitor who had to be kept in check,
and he outmanoeuvred him time and again.

It would have been reasonable to take these four widely different yet indisputable leaders as proof that the gift of leadership, if there is such a thing, is subject to nothing except the purest accident. But a moment's reflection on the nature of the hunting band makes it appear most unlikely that the leader's emergence can have been left completely to chance. It is much more probable that there is some evolutionary force at work, since clearly our species could never have survived without a leader for every hunting band; and if we reflect for something more than a moment, the logic of the hunting band can illuminate several aspects of leadership which might otherwise remain obscure.

It goes without saying that a leader is a prerequisite for a successful hunt. The prey moves so quickly and unpredictably, the situation changes so rapidly, that there cannot be a debate, a conference, a vote or an adjournment; nor can there be two different courses pursued simultaneously, nor can each individual be left to his own devices. The decision must be made instantaneously and be binding on the whole band. In fact all animals that hunt collectively have a pack leader, and current observation of our own species shows that every ten-group, every army section, football team, board of directors, committee and cabinet has adapted the ancient instinctive need for a pack leader, whether under the name of captain or corporal, foreman or chairman, to contemporary use.

So much is obvious. It is less obvious how the ancient hunting band decided which actual individual member should become leader. But it can be stated with some certainty (and many corporations would do well to reflect on this) that it did not advertise the vacancy and interview the applicants. The leader was a member of the hunting band, and if he was killed another member of the band took over: to evolve a leader seems to be instinctive behaviour, and corporation managers who worry about appointments of leaders for ten-groups are all too often wasting their time and sometimes playing with fire. A ten-group that has a group objective cannot help evolving a leader—it does not need to be told by some outside superior agency. The best such an agency can do is to confirm what the ten-group had already decided; if it appoints a different member from the ten-group's own choice, the result will be unhappiness for the leader appointed, the resentment of the 'natural' leader who has been passed over, the contempt of the whole group for those who made the appointment, their alienation from the corporation, and the impairment of their effectiveness. All too often the result is an ineffective new foreman and an effective new shop steward. It is interesting that a survey of the U.S. Army in Vietnam quoted by Lionel Tiger found that a major source of tension within individual troops 'arose from the fact that soldiers could have no hand in choosing their officers or in moving to another group if they could not respect their current leaders'.[1] The corollary of this is that if you want to form a ten-group you do not have to appoint the leader: you bring the people together, give them a stimulating and demanding group objective, and within a short time you and they will know who the leader is. This is not to say that you cannot appoint a leader, or that you cannot impose an outside leader on an existing group; only that you cannot hope to do better than the group would do on its own. Speaking for myself, if a leader has to be chosen I would rather pick him first and then let him form a group than try to pick a leader for a group that was already running successfully. Either way, the essential point is that it is natural for every ten-group to evolve and replace its own leader, and that any other method must be approached with great caution and in the knowledge that it is not the natural way.

But how did the primitive hunting band decide which member was going to be boss? The New Biology provides a very quick answer to that question: status-dominance. The urge to dominate the other members of the group, to be number one, or failing that number two or three or four or five, is common to almost all social species—birds and fish as well as mammals. It has powerful survival value for the group: when there is internal competition for survival—famine, for instance—it is the weakest, the lowest in status, who go to the wall, and the strongest who survive to breed. In some species this is reinforced sexually—females will mate only with high-status males. It is not simply physical strength that determines status—strength of will, determination, courage and what you would call 'character' in humans all contribute to this animal-dominance package. Status in the corporation is such an important and fascinating subject that a chapter will be devoted to it later in the book: for the moment it is sufficient to say that you cannot read about animal status and work in a corporation without being aware of its living force and relevance every hour of the managerial day.

But there is a snag about this simple status-dominance as an explanation of how our species got and still gets its leaders. It was evolved and refined over maybe a hundred million years for the survival of a social species. But—and this is the rub—not for the survival of a hunting species. Status-dominance in social animals serves chiefly to preserve the internal order of the group: the qualities that number one has in greater abundance than any of the others are strength, determination, courage and will-power. These qualities will also, as we have seen, make him the leader of the defence if the group is attacked, but its ordinary day-to-day function is essentially inward-looking. The leader of a troop of monkeys or apes is selected by his ability to beat up any other member of the troop who challenges him, and this method of selection is likely to produce the best individual to lead a defensive fight against an aggressor.

Hunting, however, is another matter, and to lead a successful hunt the simple primate status-dominance is not enough. The number one of a hunting species is selected by an external as well as an internal test. Can he lead the hunt to a successful conclusion? Can he regularly bring home the bacon, or the venison? Strength and courage and will-power are still important, but they are no longer all-important, and if the number one in terms of those qualities is completely unable to plan the surrounding or trapping of the prey, is utterly incompetent at choosing which antelope in the herd to go for, and keeps stalking leopards under the illusion that they are impala, then the hunting band he leads will hurtle to extinction all the more rapidly for being so firmly and decisively led. But if number two in the dominance order turns out to have a genius for knowing where the game is and how to kill it, then a hunting band which learns to resist number one's leadership and follow number two will eat and survive and breed. After all, they are something like nine against one, so although number one can by definition beat up number two, he cannot beat up the whole of the rest of the band together. Or, if they cannot depose him, individuals can detach themselves and join a better-led band.

In *The Ineffective Soldier*, a study of the U.S. Army, Eli Ginzburg writes: 'A soldier knew that he might lose his life unnecessarily because of the lack of skill or judgment of his superior, and there was little, if anything, that he could do to prevent it.

There was much talk about men who had shot or planned to shoot their officers—an indication of the tension that prevailed.'[2] This was dramatically confirmed when the Pentagon admitted that in 1970, forty-three officers were believed to have been killed by their own men. One veteran revealed to a reporter that he had killed his C.O. 'All he cared about was his goddam missions, and not the men in his platoon. We had more combat experience than he did, and he kept putting us into situations where we knew we could get killed for no good reason. It was him or us, so several of us agreed that next time we were in action we would shoot him, and we did.' (*Daily Mail*, May 20th, 1971.)

This (and many similar stories from other armies) suggests very powerfully that the hunting bands, the ten-groups which we now belong to, are the result of millions of years of tension and inter-action between the social structure of the ape troop and the logic of the wolf pack, and both are still operative within us: that when we turned from vegetarians into hunters a second selector, hunting success, came to sit at the table with the first, status-dominance, to decide which teams should go on into the next round. School provides a good illustration: small boys sort out status in a very simple animal way—playground dominance is purely an internal pecking order determined by strength and determination. But there is little if any correlation between number-one boys in the play-ground and those who go on to become number-one men in the corporation or the community; playground dominance carries no guarantee that the dominant will be able to lead projects to a success-ful conclusion when he matures and joins a hunting band. Many highly successful leaders were inconspicuous at school—they were chosen for high office by the second selector after getting no more than average marks from the first.

This does not of course mean that we have to reject the concept of the 'natural' or 'born' leader, the man whom other men follow from the playground to the grave. There is no reason why high status-dominance and outstanding success in leading the hunt should not co-exist in a single individual. But it does mean that leaders, in our species, can keep their number-one position when in a simple dominance-led species they would have been deposed. So long as we believe that they are more likely than any other member to lead the hunt to success, we support their leadership even against a more personally dominant individual. And the reverse is also true: a highly dominant personality cannot maintain his leadership if he starts failing to produce results which others can achieve. But when both kinds of leadership act in unison, the combination has a special force and magnetism. The status-dominants who are also successful leaders of the hunt can become hero-figures: Nelson and Wellington, Napoleon and Hitler, Alexander and Julius Caesar are among the most famous examples. The danger-point comes when the demands of their status-dominance conflict with the demands of the collective enterprise and leads to an ego-assertive action (like the invasion of Russia) which is destructive of the group—and is all the more likely to be pursued because of the natural leaders' power to impose their will on their subordinates by force of personality rather than force or argument: this is still one of the best routes to destruction for a corporate board of yes-men dominated by a powerful chairman. But as long as the two impulses act in unison they are a powerful combination.

All the same, the irresistible born leader, the one who must at all costs dominate any group he belongs to, is comparatively rare. For practical purposes, the leader is the one who evolves from the group because he is the one they think gives them the best chance of survival and success. Status-dominance is bound to be one of the factors that will influence them, but only one. If survival depends on strength and physical courage, the group will evolve one leader; if circumstances change and the emphasis shifts to knowledge and low cunning, it may evolve another. You may, on the football field, happily accept the leadership of a man who, at work, equally happily accepts your leadership: it is the needs of the task, not pure animal dominance, which tip the scales. Lenin, had he died in 1916, would be known to history as a fanatical Marxist agitator and pamphleteer. Cromwell, if he had died aged forty, would be known as an obscure East Anglian member of Charles I's parliaments: but radical changes of the political environment suddenly created completely new survival tasks, and Lenin and Cromwell were evolved by their groups as the most likely to lead the rest to success in the new situation. A radical change in the market has the same effect on corporations and industries: when the pop revolution struck the fashion and entertainment business in Britain in the 'sixties, it produced not only the Beatles and the Rolling Stones,

Mary Quant and Carnaby Street, it also produced a crop of high-powered executives in their early twenties, and several millionaires of under thirty.

Nevertheless, once status and hunting success have evolved their choice, another factor begins to operate. You can call it practice or experience, but its effect is to teach the evolved leader the job of leading. Leadership is a skill which, like all others, has to be learnt by doing it, and sometimes doing it wrong. Once an individual has been evolved as leader in one situation, he has an extra qualification next time in that he has done the job of leading before: equally those who have the experience of being led become less likely to contend for the role of leader next time. And it is more than just a skill or a technique: in time it becomes a role which out of custom and habit the non-leaders do not seek and the leaders expect and accept. Consequently leadership can be created as much by the empty chair at the head of the table which the others do not want to fill, as by a struggle for the throne. All the same, someone with no experience of or taste for leadership could in some circumstances find himself the natural leader: for instance in a group of much younger and equally un-dominant people where his knowledge and skills were the key to collective success.

The essential point is that leadership is not a quality at all. High status-dominance is an innate quality; skill and experience and the habit of leadership are acquired qualities; but leadership itself is a relative term. A man becomes a leader in relation to a specific group and a specific task: once he has evolved from his ten-group as its leader he can begin to learn the job, and he may go on doing it for the rest of his life, but the basis of his leadership is always that he is the evolved leader of his group. All too often the corporation gets itself into desperate trouble by not endorsing the evolved leader: it thinks it is choosing between one candidate and another, whereas in fact it is choosing between order and disorder. Nevertheless, the problem is sometimes a difficult one, as we shall see when we look at the way Corporation Man evolves his leaders.

7　When is the Leader
not a Leader?

MOST executives and senior managers will talk freely about the difficulty of selecting people to fill important jobs: how hard it is to know if you are right, how heavy the responsibility towards the man selected, the men rejected, and the corporation in which they all serve, and how grave the consequences of a bad choice. Further powerful proof of the depth of corporate concern is provided by the number of firms that earn a handsome income by specializing in management selection, and in the length of the reading list the library gives you if you ask for information. There is however another aspect, which managers talk about less freely: the enormous satisfaction and enjoyment which the selection process gives them.

Think of it: anyone who ever has to be interviewed for a job knows the trepidation and awe with which he approaches the ceremony, almost as if it were a dress rehearsal for Judgment Day. He knows the special care he takes over his appearance, the questions he goes through in his mind, and above all the nearly mystical powers he attaches to the man sitting behind the desk. If you have joined the corporation as the result of such a ritual examination, it is impossible ever to think of yourself as the complete equal of the man who interviewed you; even if you subsequently become senior to him, always at the back of your mind is the memory of that first unequal encounter, and you find he splits into two men in your imagination—two quite different men, but both equally real. So it is not surprising that the converse is also true: if you are the man behind the desk, you taste something of the power that ancient kings exercised over their suppliant subjects. Of course you are merely looking for the best man for the job, and it is just part of the day's work, and it is all completely objective and dispassionate; but there is no getting away from the fact that you have power over someone else. You are in a position to confer wealth, honour and status on one of a number of other people, and they all know it: this power to confer status is absolute proof of your own

73

status-superiority, which each candidate implicitly confirms. If he does not, if he behaves as if his status were higher than yours, that is the end of him: there is no more certain way of avoiding selection. Deference and submissiveness are not often listed as job qualifications, but those who do not exhibit them during the interview rarely get beyond it.

The consequence is that under the cloak of a dispassionate appraisal by question and answer, irrational judgments are being made on the basis of qualities which are not mentioned in the job description. Sometimes the interviewer is trying to impress the interviewee; often he is trying to get his agreement to propositions, rather than discover his views; almost always he is seeking acceptance of his authority and confirmation of his status. Many personnel experts have been appalled by the problems of selecting the right candidate in such an absurd situation, and have tried to put the process on a scientific footing. They lay stress on establishing in advance the qualities the job demands and conducting the interview to examine how the candidate rates under each of a number of relevant headings. One of them described the normal corporation interview to me as 'about as scientific as a couple of dogs sniffing each other's arses'. Their writings on the subject, though lacking that vividness of expression, are a model of enlightened objectivity and systematic common sense, and the villain of the piece is the sniffer, the old-fashioned, unscientific manager who 'can tell without any of this mumbo-jumbo' when he has found the man he wants. And yet the flaw in the 'scientific' interview is at least as grave and probably graver.

When I first reached a managerial position in which I had to appoint people to vacancies, I was convinced that one of the greatest barriers to corporation justice was the selection of people for jobs on the grounds (probably never admitted) that the interviewer liked them. I was determined that I at least would always pick the best candidate irrespective of any irrelevant personal feelings. That resolution fell at the first fence. My very first vacancy produced a candidate who by any objective measurement was noticeably better than the others, but I just could not see myself working with him without a harsh, grating sensation somewhere in the region of my colon. Nor could I see any of the rest of the team taking to him. There was nothing in the needs of the job or in his qualifications to exclude him, but all the same it simply was not possible for me to appoint him. At the time I thought that my resolution had weakened unforgivably, and I had better abandon any hopes of being a modern scientific manager. I now realize that wisdom had triumphed over intellect.

Qualifications and job descriptions would be all very well if we were appointing solitaries, but if the candidate is to join an existing ten-group then all the appropriate qualifications in the world will not counterbalance the gut feeling that he will not fit in, that he is not 'our sort'. You can try and describe 'our sort' in objective terms, but in the end you are merely rationalizing the irrational. The only way to tell is by whatever corresponds to the canine sniffing procedure, and if you do not like the smell there is no point in going any further. Nor should you try. Of course if 'our sort' describes a type extraneous and irrelevant to the task of the group, if it is based on social or religious considerations when the task is electronic circuit design, then the group is giving itself an unnecessary handicap, and narrowing its area of choice. But mostly 'our sort' is related to the sort of people who have succeeded at the task as members of the group, and although other sorts may be just as good they will not work in that group.

All the same, this irrational, instinctive feeling about people has no validity unless they are actually going to work in your own ten-group. If they are not, it is liable to lead to very grave errors. Few top managements are aware how well most groups know who ought to be given the job, and how strongly they feel about it. Frequently it is not the candidates but the interviewer who is on trial—the candidates are the questions, and since, as we have seen, it is in the nature of groups to evolve their own leaders, everyone below the job level knows the right answer: only the interviewer is in doubt. I have known a department meeting to break into spontaneous applause when their new department head's name was announced— and they were applauding the executive who had chosen correctly just as much as their former colleague who had now been so justly elevated and dignified.

I also remember a group board being exercised for months over the question of the successor for the departing managing director of a subsidiary. Should it be the technical director or the director of administration? The technical director had been with the company all his life and was one of the country's leading experts on their rather specialized manufacturing techniques, but he had a rather narrow outlook. The director of administration had joined only five or six years before, but he had run his own small family company before that. He was a much more sophisticated manager, well versed in management skills and with a much wider view of the company's problems and the larger financial context in which it operated. The management authorities would not hesitate for a moment—the director of administration must have the job; you do not appoint a man for what he has done in the past but for what he will do in the future. But it would have been a very bad appointment. The technical director was the evolved leader of the company; his brilliance at the business on which the company's survival depended was a legend: to pass him over would be not only a slight to him but also a proof that the group board did not understand what the company was about, and a clear indication that success and preferment were no longer related to the ability to lead the hunting band to a successful kill. Management courses, not successful products, were to be the route to the top in future. The group board, however, made the right choice. The technical director was given the job, the admitted skills of the director of administration were at his disposal, and once he was made to look at the company as a whole and not merely as a design-and-manufacturing entity he started to develop the new survival skills that the new objective demanded. It reminded me of a shrewd observation by my squadron commander during my army service. I was objecting to his proposal to promote a corporal to sergeant, and he asked me why. I said that he just didn't look like a sergeant to me. His reply ought to be hung on the wall of every manager's office: 'No corporal ever looks like a sergeant until he's got three stripes on his sleeve.'

One of the chief reasons why a mistake was avoided in the case of the two directors was that a group of people, not a single omnipotent interviewer, discussed the appointment before it was finally made by the chairman. This is one of the best safeguards I have encountered. The B.B.C. always has at least three, and usually four or five, people to sit together as an appointments board when posts of any importance have to be filled. I am sure that most of us who appeared before these boards were more inclined to believe that justice was done than we would have been in a one-against-one interview, and this impression was reinforced for me when I started to sit on appointments boards myself. I remember once having more or less written off a rather dull and uncommunicative candidate who had a lowly job despite good paper qualifications, when someone asked him why he had applied for this post. Still uncommunicative, he said, 'Ah, that's the sixty-four-thousand-dollar question.' And then a senior colleague of mine who had not yet asked him anything chipped in. 'No, it's not,' he said. '*This* is the sixty-four-thousand-dollar question: why haven't you done better? Here you are with all these certificates and things, and you're not much more than a clerk. Why?' I was about to be profoundly embarrassed, but the young man just grinned with what seemed like relief. It was as if a barrier had suddenly been swept away, and he became relaxed and informative. 'Do you know, that's what I keep asking myself,' he replied, and continued in such a convincing and genuine way that we were interviewing a quite different candidate, who in fact got the job and was a sensational success. From that I learnt more than the fact that it is unfair to a candidate to avoid asking him what you think is an awkward question; I also learnt (since I would certainly have appointed someone less suitable) that a small ten-group is a far better instrument for appointments than the solitary interviewer.

In an ideal world, or an ideal corporation, appointments and promotions would be no problem. Leaders would evolve from their groups and everyone would know. It would only be a question of officially confirming an accepted reality. As the years went by the younger groups would take the place of older ones, or younger leaders would take over from their seniors, and the corporate succession would evolve naturally. No newcomers would have to be appointed except at the lowest level of primary recruitment. Specialists might be brought in from outside, but not as leaders, even though they might evolve into leaders later; every group would be led by the best man for the job. But it must be admitted that in real life there are occasions when there is no evolved leader, or when the evolved leader is not up to the job. (These occasions are much rarer than most corporations realize—I would guess that bad appointments through ignoring the evolved leader are at least ten times as common as bad appointments through promoting him—but they happen.) Groups can fail, morale can drop, the task can grow or change beyond any member's capacity, a leader can quit and leave a successor who lacks the will or qualifications to take over, a leader may evolve but fail when things get tough—there are many reasons why, even in the best corporation, a ten-group may find itself with a member in charge who is in no sense the leader except on the corporation's organization chart.

The first question, of course, is how do you tell that this has happened? When is the leader not a leader? In schoolboy fiction it is easy: a leader is anyone who is 6 ft. 6 in. tall, well built, with fair, wavy hair and steady blue eyes. This, however, quickly proves to be an unreliable criterion: the fact is that since leadership is relative, it is in the leader's relationship with his ten-group that you look for the signs of leadership, or their absence: and there are certain types of leader-behaviour which must have been essential to survival from the earliest days of the hunting band.

Fundamental to every real leader is the maintenance of his own authority. A hunt demands a single, unquestioned leader, and without it, the band is doomed. There can be any amount of criticism and argument on most matters within the group, but there cannot be any argument about who is the leader. That is the surest recipe for failure, and any leader who cannot make a decision until he has 'talked to the group', meaning got the approval of one or more members of the group whom he cannot compel, but only ask to comply, is not the leader. Of course any leader will often want to talk to his group before giving an answer: but that is visibly different from having to defer to their will if it conflicts with his. It is therefore basic leadership to come down violently on any attempt to challenge the leader's authority. His decisions can always be challenged; but not his right to decide.

As well as his authority within his ten-group, the leader preserves with equal force his authority over his ten-group if it is challenged by someone outside. This is normal number-one behaviour in almost all social species. Any leader who willingly lets a superior within the corporation erode that authority is not a leader. This authority is eroded whenever members of the group have to seek authority from someone other than the leader to carry out the group's task; whenever the leader has to defer to an outside judgment on how tasks shall be allocated within his group; whenever the leader's orders to his group are countermanded from above; or whenever someone from above praises a group member for something the leader has criticized or criticizes him for something the leader has praised. If a superior wants to talk to one of the group on group matters, a leader will often start to twitch and insist on his right to be present, just as he insists on written communication to the group being made through him.

A consequence of this is that the leader will never excuse the group's failure by blaming, to his superiors in the corporation, a member of his group. The reverse side of authority is responsibility: if the leader has authority over the group, then he is responsible for what it achieves. He accepts that the group's failure is his failure. If the group is praised for success, he may single out one member as having done something meritorious, but he will not pretend (except within a convention of modesty) that the real credit belongs to anyone except the leader who trained him and set him to the task, and the same is true of blame for failure. But this personal acceptance of blame is for outward show. There is not and cannot be any such reticence within the group towards the member who let the others down. The leader is not particularly sensitive about people being easily hurt, unless it impairs their performance: the success of the hunt overrides all personal considerations, and anything that really threatens it will call forth a powerful rebuke, probably in front of the rest of the group; the leader of the primitive hunting band did not have a private office, and anyway it is important for the whole group to see what will not be tolerated. These rockets are never pleasant to receive, but if they are justified they increase respect: the admiring glee with which people recount to each other how Charlie hit the roof when he found out what had been going on is a sure sign that there is a leader around. Equally, however loyal the leader may be to his group (and that sort of loyalty is a characteristic of leaders), he is prepared to discard any member who is a permanent liability. Age, length of service and loyalty may condition where he is discarded to, but if any member is or becomes by his nature (as opposed to occasional and curable mistakes), a hazard to survival, then his continued presence in the hunting band cannot be tolerated—or, to put it in evolutionary terms, the bands which tried to carry passengers on the hunt were selected out, and we are descended from the ones which discarded them.

The third jealously protected area is authority over the means of achieving the objective. Of course it can be discussed and questioned in advance, but once a leader has said how it shall be done he will passionately resist any instruction from on high to do it differently. A change in objective as a result of circumstances is another matter — it is one of the hazards of the chase and a leader's task is to adapt to changed circumstances; but if the objective is unchanged and a superior simply imposes a different plan from the one the leader has given his ten-group, this calls forth the same aggressive response as the other authority infringements and challenges to leadership.

You will also begin to suspect a leader who asks a superior to sort out for him a dispute within his ten-group. The 'magistrate' function of leadership is as important to survival as the personal authority in which it is rooted. A quarrelling and divided band will let the quarry escape, and a leader who does not instinctively stop the quarrels and settle the disputes on his own is not a leader. It is also suspicious if he modifies his plans 'because so-and-so doesn't get on with so-and-so'. This sort of consideration makes survival harder, and as far as the leader is concerned they get on or get out.

The real leader is also accepted by his ten-group as the final arbiter of status. Just as a band cannot hunt successfully if there are constant arguments about who does what and how they do it, so it cannot tolerate constant status squabbling. In a good ten-group every member knows his own status exactly, and knows that the leader confirms it. If a junior member tries to assert higher status than the group accords him, for instance by arguing not from a fact base ('actually it started in 1964, not 1966') but from a status base ('I'm just telling you it won't work'), he is likely to be sat on by the leader very quickly. Any evidence that members of the group have a different view of the pecking order from the leader's is a sign that they will not be around for long, or that there is something wrong with the leadership.

It is, however, only the people above who need to look out for the signs that someone is occupying the position of leadership without exercising the function. Those immediately below are only too well aware of the fact: but they are also aware that the hardest and most thankless task in a corporation is to tell the higher managers in the corporation that your immediate boss is no good. In the first place, they appointed him, so you are implicitly criticizing their judgment. In the second place, maintenance of corporate authority demands that they take his word against yours. In the third place, no one much wants to employ the sort of person who is liable to go behind his back to a superior and vilify him, even (or especially) if that person is telling the truth. In the fourth place, your motives are bound to be suspected. In the fifth place, the best policy for the boss on the defensive is to destroy the character and credibility of the informer. And yet survival demands that the band must have the best leader. So what happens?

Usually, as you would expect in any hunting band, a collective challenge develops under the alternative leader. Perhaps the official leader will resist the challenge: it may be the crucial trial of strength from which he emerges for the first time as a real boss, and it may be a part of the process by which our species tests and forms its leaders. Or he may manage to hold on not from natural authority but from the authority the corporation gives him, in which case it is likely that the rebel chief and perhaps some of the others will walk out dramatically or detach themselves quietly, depending on their temperaments. But very often the natural leader takes over in fact, while the official leader remains at the head in appearance. From the outside, the official leader looks like the boss. It says he is on his door and in the chart and in the personnel files. But the real leader runs the group, and so long as the official leader accepts all his recommendations, the fiction of his authority will be preserved in public. The official leader becomes a deposed king, the one-time head of the family who is now the old man in the chimney-corner.

But while it may be true that, from the point of view of a ten-group, there is only a right leader and a wrong leader, the corporation encounters a third category: the leader who evolves but lacks the skills that leadership comes to require later on. As you rise higher through a large and complex organization, the nature of the task changes radically, and a leader evolved at the lowest level may be totally unable to cope as more and more importance attaches to understanding technical arguments, assessing financial projections, foreseeing market changes and formulating long-term plans. Of course there will be many highly qualified staff working on all this: but the leader must be able to understand them, to know how to use them, to check that he is getting the information he asked for, and to sense that something has been left out or misunderstood.

6

At the same time, he has to be an evolved and proved leader whose authority is accepted and respected—he cannot be a high-grade clerk, so to speak, who comes in at the top to run the whole corporation. But there is very little in the tasks at the lowest level to ensure that a leader who emerges there will be capable of the types of skill that will be needed later.

Most corporations solve the problem by graduate recruitment and management training, but this has many snags. It can very easily lead to an us-and-them feeling, a separation (because there has never been any ten-group comradeship) between those who do the work and those who decide what work shall be done, and result in that alienation and absence of a sense of belonging which leads to unrest and dispute. It also spawns rootless, interchangeable managers who have not grown up out of any craft or trade and who move from corporation to corporation and job to job in order to solve problems rather than lead people. This in turn encourages instrumental management.

I experienced one of the most interesting approaches to this problem during my two years in the British Army. Even my selection for management was interesting: I was summoned to a three-day War Office Selection Board, where we were divided up into ten-groups—mostly of eight, as far as I remember—and given a string of different assignments. For some we had no leader, for some we had an appointed leader; some tested the ability to organize people, others the ability to organize projects; some tested personal authority, others tested powers of communication. It was fascinating how a staff-work project, for instance, would evolve a leader quite different from the one evolved by a field-work project. I think (and hope) I would have thought it just as efficient and thorough a test if I had failed it. However, I was selected, and after several months in an officer-training establishment I was eventually commissioned and sent out all wet behind the ears to a regiment in the Middle East.

I can still recall my absolute bafflement as to what on earth I was doing in a position of authority over men of such vastly superior technical knowledge, practical ability, military experience and soldierly demeanour as the sergeants and corporals who had to salute me and call me 'sir'. They knew far better than I did what had to be done and how to do it, and to start with I could see no role at all that I could fill. The first time that in my own opinion I made any officer-like contribution was when Corporal Burrows came in very worried with a piece of paper in his hand. The problem was that we had asked all the troops to send an equipment deficiency return in triplicate to the squadron office, but one of the troops had sent four copies instead of three. Where should the fourth copy be filed? I held out my hand for the piece of paper, and Corporal Burrows relinquished it eagerly. I tore it into four pieces and put it into the wastepaper-basket. He beamed with relief, saluted happily, and went out, and I dimly saw how I might one day be of some use as an officer.

I had joined the army without much enthusiasm, but once I was in it I had to admit that the system worked: the authority of the officers was respected—even mine, which I did not really believe in myself—and for all the rawness of the second lieutenants we did provide one useful function. Because our full-time responsibility was our troop of thirty men, with our troop sergeant and three section corporals, we were always able to represent them and their case to the management with just as much force as when we passed on management's instructions to them; and by spending so much of the day with them, a young officer gained over the years an insight into the hopes and fears of ordinary soldiers, into how they reacted and what pleased or irritated them, that would always be a part of any decisions he would take later on in higher ranks. It also meant that mutiny, or 'strike' as it is called in civil life, unless the officers joined in, was a virtual impossibility with such a close working relationship in such a comparatively small group.

But why, in that case, did the army not just sit back and wait for the leaders to evolve? Why all the mumbo-jumbo of saluting and uniforms and separate messes and 'sir' and all the rest of it? I assumed at the time that this was just ancient tradition that no one had bothered to change: it was many, many years later that I met by chance a man who could explain it to me. He was (and indeed is) General Sir John Hackett, a scholar-soldier who went from the command of the British Army in Germany to become Principal of King's College at London University.

The army, he said, absolutely believes that leaders evolve. But it could never, by purely natural methods, evolve enough leaders with the technical knowledge, administrative grasp, powers of analysis and communication, and mental discipline, to fill all the positions in which those qualities were required. If the army just let the recruits with those special qualities join in the ranks and take their luck, some would evolve but others would yield precedence to better leaders who, lacking their qualifications, would nevertheless become corporals and sergeants over them. So they select, exclusively from people who have those qualities, junior officers who are not evolved leaders and some of whom quite possibly never would have been. Then they dress them up as if they really were leaders, give them all the badges and status symbols, put them in separate living quarters, and make all the soldiers behave towards them as if they were leaders. They enhance this by giving them certain formal (if not very real) authority, and making them the main channel of communication by virtue of their access to more senior officers. Also, the senior officers treat them, and expect them to behave, as if they were the real leaders of their men. In a quite narrow sense of the word, it is a process of manufacturing synthetic leaders. Under such pressure it is very difficult for them not to act like officers; like Max Beerbohm's Happy Hypocrite, they are given a mask which they wear for so long that in time the face underneath grows to the same shape: they by-pass the evolutionary process, but with time and experience they learn the skills and habit and role of leadership, and become acceptable as real leaders. As Hamlet says, 'Use almost can change the stamp of nature.'

Whether this solution can work in the corporation is another matter; but it is interesting to see that something similar has been tried. Some corporations have turned their university intake into graduate foremen, giving them a year or two in a position very similar, to that of an army subaltern, though without the trappings and the suits of commissioned rank.

But there is a different approach, which was Napoleon's. At the end of a battle or a campaign, his question was, 'Quels sont les braves?' — who are our heroes? Those were the ones to be promoted; appraisal by results, the principle favoured both by modern management theory and age-old natural selection. Napoleon of course encountered the same problem as the British Army: there was no guarantee that *les braves* could read or write. So when they were named, they would be sent off to school until they had acquired the level of skill and knowledge necessary for their new rank.

There is no reason why the corporations should not apply both principles, and indeed the Napoleonic principle, in a very limited way, is employed by many of them. But it is one thing to send a man on a three-week course, and quite another to spare him for a year or two of full-time training. As a consequence, Western society at the moment seems to be in danger of fulfilling H. G. Wells's vision described in *The Time Machine*, in which at some future date the human race has split into two species: the bright, gay, beautiful and delicate Eloi living in leisure and luxury above ground, and in the dark caves below the pale, hollow-eyed Morlocks endlessly bending over the machines that keep the system going. The enormous expansion of university education seems to be leading to a subspeciating of the working Morlocks from the graduate Eloi.

But does it have to be so? It all hinges on how we select for our universities, and I have an awful feeling that we have gone dangerously wrong. At one stage it was very easy: universities were for the reasonably wealthy, and were a finishing course for a small elite. The next stage was also fairly easy: the doors were opened a little wider to let in the intellectually distinguished, no matter where they came from. It is at the third stage that the questionable decision has been taken: to select the vastly enlarged numbers by just going further and further down the examination list; to say automatically that whereas we used to take numbers one and two in the class order, we will now take numbers three to eight as well.

Numbers one and two must always go on to further courses of the most vigorous, disciplined and demanding scholarship. But Napoleon at least would have questioned the automatic acceptance of the rest. Why should they not all go to work for two years or more and see which of them emerge as *les braves*? They could take up their university places then, and be selected not just on their school record but on their performance afterwards as well. And it need not stop there—at any stage during the next ten years or more, the evolved leaders with abilities beyond their education could take up the university places at present devoted to educating numbers six, seven and eight beyond their abilities.

In 1969 I went to a lunch with a number of senior police officers at Scotland Yard. It was a time of student rioting, and I was surprised at the depth of hostility that the students aroused in my hosts. But the reason was clear: I doubt if a single one of them had been to a university, and all of them would have done anything for the chance. And they had to face abuse and violence from students who were frittering away, as they saw it, the precious opportunity from which they had been excluded. All of them were the evolved leaders, all had begun as ordinary coppers and been promoted on merit, and they had become the elite of one of the acknowledged star police forces of the world. And the higher they rose, the more keenly they felt the lack of the broader education that no specific job training could replace. They would also, if they had gone to the university then, in their thirties and forties, have been the sort of students that harassed and despairing professors dream about. But they could not go, and many of the eighteen-year-old numbers six, seven and eight were apathetically and reluctantly occupying the places they would have filled so eagerly. Must it always remain impossible to temper the intricacies of academic selection with the simplicities of natural selection?

8   Leadership and Listening

W HERE is all this getting us? What have we been doing for the past seven chapters? As I see it, we have been looking at the way Corporation Man sets about his collective tasks, and trying to isolate from all the systems, structures, theories and techniques those elements which are the enduring essentials of human collective behaviour; the elements which go back beyond management theory, beyond political organization, beyond armies and cities and settled communities, back to the hunting life which over millions of years formed us into what we are today.

If this inquiry is leading anywhere at all, it is leading to the conclusion that there is, in the most proper sense of the word, a natural way to organize a corporation or government institution or any other human enterprise involving large numbers of people. Of course other ways are possible, just as it is possible to make elephants sit up and beg, or lions jump through blazing hoops, or bears wear frilly skirts and dance. With time and long practice and will-power you can subject them by means of rewards and punishments to your unnatural disciplines; but untamed nature is always lurking just below the surface, ready to burst out the moment concentration wanders or determination weakens. And so, while it is possible to impose an unnatural organization on a corporation, the natural organization will keep trying to establish itself; it can be blocked and frustrated, but it cannot be destroyed. And why should we want to destroy it? It is far simpler as well as far more effective to encourage the natural order instead of fighting it, to use the age-old co-operative impulses of our species as the foundation of the organization, and to think of a corporate structure as a national park instead of a circus, and managers as game wardens rather than lion tamers.

So far we have agreed (or I have, anyway) that the basic unit is not the individual but a group, nearly always a male group, which varies from three to twelve or fifteen in number, and perhaps optimizes somewhere around ten; that this group is bound together by a common objective, and that the bond of trust and loyalty thus formed can become an extremely powerful uniting force; that the ten-group needs to decide on (or at least take part in deciding on) its own objective, and to work out for itself how that objective shall be achieved; that it will evolve a leader out of its own members by a process of interaction between the needs of the task and the nature of the individuals; that the leader once he has evolved will resist challenges to his authority from inside and from outside the group; that he will quell strife, punish dangerous behaviour, discard passengers and enforce the status-ranking.

I shall suggest a little later on that the ten-group is not the only organizational form which we have brought with us out of our dim prehistory to regulate and direct our collective behaviour. But before we move on beyond the ten-group and its leader, there is one more question we need to answer: how did it make sure it came to the best decision, or—to put the same question differently—what sort of decision-making system would give a hunting band the best chance of survival? Clearly a hunting band has many decisions to make: which trail to follow, which animal to go for, how to set about the kill, when to call it a day and go home, whether to take special measures against predators, who should carry out which role, and many more. In its earliest days it had only the social instincts and apparatus of apes—the noises, signs, postures and actions which communicated in a rudimentary way certain simple warnings and information and intentions, and the responses to them; by the end of the hunting era it had extreme painting skill and a well-developed language with complex grammar and syntax. But however crude or subtle the instrument of communication, the band had to make decisions. A vegetarian life makes few demands on collective decision-taking, though it must still happen from time to time when predators attack or new feeding-grounds have to be found: but for the hunting band correct decision-taking is a daily survival necessity.

The simplest form of decision-taking is follow-my-leader. Let the leader make all the decisions, and the rest will do as he tells them. For all we know, this may have operated for many ages: but there is a better way, and it is beyond doubt that at some point in prehistory our ancestors evolved it. We have already established that hunting requires a number of separate skills: tracking, spotting, stalking, running, aiming, throwing, striking and so on. While we can assume that all members of a hunting band were proficient at all of them, we can also assume that they were not equally proficient. One would excel in stealth, one in speed, one in accuracy, one in strength. Consequently some sort of role specialization, by which each individual did most of what he did best, must have been favoured by selection: the bands which used their pool of skills most effectively would have the best chance.

But hunting is more than the application of physical skills: it also requires knowledge and judgment, and these too are not likely to be evenly distributed. One member of the band may have the sharpest weather sense, another may be the best at understanding tracks, another may have a gift for sensing which member of the herd of game will be the slowest or most stupid, and so on. A hunting band that can bring all this pool of knowledge and judgment to bear when decisions have to be made is going to make the right decision more often than the band that just plays follow-my-leader and leaves every decision to the private judgment of a single individual. Of course there can be no such debate in the heat of the chase; the leader's decisions there must be given instantly and obeyed unquestioningly. But at the start of the day's hunting, when there is no game in sight, or several herds in different directions, there is time to draw from the pool of collective wisdom.

This reflection on collective decision-making in the hunting band takes my mind back to the late 1950s and the *Tonight* programme. Of all the ten-groups I have worked in or known of, this seemed to come closest to the rhythm of hunting life. To start with, it was in the fullest sense a daily programme. We arrived in the morning with very little idea of what would be in the evening's programme. One or two items might already have been arranged, but the bulk of the programme was left empty until the day. In the second place, we were a real ten-group—a central nucleus of about six, and four or five others. And in the third place, nearly all the group, and five of the central six, stayed together for over four years keeping the same routine of a new programme every day. What is more, our daily routine followed the pattern of the hunt. We began every morning with a discussion on what to put in the programme. The editor would then decide on a provisional programme, and we would go off on reconnaissance expeditions, so to speak: we would ring people up to find if they could come on the programme, or for advice about how to treat a topic; we would arrange filming: we would investigate the availability of film clips, still photographs, cabinet ministers, film stars, preservationists and abolitionists; someone would be finding out how to get a three-ton truck into the London studio, another would be seeing if the Cardiff studio could accommodate an organ and a sixty-man choir. Sometimes a scent would go cold and we would have to meet again to think of an alternative. By lunchtime, we usually had sight of the prey: we knew what we were after, and it had become a question of getting it on to the screen by 6.50 that evening. During the afternoon the hunt would quicken, and the critical point would move from one member of the team to another: first it might be a question of getting an interviewee on to a train in Norwich by 3.05, then of getting some film to the laboratories before 4.00; next the pressure would move to the cutting rooms to get the film edited, then to the writer to finish his commentary in time; as the kill approached, the dubbing theatre became the focus of anxiety, with commentary and effects to be added to film, while the live studio items became critical as interviewees arrived and photographs, musicians, charts, props and scenery had to be assembled, plotted, lit and rehearsed for cameras; finally the studio and its control gallery became the place where the day's hunt succeeded or failed, as the programme was transmitted. Sometimes there was a splendid kill and we were all elated, sometimes our quarry got away and we were proportionately downcast. Either way, we would go off for a drink and post mortem to draw what general conclusions we could and see that successes happened more frequently in future, and that the causes of failure were isolated and eliminated.

The enormous stimulation and satisfaction of a daily routine, a new task each day and no precise foreknowledge of what it would be, prompts the reflection that perhaps one of the most unnatural of the boring elements in repetitive work is the knowledge of exactly what will have to be done tomorrow and next week and next month. The day-task comes most easily and naturally to us, and we are at our most productive and most satisfied when our group completes each evening the task it decides on in the morning. That, however, is by the way. I used the example of *Tonight* because, having now observed or taken part in many decision-making groups, I find it stands out as the model of how good decisions are made.

The first point to establish, and every committee should note it, is that only one person ever took the decisions—in our case the editor. The purpose of the rest of the group was to help him reach the best possible decision. This, I am sure, is a truth which holds for every group decision: in the end it is one man's decision, and the others' membership in the group means their acceptance that his decision when made is binding on them all. It is arguable that more delay and discord in great corporations and departments of state are caused by the delusion that committees can take decisions than by any other management myth. A committee's purpose is to help a man decide.

The second point is that the editor never decided anything on a majority vote. To give each person a vote would be to imply that each man's voice was equal, and it never was. As far as I can work it out there were always at least five variables, whose combination might differ on each topic. One was knowledge of the subject: since we dealt with almost any subject—politics, science, art, fashion, economics, films, industry, international affairs, music—the value of any individual's contribution would depend on his expertise in the subject. Another was production skill—how much experience and success the speaker had had in the production techniques that would be used. Then there was strength of feeling—was it just a casual idea, or something the speaker felt right down to the depths of his soul? Another highly important variable was judgment: did the speaker tend to be right in his assessments of what would work for the audience, was his judgment better on some topics than others, did he tend to optimism or pessimism? The fifth variable— extremely important—was executive responsibility: was the speaker the one who was going to have to carry out the idea? If so, his feelings had special significance, and if he was really opposed to an idea that he alone could execute, then he virtually had a veto.

Obviously there could be no way of reflecting all these variables by a distribution of votes, particularly since the weight of an individual's opinion would change even within a single discussion. And of course it never occurred to anyone to suggest it: we all knew it was the editor's decision and that it had to be. He was the evolved leader because we knew he was more likely than the rest of us to lead a successful expedition, and had the sharpest sense for keeping away from danger and destruction. A collective hunting expedition demands a fine and flexible grading of priorities—that route gives us the best cover but is more likely to hide leopards, this investment proposal offers the highest return but the country concerned is more likely to be plunged in civil war—and only the leader can keep them permanently in balance and adjustment. Also any plan can be modified to put more weight on one member and less on another—a stiffer production target can give an easier job to sales, a shorter time in the dubbing theatre gives the editor longer to cut the film, a brilliant piece of stalking can make fewer demands on running, and so on—and this too can only be balanced out from day to day by the leader.

But although the leader is the expert at the total objective and at the allocation of roles and priorities to achieve it, on any individual aspect of it there is always liable to be a member of the group with higher skill or better judgment or a more ingenious plan. If the leader does not incorporate these into his decisions, then the survival of the group is threatened. It is also threatened if a plan is decided on in the absence of someone with essential knowledge—the only man who knows the path through the swamp or the likely sales volume of the product at this price—or of the person who will be responsible for executing any significant part.

This is something that all of us understand instinctively. One of the prime causes of the fury that crops up again and again in large organizations is leadership that does not listen. The decision to go ahead with a product without talking to the production manager, fixing the price without talking to the sales force, abandoning a development project without reference to the department doing the work on it—these are happening all the time and arouse emotions which have nothing to do with reason, logic or consideration of the facts. In cool retrospect many years later, I can see that my fury was often aroused by a decision which was substantially correct. I can think of other cases when I accepted an unpleasant decision philosophically because I had said my say, heard other people say theirs, and realized that the decision even if wrong had been reached in the light of all the available emotions and suggestions and information. It is the demand to be heard before the decision is taken which has operated in favour of survival, and the willingness to listen first and decide afterwards which has sorted out the successful leaders from the unsuccessful.

There is another aspect to decision-taking, which is nothing like so emotionally charged but still significant: the post mortem, the reviewing of the decision in the light of its result—drawing conclusions, learning lessons, building up the store of shared folk-wisdom within the ten-group, the talk round the fire at the end of the hunt; comparing today's events with past ones and looking for common threads, passing on pieces of observation, reviewing old beliefs in the light of new evidence, offering tentative judgments for refutation or confirmation, agreeing who had done well or badly, remembering any act of exceptional courage or skill. This sort of discussion tends to be intensive and compulsive in the early days of a group when there is much new experience and little precedent, and although it quietens down with time, it always goes on, and a radically new danger or opportunity can start it up again with the old intensity. In time this body of folk-wisdom becomes a decision-making factor which restrains even the leader: it is difficult for him to go against the body of knowledge and custom in whose formulation he has taken so large a part. It is another of the reasons why the group and not the individual is the base on which the corporation rests, and why corporations should think of group promotion rather than individual promotion as the norm. To quote V. C. Wynne-Edwards, Professor of Ecology at Aberdeen University, 'In general the characteristics and functions of a society belong to it collectively and cannot be completely represented or discharged by an individual member.'[1]

Most boards of directors and committees of executives understand these two principles of group decision-making—listening before deciding, and building up a store of folk-wisdom by constant reviewing of causes and effects. What they seem to realize less often is the need for it, and the value of it, all the way down the organization. The subject-matter may be different, but the process is the same. On the factory floor it will not be long-term expansion plans that people want consultation on: it will be design of parts, control of work flow, siting of machines, advance information of workload, as well as pay and conditions and holidays; and many factories are repositories of much ancient wisdom in these matters, as well as in ignoring instructions, concealing facts and thwarting the objectives of management. In the same way the sales force, the office staff, the transport staff and indeed every group in the corporation have little pools of knowledge and experience and judgment which all too often nobody draws on. The salesmen may know, privately, that a certain discount rate is unnecessarily high in their region: the machine operators may know, privately, that setting time could be saved if two jobs arrived in a different order; the accounts clerks may know that if certain bills to slow payers were sent out earlier the monthly statement could be ready much sooner: but this sort of knowledge, shared and discussed among the groups when they meet at lunch or over tea, never gets any further. Marks & Spencer now insist that every director and senior executive visit at least one store a week to keep themselves in permanent contact with this kind of group wisdom, but many corporations leave this most valuable source quite untapped.

Why? I suspect it is a legacy from the early days of industrialization when the manager was the only man expected to think, when work was simple and repetitive, when products and production methods went unchanged year after year, and units were small enough for the boss to know exactly what was going on. But today in almost every corporation the reverse is the case. Units are larger, work is more complex; there is a constant flow of new products, new materials, new plant, new processes, new markets, new techniques, new procedures, which demand the most intensive consultation on how to fit them into the existing practices, and constant review of how they are working out and what is going wrong and what can be learnt for the future. This seldom seems to happen, and the factory does not learn about the new data collection system until after the computer has been bought, and the second numerically controlled tool is ordered without the operators of the first one being asked what modifications would improve it. You can even end up with a brand new multi-million-pound container terminal lying idle at London docks because none of the dockers will man it.

If a break like this opens up in a corporation, separating the knowledge, experience, feelings and reactions at the bottom from the judgment, plans and decisions at the top, the situation is ripe for revolt. What has happened is that in collective terms there is a leader who will not listen and must therefore be overthrown. It was the error of Charles I and Louis XVI and Nicholas II, as it was the downfall of Henry Ford. Of course the revolt may be put down, and the leader may maintain his throne by force, but if he does so he is still impairing his own chances of survival: not just because of the discontent, alienation and hostility in the ranks, which cannot help in achieving the objective and must give advantages to rivals, but because he is cutting himself off from this pool of folk-wisdom built up over the years. It is just as much a management resource as the skills and efforts of the employees. But when the break happens, when a leader or a leadership group does not come to decisions by listening but simply issues instructions and enforces compliance, it drastically reduces the size of the pool it has access to. Consequently the leadership can make a wrong decision because it lacks a certain store of knowledge or judgment, or fails to hit on an idea, which is actually available in the organization — but which it cannot get at because it has locked the door and thrown away the key. Survival depends on deciding right, and every available resource has to be brought to bear on the process of decision-making: and for the leader who has to take the decision, the ear is a more important instrument than the tongue.

9   The Hunt and the Camp

WE HAVE it on the best authority that no man can serve two masters, and it seems a fairly obvious truth until you reflect on the fact that many employees of large organizations are doing it all the time. I first had direct personal experience of this in the army. I was recruited into, trained by and commissioned in the Royal Signals, and in the course of the ten or eleven months they spent turning me into something that would pass for a Signals officer I was made privy to a great deal of tribal lore. Much of it was to do with organization and equipment and techniques, and had no great moral authority, but some of it was as binding and as transcendental as Holy Writ. I remember a picture in the officers' mess—indeed it was in almost every officers' mess—of a young lineman in Flanders who had just jointed a telephone cable that a shell had severed. The line was repaired, but he was lying on his back, white and bloodstained and dead. The title of the picture was 'Through!' At first sight it recalled almost irresistibly Oscar Wilde's judgment that no man of true sensibility could read of the death of Little Nell without bursting out laughing, but in fact the picture had great emotional significance for older members of the Corps: it expressed one of the transcendental duties of every Signaller— to get communications through at all costs. It was a duty that many of their friends had died trying to discharge, and there could be no doubt of the genuineness of their emotion. For them the painting was not a work of art but something closer to a sacred icon. If I did not come to share their emotion, I at least learnt to respect it.

That same solemnity was attached to certain other observances and taboos which lay close to the heart of the Signaller's job. Two will serve as examples. The first was rigid observance of radio procedure. It was in the nature of radio that the enemy could usually pick up your transmissions and work out your position, but they did not know who you were—for all they could tell, you might be a battalion or an army. There was strict procedure to conceal that information, and a breach of it could lose a battle, so security procedure was dinned into us as a far more holy compulsion than the Ten Commandments or the Sermon on the Mount. The other solemn taboo attached to codes and ciphers – a slip that let the enemy crack a code would profoundly imperil the survival of thousands of men, so the slip must never be permitted. All this was simple and straightforward in the training school: but what happened to the Signals officer who was attached to the headquarters of an infantry brigade? If the brigadier told him to dump his radio in a ditch and retreat, he would, of course, obey. But if he grabbed the microphone and bawled over the ether to a battalion commander, 'Listen, you bloody fool, do you know who this is, it's Brigadier Howard,' did you let him do it or switch him off when you saw what was coming? If you heard the brigade major ask a battalion what slidex code chart they thought they were using, did you let him wait for the reply or jam the frequency? Which master were you serving?

These are thorny problems, but only in theory. In practice they rarely caused any trouble. You could debate theoretical dilemmas endlessly, but in any given instance you always knew which of the two masters you had to obey. I was surprised to find how well this system of dual authority worked and for a time I thought it was peculiar to the army, but I encountered it again shortly after leaving. In the B.B.C., the cameramen belonged to a different division from that of the producers: a cameraman took orders from the producer of the programme, but again there were certain taboos. The producer could not instruct him to breach safety regulations, risk damage to the equipment, or transmit pictures of a technical quality lower than the agreed minimum standard. The application of these rules might occasionally cause frustration and irritation, and they might be adjusted from time to time, but the system of dual authority was always accepted as perfectly natural.

Since those days I have encountered the dual loyalty so often, and found it worn so easily, that I feel it has to be accepted as something we do naturally. It seems that the division is always the same: one master commands our day-to-day, operational activities, and the other our permanent, long-term obedience and allegiance. In the industrial corporation it is reflected all the way up: you respond to the discipline of the department in which you are employed, but you also belong to the corporation. Your boss can give you all sorts of tasks, but he is limited by the overriding policies of the corporation. He can stop you going to Alaska, but he cannot stop your

7

promotion into another division. He can load you with work, but he cannot prevent you taking your annual holiday. He can take away your company car, but he cannot reduce your pension. In hundreds of ways he accepts that he has operational freedom and untrammelled authority in certain areas, but in other areas his staff do not belong to him but to some different, higher and more enduring authority.

This duality reaches its final corporate expression in the relationship between the chairman and the managing director. There is no obligation on any company to make these into separate functions, and indeed they are on occasions held by the same man – but chiefly when the company is actually being formed, or drastically reshaped. At such times the short and long term are so intimately connected that they need to be united in the mind and will of a single man – the 'old man', the founder of the firm. In just the same way the founders of the new African nations – Kenyatta, Nyerere, Kaunda – have to embody both the permanent state and the government of the day until a national identity is securely established. But once that has happened it soon becomes clear in the nation and the corporation that there are in fact two jobs at the top and not one. It happens with such regularity that it can be taken as the normal, orthodox way of running any large corporation – to have one man running the entire show is the exception.

The managing director is the peak of the operational activities of the corporation. All the day-to-day and year-by-year research and development and production and sales are under his authority, and the year's profit and loss account is the index of his achievement. He stands at the summit of the corporation and looks down at all those who toil on the slopes and foothills and plains below. He marks strength and weakness, success and failure, scarcity and plenty, and decides what must be done to maximize the good and minimize the bad. And beside him, just a step higher up, stands the chairman – but he is looking in the opposite direction, not inwards at the organization but outwards at the world in which the corporation has to survive. He is preoccupied with long-term finance and relations with the capital market; with the community, and the corporation's reputation within it; with the governments it has to deal with and the laws that may be passed which will affect the corporation; with long-term shifts in technology and markets and materials which may affect the sort of corporation they will have to become in five or ten years' time.

When the chairman does turn round and look inwards, he does not share the managing director's obsession with results and return on capital and earnings per share. He cares about them of course, but they are already being looked after. His preoccupation is with decisions that may change the whole nature of the corporation for the worse. Suppose the managing director wants to sack thirty executives: in some corporations it would be accepted as a correct decision, but in others it would send a shock wave to the furthest outposts. In the latter case the chairman would have to balance the saving of salaries against the damage to morale. Suppose the managing director wanted to start up a range of cheap products and enter a new market or lower the excessively high technical standards of the corporation's engineering: the chairman might know that these decisions would do irreparable damage to the confidence of customers and the pride of employees even though the short-term profits would be impressive. Equally, a single unjust act, if it helps to avert imminent danger, may not worry the managing director too much; the chairman sees that it may make all the most valuable staff start to reconsider what sort of organization they are offering a lifetime's allegiance to, and he may think the price too high. It is the chairman who is the more worried about recruitment and training and developing managers; as with his other preoccupations these concern not so much what the corporation does or will do, but what it is and will be.

This distinction is not between two halves of a job that becomes too big for one man: on the contrary the difference is so profound that it is practically impossible to discharge both duties properly at the same time. The present and the future do not run in harness: their demands and emphases move at a different pace and sometimes pull in opposite directions, and it is rarely satisfactory if the conflict takes place in a single man's mind. If one man tries to do both jobs, one of them is likely to go by default. Sometimes it is the chairman's job that goes, and the company is driven by a brilliant and thrusting opportunist who achieves outstanding short-term results, but is eventually overwhelmed by the unforeseen changes which he himself has precipitated and the enemies he himself has made. Sometimes it is the managing director's job that goes, and the company is considerate, just and tolerant, and returns 2 per cent on its assets. There has to be a proper tension between the present and the future, and a tension requires the application of a force at each end.

As I suggested earlier, it is not only in the corporation that this duality is expressed. Historically, most of the states which reached any size came to evolve the same form of leadership. The king represented the permanent and the outward-looking aspects of the state, while his chief minister was answerable for its internal organization and short-term results. The king embodied law and justice, foreign affairs, long-term defence and the capital side of the treasury; the chief minister and his government looked after the preservation of order, the framing of individual laws, the revenue side of the treasury—tax collection and disbursements—and the balancing of national priorities from year to year. It was not only in advanced civilization that this developed: the larger African kingdoms studied by anthropologists (for example, Ruanda, Buganda, Ankole) frequently evolved this same division.[1] Indeed one of the most profound troubles of countries like Britain and the United States is that they lack a proper political expression of this duality. The British monarchy, by being little more than a formal and ceremonial office, and the American presidency, by being dependent on four-yearly elections, both leave the long-term, permanent authority, the chairmanship, to go by default. Neither the prime minister nor the president can easily sacrifice the short-term need for re-election to long-term rewards which, if they are not re-elected, their opponents will reap. Consequently the long-term office becomes a vacuum which sucks into itself generals and civil servants, diplomats and bankers, judges and scientists and industrial leaders, who have to argue behind the scenes, and without any formal or democratic authority, for the future against the present. America has one advantage over the British system, in that the state governments, by filling the managing director role in many internal affairs, leave the role of sovereignty vacant for the federal government. This emphasizes the permanent, monarchical aspects of the president's role, since he has less direct responsibility for the measures debated and the laws passed by the state legislatures.

It is one thing to observe how this duality is inherent in all our organizational systems, but quite another to explain it. We have already seen that divided authority must operate against the survival of the hunting band: how can it also have operated in favour of the survival of our species? Let me suggest an answer to that question.

When we became collective hunters, the form of organization which that activity demanded, the ten-group, was an addition, not an alternative, to our older social organization. We are the product of some hundred million years of social living, as well as perhaps fifteen million years of collective hunting. As well as the ten-group, there was the camp. The hunt was the instrument of day-to-day survival, but the camp, the home-base, was the instrument for preserving and continuing the species. The camp in the daytime was the place for the women, the children and the old men. There was work to do—collecting fruit and roots and water, bringing up the children, some rudimentary attention to hygiene and comfort— but it did not have the dangers or rewards of the hunting band. All the same, the species could die out just as easily by failure to keep the camp secure and free from disease and internal strife as it could by failure to kill the game. Consequently the ancient primate society, which had long been used to living and wandering in small groups, must have preserved what it could of that form of organization while adapting to the compulsions of the hunting life. The hunt was a special, separate, and (comparatively) recent development. When the hunters returned with their kill, they rejoined the older social organization, which had already evolved means of communal defence against predators or other marauders of their own species, the avoidance of lethal strife within the group, some means of making group decisions about which way to move on, and some sort of social conventions and regulations. All these must have existed long before we turned carnivorous, and must have continued and developed over several hundred thousand generations to reach the refinement and complexity they show when we first encounter them in history.

Every modern corporation has its camp as well as its hunting bands. At the sharp end—the factory floor or the local sales office— it is usually small: a few secretaries and other office or clerical staff, maintenance men, cleaners and tea ladies, drivers and messengers and so on: all the people who are not actually devising and making and selling the product or service that brings in the money.

But as you climb up the levels of corporate hierarchy you find—especially in the worst corporations—that there are fewer and fewer hunters and more and more camp followers. They may be physically only just across the corridor, but in all other ways they are in a different world. Many of them are women, but the modern corporation has many men in such positions as well. They are in departments with names like finance, personnel, planning, public relations, administration, registry and welfare, and however devoted their efforts, however valuable their contribution, the members of the hunting bands look on them as the 'women and children' of the corporation. Any hunter who is sweating his guts out to meet a production or copy deadline or a sales target thinks of them as to some extent a burden that he and his fellows have to carry, and I suspect there is even a submerged feeling that it is women's work they are doing. Healthy, strong, active men ought to be sharing the exertions and perils of the hunt, not skulking in the warmth and safety of the camp all day. It is very difficult to say who in the corporation is in the camp and who is in the hunting band—but only if you are in the camp. You then think of the importance of your contribution, the tax savings you have devised, the pressure at which you work and how you go home absolutely drained an hour after everyone else, and you almost kid yourself that you are really one of the hunters. But the hunting bands know with absolute clarity who are the hunters and who are the passengers. Some of the passengers may in fact prove their usefulness so clearly, in the way they make the hunters' work easier and more effective, that they will be accepted and even respected: but that respect has to be earned from the hunting bands, not in the camp. What the corporation's hunters find absolutely intolerable is the squaw-men in the camp starting to behave as if they were as important, or more important, than the men who go out and kill the game. If this false importance is endorsed by the management, the contemptuous resentment is turned upward on them. Many industrial disputes are given an extra streak of bitterness when the men making the product that makes the money see their friends being laid off so as to support an army of smart young parasites in warm, carpeted offices.

There is also a biological limit to the size of the camp which a hunting band can support: there is only so much game to share out at the end of the day. But the safety and comfort of the camp are so tempting that the danger arises of more and more people trying to find themselves a job there rather than on the hunt, and putting an ever greater burden on the hunt to support them. It is sometimes called 'top-heavy administration', and it is one of the greatest dangers to corporate survival: the corporation camp has a tendency to grow rapidly in good times, when game is plentiful, and when it gets sparse there are too many flabby stomachs to fill and a desperate shortage of trained and skilled hunters.

And yet despite all this the camp has demands which are as powerful and legitimate as those of the hunters. A marvellous area for game may depend on a snake-infested camp with bad water and sparse cover. A better camp may mean harder work for the hunting band, but this has to be accepted. A higher price may mean a tougher job for the sales force, but the alternative of abolishing the patent department may be, in the long term, a much worse way of generating the extra cash. The tension is always there, and it is the classic situation for the dramatist: the hunt and the camp, the managing director and the chairman, are both pulling in different directions, but the rope they are pulling is the bond that holds them together. The hunting band is part of the whole group which must survive as a group: if the rope snaps, both sides lose. One or the other may have to give ground, and the tension may vary from very low to very high, and a permanent point of rest may be an impossibility; but both sides have to hang on to the rope whatever happens.

This tension is felt right through the corporation, from the managing director trying to get more development money at the expense of the training budget to the salesman fuming at the time he has to spend filling in sales report forms instead of calling on prospects. I sometimes wonder if this tension is not the basis of all political division, at least in stable communities which are free from war or subjection or revolution. At the end of 1970, when I started this book, it was certainly the fundamental political argument in both Britain and the United States. In Britain the Conservatives were returned to power on a national feeling that the camp has been favoured at the expense of the hunters: too much national expenditure to subsidize health and homes and schools, too much government restriction on, and interference with, the activities of industry, so let's sweep away this massive parasitic structure of controls, taxes, commissions, civil servants, and give people the freedom and incentive to produce and export and make us all richer — let's turf some of these idlers out of the camp so that the hunters can have a bigger share of the meat they bring back and go off tomorrow fitter and more eager than before. In the United States, the feeling seemed to be exactly the reverse: we've been so preoccupied with giving the hunters everything they want that the camp is dirty and smelly, fighting and bullying are breaking out all the time, we can't drink the water because everyone is excreting into it, so let's divert at least some of the time and energy and manpower from bringing back more meat than we can eat to clearing the place up and stopping the fights and making the camp a better place to live in.

This tension between the hunt and the camp runs from the highest councils of the state down into every family, where the demands of the husband's job and the needs of the home and family can so easily come into conflict. But at some point in our distant prehistory we seem to have evolved a third force whose function usually serves to resolve the conflict, and it is a strange and intriguing evolutionary phenomenon.

Nature's requirement of every individual member of every species is that he or she should contribute to the survival and regeneration of the group. With certain exceptions (sterile castes of social insects, for example) this means the breeding and rearing of young, and when that is completed and the period of fertility is over, the individual is no longer required: he would be a passenger, a burden on the group, if he stayed around, and so he is given an honourable discharge by the natural selection board and dies off quickly and quietly. A disease or genetic defect which strikes only when reproduction is completed does not threaten the survival of the group. This however is demonstrably not the case with man — we are one of those few species whose males and females survive long after they have finished bearing and rearing children. Why? What selection advantage could favour a hunting band with old people to look after, as against the young, active, unencumbered groups with a quick death at forty to prevent the old from being a burden on the young?

The answer offered by Professor Wynne-Edwards in *Animal Dispersion in Relation to Social Behaviour* is that the hunting bands who could draw on the cultural tradition of their older members must have had a selection advantage over those who were not so fortunate. The elders were the custodians of that tradition, a mixture of knowledge, experience, memory and judgment, which was vital to the survival of the group when it needed to adapt to a new situation. The younger hunters might never have seen a really long drought before, but the elders remembered what happened forty years before. In the same way, many of Wall Street's brilliant young go-go fund managers who didn't need the oldies when the index was rising steadily were suddenly grateful for their experience and memory when they found themselves on a longer downhill slide than their own short lives had witnessed.

The presence of the elders in the camp acted as a countervailing force to the demands of the hunters; but, as men who had themselves served for a long time in the hunting band, they could understand and weigh the needs of the hunt as well as the needs of the camp. Their status and influence with the younger males would presumably be high, since they would have been the leaders of the pack when the present leaders joined it as novices, and their daily advice and warnings would reaffirm their value. Moreover, the fact that they had avoided death in the hunt for so many years was living evidence that they were experts at survival.

When we look at the ten-group in the corporation, therefore, we have to accept that it has never been a totally independent and autonomous unit. In the heat of the chase it can accept no interference, but when the hunt is over, when long-term decisions have to be made, when there are wider considerations than killing the game to be debated, it accepts limitations on its freedom of action. Equally, my corporation experience tells me, it accepts them only from those who have themselves been brave and skilled hunters, whose experience and achievement are respected and whose leadership has brought success to many hunting expeditions in the past: it does not submit to the judgments of the women and children. But if the best leader is allowed to evolve both from the hunters and from the elders, then the dual authority of the camp and the hunt, the operational and the institutional, the short- and the long-term, is easily and naturally accepted. It is a duality that will become important as we leave the single group and look at the larger and larger organizations into which it combines.

10 The Corporation Tribe

ONCE you have accepted the application of the ten-group and the camp to the corporation, you can then use it as the sole building block and construct a theoretical organization from it in the form of a pyramid. When I first stumbled on the idea of the ten, I assumed this must be what happened; and the obvious way for it to happen is for the leaders of the ten ten-groups to come together and form the ten-group that controls and regulates a group of a hundred. Then the leaders of the hundreds would come together and form a group of a thousand, and so on. This explanation satisfied me for a long time, and indeed it is very close to what does actually happen: we do, as we shall see, combine ten-groups into larger units by exactly this method.

All the same, I felt a nagging unwillingness to accept this sort of structure. The deceptive neatness was one reason—that sort of simplistic extrapolation smells more of midnight oil than flesh and blood. Another reason was that it was too easy: since a corporate ten-group can be in fact four people, you could, for example, explain a hundred as ten tens or as a 'small thousand' made up of five groups with five ten-groups of four in each. But there was a much stronger reason: I had a feeling in my bones that there was another grouping of great importance, even if I could not understand why. It lay somewhere around four or five hundred—perhaps six. It was essentially a maximum size; smaller numbers, as far as I could see, were perfectly acceptable, but larger ones were not. It did not seem to fit in particularly well with the ten-based pyramid, unless it was stretched to give a thousand as the absolute maximum, but I had to admit that it was there.

It first came to my notice in the early 'sixties, when I started to get interested in management. Several people with a long experience of industry mentioned four or five hundred as being just about the maximum size for a one-man firm, the size up to which an energetic and managerially unsophisticated entrepreneur could build his business and keep it under his control. Sir David Brown for instance, who inherited the David Brown engineering company from his father in the 'thirties, says that the reason it was in trouble at that time was precisely because it had grown from its normal and profitable size of five hundred employees up to a thousand, which was too many. Profits started to slide, the old man's tight grip loosened, and the trouble had begun. The clearest symptom of this occurred when he sacked two men who were standing around doing nothing, and then found they were a contractor's employees. In the old days he had known every man by sight.

When a number of practical men arrive independently at the same concept of an upper limit, and attach roughly the same figure to it, this evidence is not something to be dismissed just because it does not fit a theory. And when I came to think about it, five hundred turned out to be an extremely interesting number. Somewhere around four or five or six hundred is about the normal size for a village. It is also what most headmasters and principals think of as the 'right' size for a school or college: a comfortable size, the size they would be happy to run. And what about the army, where the logic of survival is at its strictest? A battalion in wartime is about six hundred, and the Romans—that most decimal of nations— had the tent of ten and the centurion for a hundred, but the cohort was not the thousand that simple multiplication would suggest, but a variable between three and six hundred. Why?

Then I thought back to my school list. At the start of each year we were all given a printed list of all the boys in the school—a total of some four hundred and fifty. It became a competition among the junior forms to see how many you could identify, and you ticked each name on your list when you were able to put a face to it. I remember feeling some satisfaction when in the middle of my second year I completed the list. Next year the unknowns were junior to me and the game lost its savour; to have gone round in one's third year sedulously inquiring the names of the new boys would have been at best undignified, and at worst suspicious. Nevertheless I had discovered that it was possible to know all of a community of that size by sight. My feeling was that at a stretch I might have been able to recognize up to six hundred or so, but a thousand, for example, would have been beyond my powers.

There is a special significance about recognizing and being recognized, and it concerns identity. I am using the word in a very simple objective sense, the sense of how many people know who you are.

This is profoundly important in a community, if only because it so radically affects what you can get away with. It might be worth slipping outside the school grounds or the factory gates if the chances are that whoever sees you won't recognize you, but if you know that the headmaster or the boss knows you, then the risk takes on a different complexion. Moreover, in a group of five hundred it is possible for the boss not merely to know you, but also to notice if you're not there. You could almost define your boss as the most senior man who will realize that you're not in today, and four or five hundred is close to the human limit for that sort of knowledge. Or imagine trying to conduct a matrimonial intrigue in a village of six hundred people: you could reckon that the time-lapse between one person suspecting and the whole village talking would be a maximum of twelve hours.

So it did seem that this grouping of somewhere around five hundred might have a genuine significance as an 'identity group' in which every individual recognized everyone else and—an important refinement—knew that everyone else recognized him. Since this seemed to be true for the whole human species, as far as I could find out, I wondered whether there might be a biological, genetic base for this phenomenon, some fact of brain composition, some limitation on our mental storage and retrieval system, that made it impossible for us to belong to an identity group of ten thousand, or perhaps even of one thousand.

The answer began to emerge when I grasped something fundamental to our understanding of any kind of organization, whether insect or animal or human: the principle of population genetics. I find it astonishing that this science, which absorbs so many distinguished scholars and bears so closely on the origins and nature of man, should have remained virtually unknown to the ordinary educated reader. But it is so important, and so fascinating, that I will try and summarize very briefly the relevant aspects.

The foundation of the science of population genetics was the realization that no species, however solitary its members might seem, could survive unless it was part of a wider population within its locality. The chief reason for this is the 'gene pool': no single pair of creatures can procreate indefinitely, and resist all the hazards to survival, from their own genetic resources. No matter how multitudinous their progeny, if they all contain the same basic and limited genes, then a plague or climatic change or food variation or new predator will wipe the whole lot out. But if they interbreed within a wider population, the greater available pool of genes and the variety of possible genetic combination and recombination give an enormously higher probability that some at least will emerge as a resistant strain, fill up the gaps, and replenish the population: moreover the replenished population will now have a much higher resistance than before, just as the rats which survived Warfarin poisoning and the rabbits which survived myxomatosis have fathered new, 'replacement' populations which are now largely immune.

This is, to the layman, a fairly simple and straightforward idea, even if a new one; but none the less it compels a very different view of natural selection. It means that nature's law is the survival of the fittest *population*, not simply the fittest individual. Indeed the individual who seeks his own survival at the expense of the survival of the group is a bad evolutionary risk, whereas selection will always favour the community in which the individual sacrifices his gratifications, or even his life, in the interests of the group; witness the baboons that Marais saw attacking the leopard. It is populations, not individuals, that have preserved and transmitted life from the pre-Cambrian oceans to the present day.

It is impossible not to reflect on the irony that after a hundred years of bitter division, Darwinian biology should so perfectly unite with Christian morality. But for the purposes of this inquiry there is one immediate conclusion that we can draw: the hunting band and the camp, on their own, could never have provided a large enough gene pool for survival. They must always have been a part of a wider, interbreeding population: there must always have been a number of camps within an area, and those camps must have been within a reasonable contact range. But how many camps? Just a handful, or a vast population stretching over hundreds of thousands of square miles?

The answer to that question involves another short excursion into population genetics. One of the fundamental problems posed by group natural selection is, what limits the total size of a group? The simple answer is food: but when you look more closely, it is nothing like so simple. Our own species has discovered in modern times what happens if you expand till you exhaust the food supply:

the neatest example was provided by the flourishing nineteenth-century whaling industry, which kept expanding for as long as they could find any whales. The consequence was the disappearance of the whales, and the collapse of the whaling industry. It is the universal problem of overfishing, which applies not only to fish but insects and plants and any life-supporting resource: there is an optimum annual crop, beyond which you start to diminish, and ultimately destroy, the resource and consequently the population the resource supports.

We shall never know how many billions of times this cycle was repeated in the history of life on earth. But somehow, over five hundred million years, the answer was found, and some populations evolved a means of keeping their numbers at the right level for optimum cropping of resources. Their means of doing so are varied —limiting breeding territories, eating newborn young, delaying mating age and so on—but the means are not in this case the relevant factor. What matters is that before it can operate the control mechanisms, the population must reach a collective awareness that its numbers are approaching the danger point.

Professor Wynne-Edwards has collected a mass of examples of how this is done;[1] he suggests that the flocking of birds, the howling of gibbons, the croaking of frogs, the scent-marking of trees by dogs and wolves, the dawn chorus, and hundreds of other signalling devices are used by the populations as a way of keeping a check on their numbers, of asking, 'How many of us are there around this place today?' Some, of course, are merely counting absolute numbers; but there is strong evidence that higher animals are doing something further: they are recognizing individual members who belong. Observers have noticed that in the great herds of zebra there are smaller groups of about a thousand who keep together, however much they may move around within the herd: and on one occasion when the herd panicked in a thunderstorm, the thousand 'population' was completely split up: but it had reassembled intact within twenty-four hours. This number, around a thousand, seems to be the 'population' size for a number of animals: the Alaska fur seal, the Uganda kob, the African elephant and a number of others all seem to form discrete populations at this limit. Obviously these populations overlap slightly, which again has survival value since interbreeding across population boundaries creates a cross-flow between gene pools; but this is very much an exception—the rule is that a population keeps itself to itself.

It seems beyond question, therefore, that the hunting bands and their camps belonged within a wider group that was itself reasonably self-contained, and had some mechanism for controlling its numbers. It also seems virtually beyond question that this mechanism did more than measure and control absolute numbers: it identified whether all the individuals were bona fide members of the group, the genetic isolate, the tribe, or whatever you like to call it. After all, communities of monkeys are quite capable of recognizing and resisting an intruder of their own species, and various experiments have shown that it takes time for any newcomer to become established as a full member—a phenomenon not unknown in the corporation. This alone would suggest the need for mutual recognition within the population; but in our case there was a special extra reason.

I mentioned earlier how territory acted as a form of population control: with sea-birds, for instance, only the pairs with nesting sites could raise young, so the population was stabilized by a 'convention', and 'conventional competition' for breeding sites replaced direct competition for food, since, as we have seen, direct competition for food involves everyone in taking all the fish they can get, with consequent collapse of both fish and bird populations. Numerous species of animals have evolved some such conventional competition as an alternative to resource-destructive competition, so many that Wynne-Edwards has defined a society as an organization capable of providing conventional competition. But in the case of our primitive and carnivorous ancestors, competition by fighting for territory could be just as destructive as overcropping the game. We were killers by trade, and to compete by killing each other would have been a sure route to genetic extinction. So the convention must also have precluded, or at least inhibited, fights to the death within the band or between bands in the population group. A brother's murder, as Claudius says in *Hamlet*, has the primal, eldest curse upon it, and if the population is to survive, then a neighbour's murder is only a little better. But who is my neighbour? There are other, rival hominid populations who in times of game shortage may descend in force and fury to take over the territory by that most unconventional and unanswerable of competitive devices, the sharp blow on the skull. Ten-groups who in this extremity turned on their neighbours within the same population, because they were unable to distinguish them from the enemy, would be at a selection disadvantage. Mutual recognition had a survival value of the most immediate kind.

If this is true, it begins to look very significant. But there is something else to look at before we come to any conclusions—three most interesting and unconnected research findings from three different continents. The first comes from genetics and France, where the marriage records were studied to establish whether there were such things as 'breeding communities' still persisting. There were indeed, and the size of them provided a remarkable discovery: they numbered, on average, eleven hundred in the mountain communities, but in Paris they were only nine hundred: indeed Theodosius Dobzhansky, one of the most illustrious geneticists, has suggested that even today most human genetic isolates— the units within which breeding normally occurs, and across which it is unusual—are numbered in hundreds rather than thousands.[2]

The second finding comes from anthropology and Chicago, and is even more relevant. Edward Hall studied the black neighbourhoods, and found that within them there were very clear territories, sharply divided from each other, though without any visible boundary. They had the unity of villages, with many friendships inside the boundaries and very few across them: parents would reprimand neighbours' children, the gossip network was comprehensive and rich, and group attitudes on subjects where they were necessary were formed and then generally adopted by the whole community. The population of these informal, unofficial city villages was on the small side—up to two hundred or so—but their spontaneous development, their internal self-regulation, and their communication network have the precise characteristics of a tribal unit.[3]

The third piece of evidence goes further back into our prehistory: it too comes from anthropology, from a study of the Australian Aborigines.[4] As one of the few surviving hunting groups, with their clear racial and geographic separation, they are likely to have preserved our prehistoric forms of organization with less change than any except perhaps the Bushman of the Kalahari—though of

course the possession of the bow makes them far more sophisticated
hunters than our earlier ancestors. Their ten-groups tend to be on
the small side, with five or six males and a total community of about
twenty-five; the small number may be the result of having the bow
to hunt with, or of Australia's unique freedom from predators, but
in any case it falls comfortably within the three to twelve limit.
However it is the wider grouping that is the interesting one. It has
been established that the Aborigines divide into 'dialectical tribes',
that is to say groups in which all individuals speak the same dialect,
but who are dialectically differentiated from all the other tribes in
the area. These dialectical tribes are also genetic isolates. What is
significant is their numerical consistency: all the tribes which were
studied over the years tended towards a constant number of five
hundred. If they fell below, the number was restored to five hundred
before too long. If they expanded they could just about contain
their numbers and preserve their unity up to a thousand, but then
they would split into two, a new dialect would gradually develop,
and a new tribe would be born.

There is one other example that must be mentioned, though it
is the product not of research but of experience. Mao Tse-tung's
agricultural revolution was based on the concept of total mobility
of labour within a commune of some 70,000 people. Each man and
woman would be told where to work each day, according to operational needs. The scheme proved impossible to organize. It was
reconstituted with the village of a few hundred, and not the individual labourer, as the basic unit: each village was allocated its
task for the day or the week. On that basis the plan worked and is
still working.

The Chinese commune, the Australian outback, the Chicago
slum, the Paris suburb; the school, the college, the village; the
cohort, the battalion, the one man firm—they all supported my own
inner sense of the size of community in which I could expect to
know everybody, and the size in which this would be impossible.
I suggest that we have a natural population size of five hundred with
a maximum of a thousand, which we have carried within us for
millions of years.

Once you start to think back to our African origins, there are
other reasons that begin to jump out at you. For instance, a tribe
of five hundred would divide roughly into ten hunting camps of

8

fifty each; the leaders of the camps could then come together from time to time into a leaders' ten-group which would collectively take decisions on behalf of the whole tribe and provide such rudimentary government and legal system as may have evolved over the ages. And there is a further point, which could have become important with the development of speech: five hundred is about the number you can comfortably reach with the unaided human voice in the open air, and a thousand is close to the absolute maximum, even for a regimental sergeant-major.

J. B. Calhoun defines any population as 'the major unit in which the lives of individuals find reality'.[5] I believe we have to accept that for our species this tribe of five hundred is exactly that, and that a thousand is the point at which it had to subdivide into two units. Of course we can associate ourselves in our minds with units of almost any size, we can think of ourselves as belonging to I.C.I. or I.B.M., to Liverpool or Chicago, to Britain or the United States. But this, as we shall see later, is a sort of notional membership, we belong only with our minds. I have lived in London nearly all my life and would certainly call myself a Londoner, but it would be nonsense to pretend that I feel for or even know about what goes on in any more than one ten thousandth of the homes that make up the city: whereas a villager knows and cares about what goes on in every house in the village. If you go away from your village, people ask each other where you have gone; I cannot pretend that if I leave London I provide $7\frac{1}{2}$ million people with a topic for conversation. A unit of five hundred or so is something you actually feel a part of: not with the compelling bond of the ten-group, but nevertheless with a membership that cannot be shrugged off by a change of mind. You know that if you leave, everyone will notice the gap you have made. A soldier can belong to this corps or that corps, this army or that army, and if it is successful he will be proud of his membership: if not, he will feel he is a member of a great regiment or battalion in a lousy formation. But his regiment or battalion membership is of a different order, it is not notional but real; it is a part of his permanent identity which he cannot disclaim in the same way. Less powerful than his section, his ten-group, it is nevertheless real and personal and human; he knows them all, and they all know him. It is the major unit in which he encounters reality. He belongs not only by accepting, but by being accepted.

The importance of the 500-unit (let us call it the tribe) to the structure of the corporation is enormous. It is impossible to assemble ten-groups into tens or hundreds of thousands without excessive multiplication of management layers, but with tribes it becomes not only possible but comparatively easy. All the same, I think we have to be conservative about the size of a corporation tribe: if a thousand is the maximum, it is the maximum for a tribe whose association is lifelong, whose membership changes not with hiring and firing but only with birth and death. Moreover, the corporation tribe disperses every evening—even its ten-groups do not go back to a communal camp. This can of course be counterbalanced by how much the different ten-groups see of each other during the day—a battalion on active service, for instance, will have far greater opportunities for mutual recognition than an insurance company in a skyscraper block—but the combination of lifelong membership and frequent opportunities for recognition is rare enough (though it certainly occurs) for us to think of the corporate tribe as around five hundred, and to accept that, whatever other groupings we may attach our-selves to intellectually or emotionally, five hundred is the largest group any of us is ever really a part of. And we shall begin to under-stand what that means in terms of the life of the corporation as we start to look at the tribe in operation.

11 The Tribal Chieftain

THE CORPORATION tribe is neither as powerful nor as pervasive a working unit as the ten-group. The impulse to form ten-groups is so strong that it will happen despite the corporation if necessary: the tribe, by contrast, is far more optional. Many successful small concerns stay at ten-group size: professional partnerships, research and development groups, consultancies, studios — these can manage very well without ever expanding or combining into a tribe. They are in fact often part of a larger informal tribe; their clients and suppliers and colleagues or rivals in the same area of business do form a larger unofficial community in which they have an objective identity, and if they are in business for long enough this network will build up into the hundreds. Equally, what may seem to be a completely separate and independent ten-group within the corporation usually belongs in the same informal way — however much it may proclaim its autonomy — to some larger unit. But these are not operational tribes in the full corporate sense, though they work well and happily.

All the same, there are two powerful reasons why an organizational structure based on separate and clearly defined tribes is of prime importance to the corporation. The first is that the tribe is large enough to be a satisfying community for those who belong to it. It recalls de Tocqueville's perceptive and charming observation about the township: 'The township serves as a centre for the desire of public esteem, the want of exciting interests, and the taste for authority and popularity, in the midst of the ordinary relations of life: and the passions which commonly embroil society change their character when they find a vent so near the domestic hearth and family circle.'[1] With the words appropriately altered, the corporate tribe provides exactly this. It is a rich network of scandal and gossip, friendship and feud, romance and rivalry, and if our language was furnished with a word that meant the exact opposite of loneliness, that would be what the tribe offered to all its members. It is large enough to be satisfying, but not so large that you cannot feel yourself a part of it; unlike the ten-group, if you belong to the

tribe you normally accept that you are part of the wider corporation. From the corporation's point of view, it is the prime focus
of loyalty for most of the employees during most of their working
lives.

The second reason is that tribal structure alone makes the management of really large organizations possible. Managing a hundred
thousand people, or even ten thousand ten-groups, is almost a
contradiction in terms: but managing two hundred tribes is quite
possible. They must, however, be allowed to become, or remain,
genuine tribes, and it is at this point that so many corporations go
wrong: they fail to utilize the nature of the tribe as a positive
instrument for corporate success and profit, and in all sorts of ways
they manage to destroy those elements they most need while leaving the others intact. It is not so much that there are rules which
they break; rather they lack an understanding of what a tribe is and
what it is not.

Because I worked in a new and rapidly expanding industry, I
have seen over the years the growth of a number of new tribes, and
I believe that watching individual tribes grow can give a valuable
insight into the nature of any tribe, however long established. Indeed one of the first questions to ask about any corporate tribe you
encounter is how and why it began, and who started it. Who started
it is particularly important. A tribe can of course be started by an
act of management, but that is not the way most tribes come into
being. By far the most common and most successful method of tribal
formation begins around the nucleus of a single dominant ten-group.
There is hardly a product group, department or factory that cannot
be traced back to an explosion at some point in the past, when a new
ten-group came together, seized an opportunity, developed it, and
expanded to tribal size. It is not hard to think of the ancient hunting
band finding a new territory with a new plentiful food supply, and
expanding their numbers in the same way, forming new hunting
bands, attracting stragglers or other less successful bands, and
building up a new tribe around them.

But whether the tribe originated in this sort of 'extended family'
or was founded as a confederation of ten-groups, it still takes its
orders and style and direction and standards from the ten-group
that leads it—the tribal chief and his council of elders. And it is
of course the tribal chief who is the key man—not only of the tribe,

but of the corporation. Since a large organization is in fact administering tribes, the good tribal chief is at once the guarantee of his tribe's efficiency and success, and the channel of communication between the corporate leadership and the multitude of tribesmen.

Great corporations can make great mistakes. A single error of judgment—like the Rolls-Royce costing of the RB 211—can destroy the corporation. A single stroke of good judgment—like Rank's alliance with Xerox—can save an empire. If you are running a giant corporation, you have plenty to do without worrying about who is minding the shop. Yet the corporation may be crumbling away beneath you, and your customers may find it out before you do. It will not be dramatic, with millions of pounds suddenly changing sides on the balance sheet, it will be myriads of tiny, almost imperceptible, failures. The car key that jams in the lock after three days, the shop assistant who does not know what she has in stock, the service engineer who says he will call and doesn't, the sullen, unhelpful girl on the switchboard, the travelling salesman who is obviously just going through the motions of selling without any conviction—all these and hundreds like them will happen from time to time in any corporation, but if allowed to multiply they can build up almost insensibly until they are a talking point among customers and the start of a long slow slide down the hill. They are beyond the direct control of any top corporate executive, but with a good tribal structure the offender will be personally known to the tribal chief and the tribal chief will be personally known to the top executive: a very different matter from six levels of corporate hierarchy.

Of course any hierarchical system will reach a point where someone on the chart has roughly five hundred people working under him; but this will not ensure that they form a tribe. The problem is to turn the man with five hundred subordinates from an official in middle management into a chieftain. The hardest part of the transformation is grasping what the difference is and seeing the need for change. The rest is still hard work, but not beyond the powers of any experienced manager.

The difference is rooted in the freedom and authority of the chieftain. He is not just one more link in the chain, with authority and responsibility slightly wider than his subordinates' and narrower than his superiors'; he is much more like the boss of his own independent firm. Nevertheless he has to be very much a part of the corporation, he has to be simultaneously separated and integrated. There are no rules for the resolution of this paradox, but there is a principle: the area of the chieftain's independent authority should be defined so clearly that both he and the corporation know the boundary line with great precision, and within that boundary no one should interfere with his operations; and wherever the boundary is drawn, he must be left with enough authority to be accepted by those under him as the personification of the corporation and the only channel through which they encounter its authority. It is this last point that lies at the root: whatever authority he may or may not have over money or policy, his leadership of his people must be unquestioned. A tribal chieftain can have very limited management authority indeed and still be a chieftain, but (as with a ten-group leader) unless his subordinates realize that for all practical purposes his word is their law, the tribal structure does not exist.

That is very abstract and oracular, but the difficulty of being more precise is well illustrated by the practices of two corporations, both employing about thirty thousand people. They have in common the reputation built up over many years of being among the best-managed corporations in the Western World. I have chosen them because of the extreme contrast in their approach; the difference will demonstrate why precise rules are so hard to formulate, and the residual similarity will illustrate the underlying principle. The companies are 3M of America and Marks & Spencer of Britain.

I became interested in 3M because of a saucepan scourer. I had known of them for some time as one of the world's largest producers of recording tapes, so it came as a surprise to find that such a large organization was interested in such a small object as a saucepan scourer: conversely, if a firm so large and successful was bothering to launch a new saucepan scourer, it must surely be very good (which it was). On investigating further I discovered that this was not just a whimsical experiment: they actually had more products than employees, and they had, as I said, over thirty thousand employees. This tremendous diversity was possible only because of dedication to the principle of forming ten-groups and allowing them to expand into tribes whenever they could link a new product with a growth market. Often it was simple adaptation of an existing product: Scotch tape adapted for surgeons, Scotch tape as curling tape for the cosmetic market, Scotch tape for masking in paint shops, Scotch tape for protection in packaging departments – if it looked promising enough, a ten-group would form and go out hunting. Equally, if a researcher came up with something new, his tribal chief encouraged him to form a ten-group and try to find a market. If he succeeded, he could expand until he became a tribal chief himself, the head of one of the thirty-odd divisions. He would be given the maximum freedom to make his own decisions about the product, its package, price, market, and production volume, to hire the staff he needed, and in fact to become virtually an independent entrepreneur within the corporation.

The Marks & Spencer tribes are the stores, nearly 250 of them, of which the largest employ several hundred staff: the store manager is the tribal chief. By contrast with a 3M chieftain he might appear to be powerless. All the goods are selected for him by the tribe of merchandisers at head office, they determine style, colour, sizes, price, and, for seasonal goods, starting and stopping times. All his layout and display and relative space for goods are laid down by another headquarters tribe called store operations. Staff wage rates are laid down, and so are procedures for dealing with customer's complaints and queries. He could hardly be more different from a 3M tribal chieftain developing new products and new markets on a very loose rein from head office.

And yet everyone in Marks & Spencer knows that the difference between a good and a bad store manager is crucial. In each area, a good store manager has scope to improve his results by enterprise and good judgment. He can pay a really good assistant more than the fixed rate. He can move rainwear to a more prominent place in a wet spell, or woollens in a cold snap. He can have more pink dresses and fewer blue ones sent because of a local preference he has noticed. He can extend the space for footwear if he sees the new range of shoes moving faster than the forecast. But more than all this, he is boss of his people; he is responsible for the efficiency and helpfulness of his staff and the focus of their loyalty. As far as they are concerned, he is the company. He is the arbiter of their disputes and the solver of their problems. This may not match the responsibility of a private owner running his own show, but it is critical, and it keeps him watching, thinking, learning and experimenting all the time.

What he has in common with his fellow chieftain in 3M is absolute clarity about his tribal boundaries, about which actions lie within his discretion and which are outside it. Moreover, it is not a private piece of knowledge which he shares secretly with his immediate superior: in each case it is known to everyone. How wide or narrow the boundaries are will affect the size of the job and the power and importance of the tribe; the presence of clear boundaries determines whether the tribe is being allowed to function as a tribe at all. In the case of Marks & Spencer, if divisional supervisors or merchandisers or store operations staff could walk into the store and start giving orders to the salesgirls about changing the knitwear display, or telling them to go and comb their hair, or ordering them to sweep the floors again, or sending them to the stockroom to get more shirts, then the tribal authority of the chieftain and the operational efficiency of the store would be destroyed. It is the manager's job. He does it well or he does it badly, but no one else does it for him.

There is a consequence of this which is equally important if the latent energy of the tribe is to be released and harnessed to the success of the corporation: there must be an objective criterion by which success and failure are measured. 'Objective' is the important word. It is not enough that someone upstairs should be pleased; tomorrow he may be angry at the same result. The measurement must be drawn from the market-place, if possible by making the tribe a self-contained profit centre, and always by setting a target in advance. It is remarkable how often industry's tribal chieftains, if allowed to set their own target, come up with a tougher one than anyone would set for them — but then it is remarkable for the same reason how interior decorators always take a fortnight over a job they say they can do in a week. A 3M tribal chief asks for his year's investment allocation in proportion to the profits he expects to make: he expects to be judged in the market-place. A Marks & Spencer store manager knows equally clearly what the turnover of his store should be, and there are his previous year's records and the results of the other stores to compare it with. In neither corporation is there secrecy about these results — every tribal chieftain knows how all the others have done and how his achievements compare with theirs.

Not every tribe, obviously, can become a profit centre. All the same it is surprising how often a market measurement can be found. It is often possible to compare the cost of a year's work by the legal or financial department with the cost of similar quality work from an outside firm of solicitors or accountants. It is also possible to put work out to such firms from time to time as a check. The same is even more true of the in-house supplier of parts: the front-line tribes should be free to purchase from outside if they get better service that way, and a part of General Motors' success in controlling such a vast empire so profitably for so long has been a resolute opposition to corporate protectionism: G.M. component manufacturers have to sell to G.M. vehicle-producing divisions on a level footing with everyone else; if they cannot compete successfully, they are selected out.

The creation of a tribe, therefore, demands complete and detailed agreement with the tribal chieftain on just three subjects: the resources available to him, the results required of him, and the limitations on his freedom of action. If he is doing his job properly, there should be no other subjects on which he has to defer to his corporate superiors. Above all, he must be the ultimate source of authority among his tribespeople. Their holidays, wages, uniforms and conditions of service may be determined by a higher power: that does not matter. What matters is that orders should be given only by him, or by someone acting on his authority; that requests should go to him; that disputes should be resolved by him; and that for all practical and operational purposes his yea is yea and his nay is nay; he is the father of the tribe.

There is one other factor which can be of great assistance: the actual authority over physical territory. A store manager, a factory manager, a headmaster, a destroyer commander—they all acquire an increase of stimulus and satisfaction by being able to walk round a place and feel it is theirs. It may not actually belong to them, but then Buckingham Palace does not belong to the Queen or the White House to the President. It is sufficient that as long as they hold the office it is under their command. Physical territory enables the manager to ask anyone what he is doing there, with the clear implication that he recognizes the man as a stranger and has the right to remove him from the premises. I have never seen territorial authority recommended in any book on management; but I have never seen a department head in a vast office block walking down the corridors with the pride and authority of a factory manager going round his factory.

The tribal structure of industry was much clearer in the early days of the Industrial Revolution. The mines and mills were mostly tribal in size, many had been established for a generation or more, and the difficulty of travel gave them a closer cohesion. Above all, they were comparatively static; it is the rate of change that has blurred or obliterated tribal boundaries in the modern corporation. A group of five hundred can become two or three thousand much faster than the human capacity for organic enlargement, and it is all too tempting to try and manage them within the original structure. Sometimes tribal logic takes over, and within a complex of several thousand people a number of separate tribes develop: a determined, efficient and truculent manager has his own ways of making sure he is not messed about. He has the inestimable advantage of knowing everything that is going on in his tribe, and why, and this is a powerful weapon to fight his superiors with. Another is the respect he has from his tribesmen. Above all he is getting the results that keep his superiors in their jobs, and the threat of walking out is the most powerful weapon, the ultimate deterrent, so long as he does not wield it too lightly or too often. Consequently you find informal and unofficial tribes which are acknowledged in fact, but not in theory. I have met such a tribal chieftain who was installing machinery costing upwards of £70,000 before the application for capital appropriation had been given approval. He knew it was necessary, he knew it would more than pay for itself, he knew the money was there, and he knew there were five jobs waiting for him in other corporations if his bosses wanted to make anything of it. But equally there are groups of thousands, or even hundreds, where no tribal structure remains. Orders are given by one authority and rescinded by another, nobody knows who he is working for, bad work is unreproved and good work unrewarded, managers are constantly saying, 'I don't know, you'd better ask X or Y or Z,' and only a few scattered ten-groups preserve their little pools of efficiency and self-respect.

Even when there is a sound tribal structure, it is often in a transitional state. The ten-groups expand, and several of them form sub-tribes within the tribe. It is often hard to recognize the point at which the division has to be made, the umbilical cord has to be cut, the new leader has to lead his tribe over the mountains towards the promised land. It is sometimes hard even to recognize that this has to be done as a deliberate act of management organization: it is easier to leave an uneasy agglomeration where the overall chief no longer has real personal knowledge of his whole tribal operation and the headmen of the sub-tribes do not have the independence and authority to do their job as they want to. It creates the friction of the young man who is grown up and earning his own living but still staying at home with his parents. Respect and affection do not diminish the friction — on the contrary, they prolong it. A time comes when the break has to be made, the young man has to leave home, the intermediate manager has to be established as the head of his own department, and a new tribe sets off.

And yet, in a situation where markets, technology, processes, and materials are changing so fast, the tribes are the most powerful force for stability, for making sense out of the change, for assimilating and turning to use and profit the valuable innovations, and discarding or modifying the others. But tribes, unlike new machinery, do not arrive overnight. They may be formed in a hurry, but it takes time to form ten-groups, to weld their knowledge and expertise into a body of tribal wisdom, to agree tribal frontiers, to sort out internal relationships, to establish standards and principles, and to confirm the status and authority of the chieftain. But when this has been done, when a tribe has had a number of years to establish itself, it can be a corporate asset at least as important as cash or plant. It is a cliché to say, 'Our people are our greatest asset,' especially when we all know that some of them are our greatest liability; but a successful corporation tribe that has been going for a long time establishes traditions, standards, a reputation, a depth of relevant knowledge, experience and memory, and a capacity for adapting to and cashing in on change, which are indeed an asset. But they are not held by any single person, like, say, the ability to speak Japanese; they are a fixed asset vested in the whole tribe — an asset which can continue to provide profits but cannot be exchanged for cash. Of course there can be bad tribes, they can be badly led, they can lose touch with the market, they can become ingrown and blinkered and inflexible; but very often the capacity for regeneration is there if it can be stimulated and the barriers removed. And this repair and regeneration of the tribes ranks with the formation of them as one of the prime tasks of corporate management, just as the destruction or dispersal of a successful tribe in a merger or takeover or corporate reorganization, because of the logic of administration or accountancy, can represent a loss to the corporation which it is beyond the wit of any administrator or accountant to make good. But if we are to understand what it means to build tribes and maintain them in good health, we shall have to look more closely at the inner workings of the corporation tribe, and at the stresses that can threaten its survival.

12 Tribal Unity: Rebellion and Civil War

IT IS much easier to isolate the tribe as a single discrete organism than to open it up and see what happens inside. To the outside corporate world it is, or should be, an independent entity. Something goes in one end, something else comes out the other. If it is a manufacturing tribe, it is raw metal and castings, wire and sub-assemblies, coolants and lubricants, and paint and electric power that go in, and finished products that come out. If it is a store, cases of consumer products go in, and bags full of cash come out. If it is an infantry battalion, fuel and food and ammunition go in, and newly acquired territory comes out. If it is a school, raw, untreated, unprocessed children go in and refined, processed, certificated children come out (at least that is the current theory). With service organizations, government departments and so on the input and output are less visible and measurable, but even there a good tribe will have a clear role and those who control it will know if it is functioning well or badly, and if it is going well they will be happy to leave it alone.

Tribes, however, do not always function well. Sometimes the reasons are outside tribal control—a shift in the market or a new technology or a change of government policy may take away their livelihood almost overnight. Sometimes the reasons lie in the inadequacy of individuals or ten-groups—failure to take decisions in time, inability to plan the work and control the people who are supposed to do it. Sometimes the reasons are to be found in the corporation—too much interference, too little guidance, decisions delayed or taken without full information. But when all these occasional variables have been removed, there remain certain permanent factors in the constitution of tribes which make the tribal chieftain's task harder or easier, and influence the tribe's collective behaviour. Very little useful discussion of the internal workings of a tribe can take place without reference to them.

The first consideration is the balance of tribal population between male and female. An all-male tribe is always liable to bouts of collective aggression, whereas a reasonable proportion of women working with the men dilutes the concentration of aggressive energy, and makes the chieftain's task easier. If the tribal population is almost wholly female, the dangers of explosion are very small indeed. A strike is the ultimate expression of the collapse of the corporation's tribal system (though it may also express a flourishing tribal system within the union) and it is historically the all-male tribes in mines and docks and car factories which have provided the longest and bitterest strikes, whereas strikes of all-female tribes are extremely rare.

The strength of collective aggression rises with numbers, so absolute size is the second important factor. A small tribe of one or two hundred is far less of a problem than a tribe that is rising up towards a thousand and beyond. But there is a third factor which can enormously diminish or intensify the importance of numbers, namely their concentration or dispersal. If the people are in small groups and widely separated, with little or no chance of forming larger groups, then the problem is much less than if they are concentrated in one place. Every schoolmaster knows that forty or fifty boys in a single group in the playground is something that has to be investigated at once, whereas ten or a dozen can be left alone. Every factory manager knows that a knot of forty or fifty men together on the factory floor during a tea break needs the same urgent investigation. A work situation which encourages that sort of spontaneous congregation is far more inflammable than when it takes a lot of pre-arrangement.

The easiest tribes to control, therefore, are small, widely dispersed and chiefly composed of women: stores, schools, banks, offices, hospitals. These factors are of course no guarantee of enterprise, efficiency or success; the work can still be extremely badly done. What they mean is that the simple fact of organizing people is not one of the major problems, and therefore the internal structure is not critical. Many different groupings and sub-groupings can work perfectly well, depending on the nature of the job.

At the other end of the scale is the large all-male tribe concentrated into a small area, with plenty of opportunities for mingling in large numbers. This has to be recognized as an inherently explosive situation, and in this situation more than any other the corporation is in danger of losing control. The first safety-valve is a proper structure of ten-groups, with none of them getting too large: if they can be divided up so that the groups correspond to an operational function, so much the better; but if not, then the evolved leaders of the natural social groupings, the informal ten-groups, need to be given proper recognition and representation. There are many decisions which are not operational — holidays, shift working, conditions of work — which can easily cause grievances and build up a head of steam. If each ten-group has an acknowledged identity and an official spokesman or representative, the steam can find an outlet. It can also help the sense of belonging, of being part of the tribe, if each ten-group has its own territory: even a group of machines arranged in an open square instead of along an endless line can help to build this sense of group identity, just as it is easier in cities to create a sense of community among the houses round a square than among those along a road.

With a tribe of this composition, the further groupings of ten-groups become extremely important. In theory, the leaders of ten ten-groups ought to form a ten-group of their own to sort out the work of a hundred. In practice this rarely seems to happen: the next grouping seems to work out at thirty or forty, three or four groups, with someone in charge who is not (though probably was previously) a full-time leader of a ten-group. He is the foreman, the subaltern, the supervisor; and just as this size of thirty or forty corresponds to the size of the camp to which the hunting band returned, so he corresponds to the head of the elders who does not go on the hunt himself but who is the final arbitrating authority between the needs of the camp and the needs of the hunt. He is the most underrated figure in the corporation. Just as the tribal chieftain is the key man in the wider corporation, the link between the highest level of planning and the real events on the factory floor, so the foreman is the link between the chieftain and the hour-by-hour progress of the tribe's efforts. He is the pivot. All information and instructions reach the ten-groups through him, all the problems and resentments and long-term worries of the ten-groups are interpreted, evaluated and then expressed by him to the chieftain. So long as he and his dozen or so colleagues in the tribe are respected and trusted by the ten-groups (they do not have to be liked) and are fully in the confidence of the chieftain and his council, the tribe is properly bound together. If not, that is the point where the break comes and where the union starts to build its alternative organization, its own revolutionary tribe.

If the foreman or supervisor is the naturally evolved leader from the three or four ten-groups' leaders, then half the battle is won: an outsider superimposed on the groups has a tremendous task to get his authority accepted and is all too likely to be treated as a joke or an irrelevance. It is much easier to forge the link in the other direction, to take someone who is respected on the shop floor and weld him into the tribal leadership structure. What is more, there is an instrument for doing this, though it is nearly always neglected. The man who saw the way most clearly, though at a far more exalted level, was Alfred Sloan. He recognized that at the very top of General Motors there was exactly this danger: a fatal separation between the long-term planning and the day-to-day operations, between the board and the executives, the future and the present, the camp and the hunting bands.[1] And so he established a regular meeting between the divisional heads — Chevrolet, Buick, Cadillac and so on — and the government of General Motors, his own four-man executive committee. No decisions were ever taken at this meeting; that was not its purpose. Part of its purpose was to enable those who were planning the future to have a sense of the current mood of the divisions — were they chafing at restrictions and bursting to go, or feeling overstrained and hoping for a let-up? Part of it was to test out new ideas on the practical men. Part of it was to find out how past decisions were working out in practice. Part of it was to lift the eyes of the divisions from the floors of their factories up to the horizon, and see where the whole enterprise ought to be heading. Part of it was to keep each side aware of the other's problems and aims.

This meeting between warriors and statesmen is needed at every level in the corporation, but at none more urgently than the lowest, when the foremen sit round with the tribal chieftain and his elders. It is also the easiest meeting to neglect, since it is not related to the day's operations. And even when it is held, it can too easily degenerate into a string of detailed trivia ('Item 34, the cold tap in number 2 washroom ... '), or simply become the boss's briefing session, where he issues his orders. At least half the purpose of the meeting is for the boss to shut up and listen, and half the agenda should

9

normally be decided by the foremen; the boss should raise on his own initiative only those questions that require a decision from him.

There is very often another problem: many tribes have to divide into sub-tribes for operational purposes, and groups of foremen may report to a departmental manager; a tribe may well contain four or five such managers, and they will necessarily form the chief's operational group for most practical day-to-day purposes. But these departmental managers can also form a barrier between the chief and the foremen, since he will not need to meet them operationally; they will get their orders at one remove. This in fact makes it necessary to hold the meetings with them more frequently than if he were in direct operational contact, but in practice (and especially if the intermediate managers do not understand the difference between the hunt and the camp) it works the other way: he talks to the intermediate managers instead of the foremen.

This meeting, of course, if properly conducted, serves another purpose. Not only does it enable grievances, ideas and problems to rise up to the top—it enables people to rise as well. Most tribes are run by a ten-group, which often seems to work out as the chieftain with two or three elders (finance, planning, personnel) and the three or four operational group managers, perhaps with a works manager in a managing-director relationship to the chieftain's chairmanship. This occasional wider meeting, where they collectively meet the whole group of foremen together, is perhaps the only opportunity to form a tribal judgment (as opposed to a number of separate private judgments) of who are the coming men and what is the real status-ranking of the foremen. One of the prime causes of disaffection, sedition and revolution is blocking the upward route of the best men, the men with ambition, status-dominance and a popular following. The fortunes of a factory or a kingdom can hinge on whether such men are allowed to become gamekeepers or forced to be poachers. At each level this meeting is the arena in which they first show their mettle.

These three factors—numbers, concentration and male-female balance—determine the danger of a horizontal division within the tribe, a fatal separation between the top and the bottom, between the managers and the men. There are, however, three other factors which when they become critical can create not a horizontal but a vertical division, not subversion and revolution but baronial warfare: in short, conflict between rival groups within the tribe.

The first of these is change in the volume of tribal activity and prosperity: as long as the volume remains constant, the existing boundaries between ten-groups or other subdivisions of the tribe remain unchallenged, but if the volume of work either contracts or expands with any rapidity, the boundaries come under pressure. With expansion, a small group is likely to grow bigger and start to assert itself, new men become important and older ones resent their assertiveness, and friction begins. ('Why the hell do we have to clear our plans with them? We're bringing in twice the business they are. Let them clear their plans with us.') With contraction, the groups see their importance and even their jobs disappearing, and each tries to keep hold of the work that will continue, or grab some from somewhere else. Of the two, expansion is by far the more liable to cause strife, since in a contracting situation few people will press a quarrel to the point at which they become a nuisance, because nuisances are so easily disposed of: but when business is expanding the nuisances are often the most necessary to the future prosperity of the whole tribe, and they know it.

The second of these factors is change in the type of work. Even when the volume remains fairly constant, there is sometimes frequent change in the sort of tasks the tribe has to undertake. If the factory simply turns out ball-point pens year after year, responsibilities become clearly defined and universally accepted: if it is constantly having to adapt to new products and processes and materials and machines, the weight of responsibility is likely to shift around, causing much the same friction as the increasing volume of work which so often accompanies it. And the third factor concerns the antiquity of the tribe: if they have all been together a long time, they can adapt much better to these shifts and innovations than a group which has been newly formed or rapidly expanded to twice its original size or even larger. The easier of the two extremes here, therefore, is the old-established tribe which is still doing much the same sort of work in a fairly constant volume. In such a situation there is unlikely to be any serious clash over function and jurisdiction and boundaries of responsibility. At the other extreme is the newly formed or suddenly expanded tribe with a growing volume of work of a constantly changing kind: and this brings a major problem.

The problem is rooted very deep in our animal nature. I have already referred to the territorial instinct, the inborn compulsion to acquire and defend your own exclusive territory, which is common to many species including man. I have found in the corporation something that I can explain only in territorial terms even though it is not strictly territorial. It is a kind of territorial defence of role or job, and although it certainly operates within individuals, it is at its most powerful in groups: 'my department's responsibility', 'my salesmen's area', 'my union's job'. A hunting band, after all, would defend its camp, but it would also resist intrusion into its hunting area even by other bands from the same tribe. On the other hand, an intrusion without hunting intent into a part of the area where there was no game would be unimportant: the significant factor would not be territory as such, but a threat to compete for the same source of food. The result is something I can only call a quasi-territorial response, a defence of your means of livelihood calling upon territorial instincts but not precisely or exclusively territorial in its application.

Once a ten-group or tribe or any other grouping within the corporation is given a clearly defined task and an area of responsibility, it has the title-deeds to a piece of quasi-territory: but a changing situation will constantly call the boundary line into question, and if it creates uncertainty or overlap it will provoke the most formidable animal reactions from Corporation Man. Troops of howling monkeys have a way of standing each on their own side of the territorial boundary and howling at each other in fierce and deafening concert: departmental managers and craft union officials often behave in a very similar way.

In my B.B.C. days the classic quasi-territorial boundary, the Gaza Strip of the Corporation, lay between *Tonight* and *Panorama*. *Tonight* covered current affairs in the widest terms and at every level for five nights a week, whereas *Panorama* dealt once a week with events of the highest national and international significance. If an important public figure was suddenly in the news, which programme should he be invited on to? If *Tonight* had a topical reason for dealing on Friday with a subject *Panorama* had spent days preparing for the following Monday, who should have preference? If both programmes wanted to send a film crew across the world to report on an important event, should the B.B.C.

duplicate its efforts or give preference to one or the other? On each occasion the howling monkeys emerged and went through their conventional rituals, and observers would have thought the division was irreparable. But six miles away in Alexandra Palace there was another complete tribe which occasionally raided the tribal quasi-territory which both programmes shared. It was called News Division, and was a danger to us all. In times of news urgency it might even demand immediate use of film that *Tonight* or *Panorama* were planning to use in a day or two's time, on the grounds that it could thus scoop the competitive commercial stations. If we transmitted a feature which upset an important institution, they would search vigorously for errors in our treatment so as to accuse us of endangering their news access in the future through incompetence. They would even try and establish situations when we had to apply to them for permission to film events or interview individuals. In these crises, the differences between *Tonight* and *Panorama* were forgotten, and we would present a united front to the common foe. We realized that if they won those battles, the two of us would be left squabbling over the bones and offal while they devoured the meat in their cave in Alexandra Palace.

Was this competition to the advantage or disadvantage of the B.B.C. as a whole? The answer is that it could be either in any given case. Quite often *Panorama* or *Tonight* would move so fast on a news event in order to get in before the other that the programmes of the commercial television companies would be left standing. Quite often a part of the driving motive behind an item was to show the other programme how it ought to be done. Sometimes this professional competitiveness would provoke ingenious economies to show that 'we can do it cheaper than they can'. In all sorts of ways the competition could be healthy and creative. But there was no guarantee that this would always be so; if an important piece of film were offered to the B.B.C. and the two programmes started bidding against each other for it, that could do the B.B.C. no good, though the owner of the film would be happy. If the Prime Minister found five rival B.B.C. programmes all pursuing him and asking him not to go on the others, it could not help the B.B.C. management's posture as the single united national instrument of broadcasting: nor would it help any of the programmes if he chose to appear on commercial television because he was fed up with being pestered to make the B.B.C. management's decisions. It could not help if one programme forced the other to hire an outside film crew rather than lend it one of its own that was not working that day. Consequently neither a ban on all internal competitiveness nor a total free-for-all could be the answer.

An equally passionate quasi-territorial battle was fought out in Whitehall shortly after the election of the Labour Government in 1964. The Treasury, the most powerful of all the ministries, had historically controlled all government expenditure, long-term as well as short-term. The Labour Government believed this was too much conflicting responsibility for a single ministry, and set up the Department of Economic Affairs to take over the longer-term part. To the politicians it may have seemed a simple and sensible piece of administrative reorganization: to the Treasury it was a monstrous and intolerable assault on their ancient quasi-territorial rights. They fought with the desperate passion of men defending their homeland, and in the end they won. The D.E.A. never managed to prise out of the Treasury the control of longer-term investment they needed, and were left with the dregs of economic power—regional planning, the control of prices and incomes—while the Treasury went on drinking the wine.

And yet despite the emotional intensity of the quasi-territorial responses there is no guarantee that the existing boundaries are the best ones to serve the corporation's ends. A manufacturing company which was in grave trouble with its customers because of bad workmanship decided that the trouble lay in quasi-territory: the manager responsible for meeting delivery deadlines was also responsible for inspection, and, with frantic customers and salesmen on the phone demanding instant dispatch of the product, it was always inspection that was scamped. So they removed inspection from his authority and set up a quite separate inspectorate reporting straight to the director of production, with the not surprising result that complaints and returned products dropped dramatically.

And of course border conflict can be to the corporate advantage; the competition between Birds Eye frozen peas and Batchelor's tinned peas is more rather than less intense because they are both part of Unilever. And yet if Birds Eye and Batchelor's were to start competing by privately knocking the other product, retailers might decide to move over to some third supplier outside the corporation. So do you encourage border conflict or discourage it?

This is one of the most common of management dilemmas; publishing houses constantly encounter it between their various magazines and newspapers, government departments meet it all the time. They realize that it can be a positive source of alertness, efficiency and enterprise: from the corporation's point of view it provides the ideal form of 'conventional competition' when it works, since whichever group wins or loses, the corporation itself goes from strength to strength and constantly improves its stock by expanding through the victorious groups and economizing in the unsuccessful. A large part of the success of General Motors was due to their seeing the logic of this kind of internal rivalry earlier than most people. But when it does not work it can be damaging and divisive, as rival departments try to encompass each other's downfall. So what should you do?

Obviously there is no simple rule, but most people seem to have hammered out certain principles. The first, I would say, is to abandon the fiction that we are all a big united family, sharing our delight in each other's success and our disappointment at each other's reverses. The tribal chief must expect rivalry between the ten-groups and sub-tribes, and expect it to manifest itself in competition between the leaders: equally, the corporation must expect tribal chiefs to compete against each other. It is in the strictest sense natural behaviour; competition between individuals and groups for each other's territory is common to many species and ensures that the weak and irresolute and unfit are kept down while the strong and determined and courageous survive and expand. Since group competitiveness has got us this far, there is little hope of outlawing it successfully in the corporation, and a great deal to be gained by channelling it in the right direction.

The second principle was best enunciated by Robert Frost (or, more accurately, by his neighbour) in the poem 'Mending Wall': 'Good fences make good neighbours.' His insight has recently been confirmed by a psychological experiment designed to find how people get on each other's nerves when forced to live in each other's pockets for long periods. Several pairs of sailors shared small cabins for several weeks, and it was found that friction and quarrels were lowest where they agreed early and clearly which space and seats and cupboards and table area belonged to which. Lack of certainty and definition was the prime irritant. Corporation Man needs exactly the same clarity and certainty, and an important part of the tribal chief's job is to see that these fences are firmly established and in the right place to further the success of the whole tribe. It is one of the most important of organizational tasks, and failure comes most often through drawing fences round functions which are part of a single entity. It can too easily result in production competing with engineering by proving that making up the design takes twice as long as the designer said, and sales competing with them both by proving no one wants to buy it. Fences round complete products or projects or sections of the market stimulate the right sort of competition. It was interesting that whereas the fence between *Tonight* and *Panorama* was in principle an extremely good one, a bad one started to be constructed within *Tonight* while I was there and chiefly because of my own failure to realize I ought to do something about it. The fence divided the film directors from the film editors: because of the speed of the programme and the volume of film used, there was rarely time for directors to meet film editors, let alone supervise the cutting of their films. As a result, resentment started to grow on both sides: the directors thought the editors were ruining their masterpieces, and the editors thought the directors were shooting too much useless or aimless film, and both lost enthusiasm, satisfaction and incentive. Obviously I should have teamed up each director with his own editor, made sure they met as often as possible, and held them jointly responsible for the final result. Instead, I allowed the bad fences to go on making bad neighbours.

There is a third principle which follows from this, namely that just as everyone has to be absolutely clear where the boundaries are and where overlap and quasi-territorial infringement are forbidden, so it must be equally clear where competitiveness is permitted and encouraged, and this too must be constructed to further the tribes' interests. Robert Frost's neighbour was right, but Frost was right too when he said, 'Something there is that doesn't love a wall, that wants it down.' Any group needs room to expand, to test its strength, to break into new hunting grounds. It must not be completely hemmed in — there must be a gap in the wall, a place for locking antlers with the others in conventional competition.

It would have been perfectly possible for Alfred Sloan, when establishing his five main car divisions to correspond with five different market levels (Chevrolet, Oldsmobile, Buick, Pontiac, Cadillac), to lay down that the top price in one division should stop short of the bottom price of the next; instead he encouraged overlap at each end, so that as a customer approached the top of the range in one G.M. division, the next division up was competing for his custom at the same price.[2]

Nevertheless, with the best designed fences in the world there are still going to be disputed frontiers where the warfare does nobody any good and a line has to be drawn. The best guidance here comes from observing Professor Carpenter's Rhesus monkeys. He took 350 of them from various parts of India and released them on an island in the West Indies. There was plenty of food, plenty of room and no predators, yet within a year they had split up into groups and each group had established a clear territorial area — an exclusive space where no other group was permitted to trespass.[3] My experience of the corporation suggests that the same thing happens there too; groups work out their own frontiers with each other, and too much or too rapid intervention by the chieftain can make him spend most of his time in arbitration. When *Tonight* was disputing with *Panorama* and had no real case, I knew it in my bones and I am sure it came out in my voice. Equally when I felt so strongly that I was prepared to take the matter up to the Director General if necessary, this too was clear from my demeanour and *Panorama* retreated with the appropriate threatening or derisive gestures. Observers have noticed how a monkey who has trespassed on to a neighbour's territory behaves with the furtive guilt of a schoolboy raiding an orchard, and hurtles out in the same way if he is spotted. Corporation Man, or Corporation Manager, has just the same sense of guilt and nearly always knows when he is on his own territory and when he is trespassing, just as he knows when his neighbour is burning with a passionate grievance and when he is just trying it on. A judgment from the chief of the tribe works only if it confirms what both of them know in their hearts anyway, and very often the dispute is better settled by offering to give a ruling only if they cannot agree by negotiation within a limited time.

There is one other weapon at the disposal of the chief: the meeting between the warriors and the elders. It can be very difficult for him to be constantly in single combat with a territorially aggressive leader, particularly when the boundary dispute becomes, as it too easily can, a challenge to the chieftain's authority. It is true that the warriors and elders meeting is concerned with issues that unite the tribe rather than those which divide it; but in fact the unity of the tribe is threatened if one of the headmen is constantly marauding his neighbours, and the united condemnation of all the others, particularly if they have been welded into an effective ten-group, is too powerful for even the most egocentric expansionist to defy. The wise chieftain will, however, privately assure himself that such united condemnation will indeed be forthcoming before he raises the issue.

13 Status and Hierarchy

REBELLION and baronial war are the two most obvious consequences of weak tribal leadership or inadequate tribal structure. There is however a third; it is less spectacular but much more pervasive, and is a far more personal source of anxiety and friction than the other two. It concerns status.

Of all the driving motives inside Corporation Man, his concern for personal status within the corporate hierarchy is the least understood. There seems to be a generally accepted view that the desire for status is comical and unworthy, and that status-seeking is the mark of the worst sort of organization man. Everyone subscribes to the pretence that status considerations do not operate. 'I just need a larger office because I have to have meetings of twenty people'; 'It's not the size of the car, it's the silence of the engine I need because of the dictating I do while I'm driving'; 'A carpet gives much better sound insulation than linoleum'. But in fact, so far from being shameful or unnatural, the drive for status is one of the principal tools of evolution and natural selection not only in man but in a wide range of other species, and in particular those species which go around in groups; indeed, it is doubtful whether there is any animal society that does not have a status hierarchy. Baboons, jackdaws, monkeys, hyenas, antelopes, rats, hens, sword-tail fish — the list goes on and on, and man has his place in it as clearly as any of the other animals. The function of status is to select for survival the best individuals in the group — the best both individually and for the group. When food is short, the status-dominant will eat and the weak will starve. When females are hard to come by, it is the status-dominant who will mate and breed. Equally, when disorder breaks out in the group it is the status-dominant who move in and quell the strife, and when the group is attacked the status-dominant head the defence. A driving force which has been one of the instruments of our survival for so many millions of years is not going to disappear because it clashes with corporate organization theory.

All the same, there is a profound difference between status in animal communities and status in the corporation. It is very rare for animal status-rankings to change once they are established, except with the normal processes of maturity, ageing and death. Contemporaries usually sort out their pecking order early in life and keep it thereafter. Life in the jungle is not a status struggle – rather, it is the reverse. Animals know their own status and the status of all the others in the group; the leader evolves and maintains his leadership, the others all know their respective places, and although occasional challenges and squabbles develop the normal consequence is stability, security, and – in both senses of the word – order. It is the large numbers, the anonymity, the changing forms of organization and the frequent new groupings and relationships which make corporation life so much more anxious and insecure than life in the jungle.

The unit of the corporation which comes closest to the fixed and secure status-ranking of the jungle is, without any question, the ten-group. I cannot recall ever encountering a ten-group in which status manoeuvring or dispute was ever a significant factor. Occasionally the arrival of a new recruit might cause temporary disturbance, but he would quite soon find his ranking or depart. It is this complete certainty and security about status that makes it so satisfying to work in a ten-group – and there is the added advantage that you also have a clear status within a wider circle by virtue of your known membership of that ten-group. 'I'm in Number 3 Platoon, B Company,' gives you immediate identity within a regiment of six hundred men: you have your own established status within your section and platoon, and the platoon has a distinctive identity within the regiment. This internal status balance of the ten-group has been used with extraordinary effectiveness by I.B.M. in their factory at Greenock in Scotland. It employs nearly two thousand people, and there is a leader to every ten workers; and each leader determines the relative payment of the men under him by grading them from A to E. According to reports, the result has been extreme harmony and a very low level of dispute and discontent over pay. Certainly the idea of pay differentials being fixed by each ten-group leader has a great deal of natural common sense behind it.

The ten-group is the only unit in which status is almost invariably secure. All the same it is by no means impossible (though it is less common) for this same security to extend to the sub-tribe and even the tribe. Carveth Read in *The Origin of Man* quotes one

of the most basic statements of status security from the memoirs of
an American pioneer: 'All along the frontier between Canada and
the United States everyone knew who he could lick and who could
lick him.' In a long-established and self-contained corporation
tribe, the tribesmen have much the same security. They know who
rates higher than them and who rates lower, and they know that
everyone else knows; consequently they do not have to keep assert-
ing anything. This may well be yet another reason why five hundred
or so is the normal limit for an effective corporate tribe: it is difficult
to know who you can lick and who can lick you if the number rises
much higher. Of course within the tribe the ten-groups will have
their own status-rankings, and in a changing situation these can
alter and cause exactly the same friction and division as disputes
over quasi-territory: if, for instance, the manager of one department
finds that his job is graded lower than that of a manager of another
department which he believes to be no higher than his own, the
stage is set for a battle in which group status and personal status are
inextricably intertwined.

It is as numbers grow larger and tribal boundaries become less
clearly marked that status becomes more and more of a problem in
the corporation. It should of course be a straightforward matter,
being graded in direct proportion to each individual's unique
personal contribution to the survival and success of the group. In a
ten-group this is what it does indeed reflect, and in a completely
self-contained company of four or five hundred the group status
would reflect reality in the same way: everyone would know which
of the different groups—the manufacturing groups, the assembly
groups, dispatch, sales, design, accounts and so on—carried most
responsibility for the success of the firm and would be the hardest
to replace, and status would be determined by operational imperatives and the logic of survival. There is no point in the accounts
group trying to get more money than the sales group when everyone
knows the sales boys are keeping the firm alive by busting their guts,
whereas you could pick up a new set of accounts clerks tomorrow.
There is no point in dispatch trying to get the summer holiday date
moved if it is the one that manufacturing and assembly have asked
for, for the same reason. And everyone knows there is no point:
they know what the answer would be, so the question is never put.
This sort of stability, however, depends on everybody knowing

how much weight he and everybody else are carrying in the task of collective survival. In the primitive hunting band it must have been perfectly clear, and the relative dominance of the different hunting bands within the tribal area must have been equally firmly settled, even if it was revised from time to time in border clashes or by fiercer and more lethal conflict. But in the higher reaches of a great corporation, particularly when there are no clear tribal divisions, who knows how the weight of his burden and the success with which he bears it compare with the others? It may be clear enough within his own department, but there are many departments, and their functions are so interlocked and interdependent that it is impossible to judge them separately. And yet Corporation Man desperately needs to know his own status, to know the status of everyone around him, and to have his status known by them. In addition, his evolutionary nature has given him an urge to gain the highest status available to him. What is he to do?

It is, of course, a problem we have already encountered. We know that a society is defined by its ability to provide conventional competition for conventional prizes. In the small status-secure company the convention was unique contribution to profitability and long-term survival. In the giant corporation it is only a question of discovering what are the conventional prizes, and what are the conventional ways of competing for them; these become immediately obvious when you look at the people around you, above you and below you and see what distinguishing marks the higher have in common with each other, how these differ from the lower, and how they got them. Then you go ahead and compete.

This procedure would be perfectly satisfactory, given one condition: namely that the corporation had deliberately constructed its conventions of competition and reward so as to improve its performance and increase its chances of survival. The corporation, however, does not do so. The source of all the friction and anxiety is its pretence that it is not respectable to be concerned with personal status; that people come here to do a job, they get paid for it, and they can keep the status struggle for home and the Joneses. No single private individual I have ever met in any corporation believes this, but the corporate attitude enshrines the creed. The consequence, however, is not an absence of status display within the corporation—the instinctive drives of Corporation Man are too strong. The consequence is a whole range of badges and signs and displays which develop at random and by accident, and then come to acquire status significance and so are jealously competed for, even though no one in the corporation ever intended them to become indicators of status. It is to these that Corporation Man looks (unless he is in a small and exceptionally status-secure tribe) for evidence of how the corporation rates him, how it rates those around him, and how the corporation's expressed ratings compare with his own.

The first place he looks is his pay cheque. Since salary is one of the simplest ways in which the corporation conventionally grades its staff, it is a quick and reliable guide. It is, however, often extremely hard to find out other people's salaries. Nevertheless when it does emerge that a colleague you rank below yourself is being paid more, the discovery strikes at the very heart of your security, identity and self-respect. I have known some terrible corporate battles over money, but none of them have been motivated by the money as an absolute. If you are concerned over money as an absolute, you can — assuming you are underpaid — always leave and go to another company. You only fight if you want to stay but have received an affront to your status. Always the cause of anger is money relative to the money someone else is getting. This, however, cannot be openly stated, so the battle is fought in disguise, and the argument rages around the difficulty of the work, the time it consumes, the level of responsibility borne, and comparable salaries in other corporations (where they help the case). The B.B.C. had a grade for every job, and we went through unbelievable contortions to get a job regraded simply because it did not reflect the higher status of its actual incumbent. All too often the regrading was effected just as he was moving on elsewhere, but the fiction of the job's importance had to be preserved and as a result a low-status successor found himself with a grade and a salary beyond his deserts.

Salary is in fact a very poor instrument, if used on its own, for the corporation to employ as its internal status index. One reason is that money is the prime instrument of corporate survival, and if employees are encouraged to compete by seeing how much of it they can take home, the competition is damaging: the kingdom is using the gold in its treasury for medals and challenge cups instead of defence and expansion. And there is another reason: a sudden need for rare skills may put up the market value of comparative newcomers—systems analysts and programmers, for instance—whose personal status is nothing like as high as the salary they can command. This can cause deep grievance among men of higher status if they have been brought up within a convention where salary was a direct expression of status.

But of course salary is not the only conventional prize in the status race. There is another of equal or even greater significance, which is perhaps even more damaging than salary when it becomes a source of status conflict. It is function, the actual job you are given; and the battlefield is the corporate or divisional or company organization chart. The organization chart causes more agonized exasperation than any other piece of paper, and for a very good reason: it is drawn up in good faith by men who are trying to arrange the most effective means of deploying the corporation staff for success in the survival battle, but everyone on the chart is looking at it as evidence of how the corporation judges their status, and they see the lines and boxes as conventional prizes for which they are invited to compete. Again the naked status argument has to be clothed: this time it wears the guise of operational theory. 'If I have to go through the controller, it will cause the most appalling delays'; 'If he reports direct to you instead of through me, we're going to get the most ghastly crossed lines'; 'Won't it simplify the lines of communication if all those twelve come under me—wouldn't that make your span of command more manageable?' Or more menacingly, 'If I have to clear everything with him, then the job can't be done, and that's that.' The poor, well-meaning fellow who drew up the chart does not know what has hit him: he had no idea the corporation contained so many passionate experts on the theory of organizational structure. But every compromise he makes to soothe ruffled feathers is a compromise of operational efficiency: and after he has been through the performance once and got it over, he privately vows never to do it again. The existing organizational structure will have to serve unchanged for the rest of his career.

Salary and function are unquestionably the two most significant status indices in most corporations, but they both suffer from the same drawback: they are difficult to display. You cannot really have '£5,275 p.a.' embroidered on your tie, and even if your card and office door say 'Chief Assistant to the Deputy Controller of Light

Engineering Operations, South Eastern Region', its precise import in status terms does not instantly leap to the mind. And yet visible status badges are extremely important in many animal species, since they obviate the need for aggressive status behaviour; with a badge of some sort, status is instantly visible. Among vervet monkeys the status of adult males in the troop is demonstrated by the colour of the scrotum—deepest indigo for number one, shading down to the palest pastel blue for the monkey at the bottom of the heap. It means that a quick glance shows each member whether to push in front or stand back. Number one gets all the food and females and deference he wants, then number two gets his turn, and finally the last one gets the left-overs, if any—the females are not interested in him and all the males shove him out of the way. This observation was confirmed when an experimenter removed the lowest-status individual and painted his scrotum an even deeper indigo than number one's and returned him to the troop. No human act could ever come closer to the magic of Cinderella's fairy god-mother: suddenly all the males deferred to their transformed brother, all the females clustered around him, and he had all the best food and as much of it as he wanted. The poor little chap suddenly found himself living out the wildest fantasy of every neglected clown from Bottom the weaver to Charlie Chaplin. I have never found out what happened when the paint wore off.

Since the corporation does not believe in competition for status, it obviously cannot admit that it deals in status badges; in fact, of course, every member of the corporation knows that it is a treasure-house of them. The only acknowledged form of corporate display is the tie, and perhaps blazer or tie-pin or cuff-links, simply denoting corporation membership. This in fact is usually a low-status badge, worn by those who are proud to belong to the corporation at all: higher-status Corporation Men have more to say about themselves than that, and sometimes form higher-status groups—even with ties and cuff-links—within the corporation. In my B.B.C. days there was just such a club formed by those who had run the B.B.C.'s famous overseas news service during the Second World War in Bush House. They called themselves the Bushmen, and held occa-sional dinners and sporting events, but the chief attraction for members was the status by association, and the means of displaying it.

10

The real status badges, however, are less formal and contrived. I remember the day I became head of a department, and exchanged my measly green windscreen badge which allowed me to use the general car park for the proud red badge of the senior executives' car park. I remember going to lunch for the first time in the senior executives' dining-room, and the slightly exaggerated geniality of the welcome from colleagues I had known for many years and who would hardly have noticed my arrival in the bar of the club downstairs. I remember the official from the accommodation department who brought me a slide viewer with pictures of the new range of office furnishings I was now entitled to. I also remember two moments of deep shame. One was when I found my red leather chairs did not go with the carpet, and asked for blue ones instead, and the other was when I asked for a waitress to bring coffee to my office: on both occasions a junior official had to convey to me, in an agony of embarrassment, that blue chairs and waitresses were badges of a status higher than mine. Since one of the rules of status is that you can allocate relative status only to your subordinates, never to your superiors, I had violated a convention instead of competing within it and so we both lost face.

All the same, this introduction to a system of allocating status badges within the B.B.C. which I had never been consciously aware of before started me thinking and inquiring outside the B.B.C. Quite quickly I discovered that corporations have a complex honours system with at least a dozen different orders and any number of grades within each order; not every corporation has all of them, but few are without some. There is the secretary, ranging from access to the pool, through a secretary in your office, then a secretary in a separate office, to two secretaries and finally an assistant with her own secretary. There is title, from foreman through various grades of manager to executive and then director. There are flowers, from zero when your secretary has to bring her own, through rubber plant and then flowering plant, up to fresh cut-flowers provided every day. Office area is another, from cupboard size to ballroom size, and office furnishing from light oak and lino through endless gradations to fitted Indian carpet, Sheraton or Chippendale furniture, and genuine Impressionist paintings. (In the Civil Service wall-to-wall carpeting is reserved for a certain level of seniority, and if a junior takes over the office someone comes and turns the carpet back two inches from the wall before he moves in.) Then there is stationery, rising from thin printed to thicker embossed and culminating in something very like cardboard, embossed with your own name. Drinks are another order, from the pub across the road through the executives' club, then the office cocktail cabinet, up to a bar with a waiter in a corner of your office suite. The Order of the Bath, in the corporation, starts with sharing the general concrete-floored lavatory, progresses through various grades of more refined toilet facilities, until you have a key to the executives' washroom and finally a complete suite with bath and shower in your own office. Tea and coffee start at the vending machine in the corridor and go through trolley service to room service, while the receptacles progress from thick canteen cups to fine bone china and silver coffee-pot brought in on a silver tray by a butler. Where you eat is another universal badge, with grades rising from a special table in the works canteen through a range of more elegant and exclusive dining-rooms, until a butler serves lunch in the dining area of your office suite. The grade of company car provides a long series of different grades from second-hand Mini van to this year's Rolls-Royce, and the place you put it goes from the street, through the company car park, to a reserved space in the company car park, then to the directors' car port, until finally you do not have to know since the chauffeur always drives you to the door in the Rolls and is always waiting there when you come out.

The precise conventions will of course vary from corporation to corporation: just as the sovereign is the fount of all honour in Britain, so the chairman or president or chief executive is the fount of it in the corporation. If he believes it is wrong to have drinks on the premises, he does not have to ban them from offices: they will disappear, except as a badge of nonconformity or rebellion. If he thinks directors and executives and managers should eat with the rest of the staff, the order of private dining-rooms will vanish from the honours list. If he uses a Rover instead of a Rolls there will be a corresponding reduction in car luxury right down the list, and the economy will be many times greater than the few thousand pounds he saves on his own car. All this, however, affects only the type of status system which operates in his corporation: he cannot avoid having a system even if he were foolish enough to want to.

The beauty of all these corporate status badges (and there must be many others) is that they have developed without the intention and often against the will of management. But management's wishes are irrelevant beside man's ancient evolutionary compulsions, and they demonstrate more clearly than any theoretical argument the power of the status instinct and need for display. It is equally noticeable when there are no visible marks of status how conversation is used to demonstrate it — careful mention of high-status groups or people with whom the speaker is or has been associated, criticism or condemnation of people whose status is lower but who seem to be trying to move up, threats or promises of action in order to show the speaker is important and influential enough to take that action, use of Christian names when referring to high-status figures — where there is no other indicator, these signs pop up all the time until relative status is properly established. Ironically, the waving of status flags is usually itself an admission of lower status: you do not try and register your status with your inferiors; you simply snub them if they try and behave as if they were your equals. But whether by badges, conversation, salary or function, or all four together, Corporation Man needs to have his status established and accepted.

Why, then, is the corporate honours system so often shrouded in secrecy, embarrassment and pretence, and allowed to become a focus for tension and resentment instead of a source of pride? Almost certainly the trouble springs from a failure to make the crucial distinction between the hunting band and the camp, the day-to-day operation and the corporation as a permanent institution. Corporations which establish the difference, and make it clear that there are two routes and not one to recognition and reward, save themselves endless difficulty. Success on the hunt brings its own rewards in fame and bonuses and operational authority, but these are essentially for specific performance in a specific task. Next year may be different. Corporate status, however, is something more permanent, not tied to a specific job. It is the status-order of the camp, and although it can change with time the adjustments are normally gradual and infrequent. This permanent nature of status is of course recognized by a number of institutions. The armed services have it clearly established and displayed through rank, with special merit in the hunting band separately distinguished by medals and decorations: you do not make a corporal into a colonel for gallantry, though you may give him the V.C. Japanese corporations tend to be very clear and logical about it: Toyo Rayon for instance has thirty ranks which are related not to function or job but to seniority and qualifications. Promotion is automatic after a certain time, but high fliers can be promoted earlier, just as they can be given jobs, on an acting basis, with authority above their ranks. Unilever, too, has an extensive grading system on the same permanent basis, an expression of camp status rather than hunting success. It is extremely important that this status-ranking should reflect the general view of relative status, and that it should be made known to all those who are included in it. It is also important that there should be plenty of different grades both to reflect fine distinctions and to give everyone a good sense of steady progress. And of course it is vital that exceptional progress up the ladder should reflect, and be seen to reflect, outstanding service and loyalty to the corporation over many years—a recognition of permanent qualities and not single achievements. It is this ranking that should be marked by the various grades of honours in the corporate honours system.

Once a permanent status-ranking is published (annually if necessary) a great deal of the steam is taken out of the salary struggle. Each grade will presumably carry a salary or salary range, and this will be the salary guaranteed to everyone in the grade, even if their efficiency is minimal: it will also be the salary for pension purposes. Any higher sum can in fact be paid in a given year for special merit or responsibility or scarcity value, but it will have no effect on the status of the recipient, though of course continued success will move him faster up the ladder than his contemporaries.

Established status-ranking also takes much of the heat out of the organization-chart battle. On a reconnaissance into enemy territory a brigadier will happily take operational orders from a corporal who knows the ground: when they get back, the brigadier is still a brigadier and the corporal is still a corporal. Operational needs often entail a junior giving the orders, or being given authority equal to that of men who are senior to him, if he is the only one with all the necessary skills or information; and many corporate projects would be much easier if the services' sort of short-term flexibility could be achieved. As long as camp status and hunting-band function are tangled up together on the same chart, this flexibility looks like an assault on status and is impossible. Once that threat is removed, it starts to become a possibility.

There is one other instrument which few corporations use as explicitly or as frequently as they could, though as we have seen, the army employs it regularly: the citation for gallantry. Just as status in the camp has to be displayed some way or other, so does success in the hunting band. An important assignment and a high 'acting' salary both enable the successful young hunters to know they are recognized, but they are not easy to display. All too often the display is carried out in conversation by saying how pathetic and hopeless everyone else is, thereby illustrating Sir Thomas Browne's observation in *Christian Morals*, 'He who discommendeth others obliquely commendeth himself.' A proper citation system whereby achievements of exceptional merit are described in the corporation newspaper or magazine (with photograph) or put up in weekly bulletins on notice-boards, can satisfy the desire for fame and recognition without disturbing the status system or stimulating aggressive, assertive behaviour. If the brave hunter knows that everyone has heard about his triumphs, he does not have to keep recounting them: he has been awarded his conventional prize without having to claim it.

14 The Folk-Culture of the Corporation Tribe

IN THE autumn of 1968 I paid a visit to the school I had left twenty years previously. It was an interesting experience, since it was not, in any physical sense, the school I had left; it had moved to completely new buildings in a different part of London. Nor was it the same school in terms of people; only two or three of the sixty-odd teaching staff were still there. And yet it was easily recognizable as the same school—the same balance of subjects, the same attitudes to learning and games and the arts, the same academic reputation, the same tolerance of eccentricity, the same relationship between boys and masters; the conformists were the same sort of conformists and the rebels the same sort of rebels. Anyone from outside, for instance in a university, would have described the school in almost exactly the same terms that his counterpart in my day would have used.

Quite clearly there was something about the school that outlasted people and buildings; something that kept it different from other schools, and different in the same way, despite a pupil turnover of 20 per cent a year and a staff turnover of about 5 per cent, and despite changes of physical environment. I asked the headmaster how conscious he was of this enduring quality, and his reply was extremely enlightening. He had come to the school some six years before and quite soon had decided that changes were necessary. The chief instrument by which a headmaster can change a school is in the appointment of staff, and he took the opportunity of some vacancies to introduce a new kind of schoolmaster, of the sort he felt was necessary. These were excellent men with good records, but the experiment simply did not work. They did not get on with the boys or in the common-room, they were frustrated and unhappy, and quite soon they left. The headmaster realized that, although it was not impossible to change the direction in which the school was going, it was impossible to change it very much or very rapidly. It was almost like an organic transplant—anything not

151

very similar in cellular structure would be spontaneously rejected; any new organ had to be within the acceptance limits of the host.

I quote this particular case because the change of location emphasized it for me, but in fact it is true of every corporate tribe that stays reasonably intact over a period of time. This enduring quality is sometimes referred to by shorthand phrases like 'tradition' or 'continuity' or 'group identity' or 'cultural transmission', but these are often used to avoid the effort of analysing the separate elements that compose it. However, if we are to understand the corporate tribe, that analysis cannot be postponed. So far we have dealt with the biological, evolutionary factors that ten-groups and tribes all have in common: maximum size, leadership, structure, aggression, territory, status and so on. But it is also important to understand what makes tribes different from each other. Many categories of difference are widely discussed in management literature – type of product, annual turnover, profitability, capital intensiveness, manufacturing methods – and all of them are significant. But this cultural tradition and continuity is at least as significant to the success of an enterprise, and because it cannot be quantified it does not follow that it cannot be clarified.

I shall be talking about these elements of cultural tradition as they appear in the context of a single tribe, a factory or small firm, or a school or other institution around the tribal size of five hundred. After all, it is within the single tribe that we all have direct experience of a cultural tradition. And because it has its origin in the time when the tribe was the largest permanent operational unit we knew, it is still in the community of tribal size that it operates in the most visible and natural way.

But although we shall be examining these elements of cultural tradition at tribal level, they are in fact the same ones that give unique identity to a larger company, to a giant corporation, or even to a nation. When we say, 'What is Ford like to work for?', 'What is I.B.M. like to deal with?', 'That's typical of Du Pont', we are assuming a continuing identity going right through the corporation and back over many years. In so far as we can generalize about nations – 'just like the Italians', 'typically German' – it is this same cultural tradition, not a specifically Italian or German combination of genes, that we are referring to. It is something you build up over many years, and can destroy overnight. It is what you have to change if you take over and incorporate another tribe. It can be a bastion of defence or an obstacle to advance. It is almost impossible to teach, and almost impossible not to learn. At the lowest level, it is what keeps a firm in business; at the highest level, it is what has preserved and developed all the civilization we have.

This culturally transmitted tribal identity is of course a single unity, and the separate elements are all interconnected and inter-related. Nevertheless they take separate forms within the tribe, and can easily be looked at separately. The first and most obvious is the tribe's external identity: the position it occupies among other tribes, the reputation it has built up, the behaviour it stimulates or inhibits among those who encounter it. When you start up for the first time, the options are wide open. Suppose you open a chain of restaurants; if you are to succeed, you must carve out a special niche for yourself, you must exploit what marketing men call a market gap. You can offer Continental food, or a relaxing, leisurely atmosphere, or good value at low prices, or unique speciality dishes, or very quick service, in all sorts of permutations and combinations. (In fact you will probably be expanding on the basis of a formula that has worked for a single restaurant.) But once you have got your chain going successfully, it is a chain that binds you. Your customers come for the sort of food and price and atmosphere you have encouraged them to expect, and you cannot significantly alter any of them without losing their business. Suppliers have a picture of your nature and needs in their minds, and come to you with new products and services selected to fit into that picture. The staff who stay with you do so because they are happy with the pay, conditions, treatment and management climate you have created, and those in turn condition the new staff who apply. Your rivals, too, come to give implicit confirmation to your niche; they accept the strength of your market-hold on the central part of your business and compete only at the perimeter—the upper or lower income end of your market, casual snacks rather than main meals, the youngest or oldest range of your customers, and so on. All the options that were open at the beginning are very nearly closed: the niche you cut for yourself becomes the mould which forms your identity and shapes your future.

This of course was precisely the headmaster's problem. The external identity of the school determined the sort of parents who sent their children to it and the reasons why they chose it in preference to other similar schools; it was the idea which united the old boys and guided the policy of the governors; it was the reason why the present staff had applied for their jobs and the older ones had stayed on instead of going to other schools. A sudden change of that identity would have been a massive breach of confidence and would have provoked tremendous resistance from every group which combined to form the total community.

It would have been different, of course, if the school had been failing. A part of any tribe's external identity is its status among other tribes, and like personal status it is very close to the business of survival. If possible it must be enhanced, but at least it must be preserved: as long as that happens, most people are happy with the identity that secures it. If it starts to slip, they try for as long as possible to pretend that it is not happening, or that it is a temporary reverse, or that nothing can be done about it. But in time the self-deception becomes harder and harder, and rebellious ten-groups clamour for the removal of the group that has presided over the decline; if they fail, the slide may go on to extinction, but if they win, then all sorts of changes and innovations become possible which were unthinkable in the days of success.

The second element in the culture of a tribe is very close to the first: it is the internal status system. The principle of an internal status system is of course universal to all tribes, and we have already seen, in Chapter 13, how status operates in the corporate community. But the individuality of tribes lies in the different people, groups, functions, achievements and personal qualities to which different communities accord highest status. In one firm it will be the scientist, in another the salesman: in a healthy firm the status-ranking will follow the priority order of importance to the firm's success and survival. The convulsion comes when the conditions of survival change faster than the normal organic change of the individuals on the status ladder. Many manufacturing firms by the start of the 1950s had survived for generations by efficient, dependable, low-cost production, and their tribal status hierarchy rose out of the production line. When the sudden change from production-orientation to market-orientation struck the manufacturing world during the 1950s, it rapidly separated the conventional high-status skills from the actual skills needed for survival.

Men who had had respected and successful professional careers, and had climbed to the top of the ladder entirely by their skill and knowledge and experience in organizing production, were suddenly made to realize that that skill was only of secondary importance. They had to vote not to buy the superb new German machine-tool, but to invest the money in a bunch of fancy boys who talked about brand images and consumer motivation and depth research. No wonder so many of them failed: it is not a simple matter of open-mindedness and seeing facts—it strikes at the heart of a man's status and self-respect.

Almost exactly the same thing happened in the B.B.C. when television started. The prestige of B.B.C. radio during the Second World War and immediately after it had been enormous: it was the prime instrument of national unity, and men became famous all over the country simply by reading news bulletins. Moreover, by broadcasting truthful and objective news on their overseas services even when it was bad news for the Allies, the B.B.C. gained a reputation overseas which still makes it the most respected broadcasting organization in the world. And then television started, and inexorably the audiences moved over to it. Of course a great many radio producers and broadcasters moved over with them, but some—and above all the most senior—remained behind. I was constantly astonished by their bitterness and hostility towards television, their stream of anti-television jokes, their refusal to see any merit in television or any limitations in radio; but of course what they were suffering from was a mortal blow to their status through no failure of their own but simply because of a sudden shift in technology, and a consequent shift of survival priorities to a range of skills which it was too late for them to acquire. I discovered later that this was by no means an exclusively British phenomenon: one of America's leading radio commentators became physically ill under the stress of television: he suffered from acute skin sensitivity and had to wear gloves the whole time, until he had successfully learnt the new skills and established himself in the new medium.

The tribe whose long-established status structure is tied to the wrong skill is a problem for any corporation (unless it is the leader's tribe itself, in which case the problem is transferred to the shareholders), but the B.B.C. stumbled on the answer. I honestly believe that if there had been room for television studios in the radio head-quarters at Broadcasting House, British television would now be dominated by the commercial networks. B.B.C. television would have grown up in the shadow of radio, and as a rather vulgar appendage of it; it would have been dominated by the radio hierarchy, and radio would have remained the best route to the top for the ambitious and successful. Consequently the start of commercial television competition in 1955 would have been too much for it, and since radio was still free from competition it would have been to the improvement of radio rather than to fighting commercial television that many of the top people would have bent their energies. But that was not how it worked out. The nearest space for studios lay across several miles of London, in the old Alexandra Palace, and when bigger premises were needed, those too were several miles away in Lime Grove. It was physically impossible for anybody looking after a radio department to exercise authority over television programmes as well. As a result, a completely new tribe was born, with its own territory, its own technical facilities, and its own audience. It was peopled by the innovators, the adventurous, the people impatient with the hierarchy and the restrictions of Broadcasting House, and there was also an element of impatience with the middle-class assumptions of B.B.C. sound radio. Consequently when the new, young, aggressive commercial television started up in 1955, it found itself competing not with old Auntie from Portland Place but with her new, young aggressive nephew—and the nephew had several years' start. It was only when commercial television began that the elders in Broadcasting House realized that if it wiped out B.B.C. television, then their great dread, commercial radio, would be irresistible. But B.B.C. television more than held its own. The device of starting a new tribe for the new skill, instead of trying to incorporate it into the old one, had saved the citadel—even if only by a geographical accident.

These first two elements of a tribe's cultural tradition—its external identity and its internal status system—are closely bound up with the third: the means by which leadership operates. Every tribe has to have a system by which it determines what shall be done, who shall do it and how it shall be done, and some way of making sure that it has been done properly. This system is bound up with territory and quasi-territory, since most of the time the leadership operates through the jurisdiction of those who have established their authority within certain boundaries. No one ever draws this territorial map of the tribe, but it is a powerful reality. Anyone can reorganize lines and boxes on a chart, but actual internal territory is far less easily changed. People quickly find that if George says yes, it's yes, and you don't have to ask the manager, or that if you can get Mr Wilkins on your side then the project will go through. This is what Elton Mayo called 'informal organization' and it is fully discussed by Rosemary Stewart in *The Reality of Management*; it grows up slowly and changes gradually, and time and again it saves the formal organization from grinding to a halt. It has a remarkable talent for coming unscathed through endless top-level corporate restructuring. I remember reading a children's story about Teddy and Andy-Pandy: they were planting seeds in the garden, and then fixing the packet in the earth with a stick, as a label to mark which seeds were in which place. But the next day Teddy thought of a better arrangement, so he swapped the nasturtium label with the love-in-the-mist label. The next day he improved it again by switching the candytuft label with the marigold label. Several times he changed the labels around, and then waited for the flowers to come up. He was furious when they all came up in the place where they had originally been planted, instead of where he had put the labels. 'Stupid things—can't they read?' he asked. I was in the middle of a corporate reorganization at the time, and I realized that it was a pure Teddy and Andy-Pandy operation: labels were being moved around with impressive decision, but the flowers were going to come up where the seeds had been planted long before; the informal organization, the real instrument of organizational achievement, was totally unaffected.

The tradition of leadership style goes beyond quasi-territory and the informal organization tree: it affects the way decisions are taken. Some tribes believe in fixed, formal meetings, others in casual dropping-in. Some believe in telling the chap what you want and leaving him to get on with it, some like to clear the lines in advance. In the former you are liable to get a rocket for seeking guidance— 'For God's sake use a bit of initiative and don't keep pestering me!'; in the latter, a bit of initiative will bring a rocket from the other direction—'What on earth do you mean by issuing these safety regulations without my authorization?' Neither style is either right or wrong in itself; it is a part of the leadership tradition and has to be learnt by every newcomer.

The fourth element is one of the most interesting and significant of all. It is the central faith. Whereas the other elements take time to grow up, the central faith is there from the start. It is the belief at the root of the business, and I call it faith because it rests on a number of unproved assumptions. 'People want quality'; 'If you can make a better mousetrap the world will beat a trail to your door'; 'It's not the product that matters, it's how hard you sell it'; 'If you want to stay in business, you've got to deliver on time'—all these expressions of commercial and industrial dogma spring from the central faith of the tribe. The faith usually starts from the leader of the central ten-group around whom the tribe grew up, and it can be the unifying idea of anything from a small partnership to a giant corporation. Most businesses start from an act of faith, a risk which comes off, an inspired guess about a market gap. Thereafter the faith which made the man or group take the risk becomes the central belief of the tribe. Equally, a near disaster in the early days can create an image of the devil which is quite as distinct as the image of God: 'Never again will we . . .' I.B.M. has a devil—the employment of too large a proportion of the local community in their plant, dating back to a traumatic early experience, and many companies are still encountering different aspects of the Evil One. The devil in Marks & Spencer—or one of his faces at least—is profit-seeking: the central faith on which Simon Marks built his firm was that science and large volume sales could give ordinary people much better quality goods (especially clothes) than they were being offered, and that they would be willing to pay a little extra for something a lot better. The faith was amply justified, but in the early days Marks and Sieff had to combat the image of sharp traders on the make: they did so by extreme honesty and straight dealing and an ethos of service to the community which still animate the whole firm, and the slightest suggestion of sacrificing quality for gain still horrifies them.

A good way to find the central faith of a tribe is to get its members to see who can formulate the biggest blasphemy. In Marks & Spencer it would be, 'So what if it falls to bits when they get it home—we've made our profit, haven't we?' In the B.B.C., 'I admit it wasn't really true, but the motor manufacturers' association P.R.O. was very keen we should say it.' In Rolls-Royce, 'It's a lousy bit of engineering but it will sell like hot cakes.' At Sotheby's, 'It doesn't look like a Tiepolo to me, but if you say it is, I'll have to take your word for it.' Almost any corporate tribesman can formulate his own for you, provided he still retains a modicum of philosophical detachment: indeed it is a mark of a unified corporation that its central faith should be clear enough for a good blasphemy to be easily found. And the separate tribes in the corporation, like monastic orders, have their own special emphases within the central faith: a special *Tonight* blasphemy would have been, 'Who cares if it's an advertiser's hand-out—the morons will lap it up.'

With such a variety of central faiths, you might expect more religious warfare between, for instance, the strivers for quality and the seekers of profit, and of course between highly competitive corporations these are emphasized—religious difference becomes an aggression focus of the sort described in Chapter 5. But the philosophical difference is in itself very small—after all, the quality people have to make a profit, and the profit-hungry must reach a certain quality. Marks & Spencer has a brilliant profit record, even if it disparages this as an objective, just as most successful profit-oriented firms turn out good products. The worshippers of Venus do not deny the divinity of Apollo. Indeed the classical gods, in a sense, represent most of the types of central faith and all have their own worshippers among modern corporations. Mars, the god of war and tough competition and price-cutting, clearly inspires the aggressive corporations like Tesco. Mercury, the traveller and messenger of the gods, has always seemed to me the symbol of Coca-Cola, carrying the good news of the all-American beverage to the uttermost corners of the earth. Venus finds most of her acolytes among Italian corporations—Ferrari, Farina, Ferragamo—with their emphasis on elegance and beauty. Juno, mother of the gods, looks after the family with good things and a sense of service—Boots and Sainsbury's, for instance. Apollo, god of the muses, represents quality and status—Harrods and the Rover car company and the Swiss watch companies. Vulcan is for those who concentrate on manufacturing skill, like the Plessey corporation, and Athene, goddess of wisdom, for the highly research-oriented corporations like I.C.I. and Bell Telephones. Jupiter, the father of the gods, is of course General Motors: corporate management at its most Olympian. But different as they are, none of them are in opposition: there is room for them all in the corporate Pantheon.

The central faith is so strongly held and so deeply felt in most good corporations that it is wise to accept it as effectively unchangeable. This might seem to be a grave obstacle in times of rapid change, a force for reaction and a danger to survival. So it can be, if change is represented as abandoning the faith and going over to the devil, and of course there will always be those who do try to resist change on that pretext. But the great advantage of the central faith is its vagueness, and (if you employ the sort of skill that the Jesuits have refined over the centuries) there is very little, apart from deliberate confrontation, that cannot be shown to be in accordance with orthodox belief.

This brings us to another of the elements of a tribe's cultural tradition, doctrine. Doctrine is applied faith, it is the way in which the central belief is interpreted in practical situations. Formulation and revision of doctrine is one of the most constant and important of tribal tasks. Faith is beyond argument and challenge: you accept it or you get out. But doctrine can be argued about, and the body of agreed, accepted, shared doctrine is one of a tribe's most valuable invisible assets. That the B.B.C. news should be impartial is an article of faith. But if it receives film from the North Vietnamese of the aftermath of an air raid by the United States, should it show it as news or reject it as propaganda? Should it show it, but say it came from the North Vietnamese? If so, should it also say that the American film was supplied by the Americans? Or take our restaurant chain: we guarantee that meals in our restaurant do not cost more than £1. The best value for the money is an article of faith. But when prices rise, should we raise it to £1·25, or reduce the size of portions, or get the extra money from a surcharge on wine, or introduce a two-tier menu, or what? All these are doctrinal points. Doctrine grows up round every activity; accounting, personnel relations, marketing policy, manufacturing standards, salary scales—there is no recurring activity in the corporation without a body of guiding doctrine shared among a ten-group or sub-tribe or tribe.

Part of the central doctrine of the corporation concerns the nature of its business. What business are we in? We make cars and trucks. Should we make motor bikes? Hovercraft? Tanks? Should we move up to the luxury end of the market? Down to the economy end? Should we start our own electrical subsidiary? Ought we have fewer dealers? The questions are endless, the answers promote the question 'Why?' and eventually the 'Why?' leads you back to the central faith, and the doctrine is established. It is, however, never permanently established, and new facts or considerations can always reopen a doctrinal discussion. The danger point comes when doctrine fossilizes, and people regard it as religion: 'We must never put on a 60 per cent mark-up,' rather than, 'We must not make an excessive profit.' The latter is an article of faith, and agreeably vague, whereas the former is a precise doctrinal application which must be susceptible of revision. In a changing situation, the constant questioning and re-examining of tribal doctrine becomes a survival necessity. New experience and new information are the food and drink which nourish the body of corporate doctrine. They are sifted and assimilated by a process of conversation, argument and discussion as if in a collective mental digestive system. Much is expelled as waste matter, but the important elements are extracted and circulated to renew and revitalize the cells.

Distinct from doctrine, though related to it, is ritual. Most corporate tribes are rich in ritual — it is (and always has been) a good way of ensuring that things get done in the right way time and time again, even if people do not know why they are doing them. Throughout the tribe every day ritual forms are filled in, ritual procedures are followed, ritual meetings are attended, ritual maintenance is carried out, ritual safety precautions are observed. Ritual grows most luxuriantly out of priestly staff departments at headquarters. Lacking direct authority over people, they seek power by working on the vague and irrational fears of those who possess that authority. When the ruler's chief fear is of labour unrest, the personnel priest has power. When it is lack of control over expenditure, the financial priest tightens his grip. When he is troubled by the poor shape of the corporate image, the priest of publicity and public relations extends his domination. Sometimes the ranks of the established church are swelled by the mendicant friars with their begging bowls — the firms of management consultants selling indulgences with names like 'M.B.O. package', 'D.C.F. programme', 'Long-range planning', which tempt the fearful sinner to buy his way to salvation. All the priests and friars operate by cornering a part of the ruler's authority to institute ritual observances for all time: expenses forms, budget proposal forms, capital appropriation forms, holiday application forms, fire alarm tests, weekly safety inspections, daily maintenance schedules, daily clocking-in routines – these are a part of every tribe's existence. Some are useful and even necessary, but they are a constant danger; they always go on long after the need for them has passed, and no one ever questions them. When I was at the depot regiment in the army, one of the clerks in my office spent his entire working life at an ancient ritual: for every soldier being released from the army a small flimsy form was sent from the War Office, and he typed certain details from that form on to the man's record card. My only long-term contribution to the army was to buy him a stapling machine from petty cash and let him staple the flimsy form to the record card. His week's work was thereafter accomplished in an hour and a half. It could have been done any time in the previous ten years, but the ritual pre-dated cheap stapling machines, and no one had ever regarded it as needing critical thought and evaluation. The real trouble with rituals is that people come to depend on them: they give a sense of work well done, a useful contribution made to the general good, while being totally undemanding once they have been mastered, even if they contribute nothing at all to the reality of corporate survival and profitability. They are a source of comfort and security, stable points in a confusing world. When Marks & Spencer had their blitz on paper work, some store managers could not bear to part with their ritual sales record forms and went on completing them secretly at home.

The seventh element of the tribal culture is a shared concept of the right and wrong way to behave. It is not particularly related to the social code of the world outside, though this comes into it in a marginal way: do you call your superior 'sir' or 'Harry'? Whichever it is, you will soon find out if you choose the wrong one. The tribal code covers nearly all the working details of the tribe – what sort of omission deserves a telling-off, and what sort merits the sack; what represents fair behaviour by a foreman, and what is unfair; what is exceptionally friendly or unfriendly; what happens to you if three jobs in a row all fail inspection; whether it's the supervisor's job to bring round the next drawings or the operator's job to go and get them from his office; whether it was right to make

Jean type the whole page again because of two little mistakes; and an endless series of tiny moral judgments which make up an agreed code of conduct. A sudden expansion or influx of new people, particularly at the management level, can radically upset people who have been used to the security of a moral code that everyone subscribed to (even though individuals frequently deviated from it). It is not necessarily a question of the discipline becoming more strict—it is just as disturbing if it becomes less strict: the details of the code of behaviour are not important and they vary greatly from tribe to tribe, but the code itself is an important force in holding the tribe together.

Another vitally important element that grows up within a tribe is its internal communication system. At the tribal level this is nothing to do with memos and circulars and notice-boards and house magazines, and owes nothing to presentation techniques. At its most basic, primitive and animal level, it is the means by which the members of the tribe separately and collectively control and regulate tribal conduct, and enforce the code of behaviour: it is a sort of nervous system, constantly picking up signals and reacting to them. It communicates warnings if anyone's behaviour is getting too far out of line, and appreciation if it conforms. It passes the message about whether a newcomer should be accepted or excluded, or whether judgment is still being formulated. It is communicated at least as much by look, gesture, body attitude and tone of voice as it is by symbolic language. Every member of the tribe has a dual function in this communication system: as a receiver he gets the message to conform, and as a transmitter he passes the message to others. This communication network is so instinctive, to those who are part of it, that a tribal chief will know at once if something is wrong—he will pick up a message of aggression or alarm or discontent without any factual information at all: he may call it 'atmosphere', but in fact it is a compound of many small things that are or are not happening, a wide variety of audible and visible signals which add up to an unmistakable message to anyone who knows the language.

This is why the communication network functions so badly in most office tribes: most office blocks are designed to stop anybody from noticing who is talking to whom and in what tone of voice, from seeing who is in and who is out or how long that meeting has been going on and whether they are sitting back in their chairs or leaning forward, and all those tiny impressions which add up to a priceless store of current information. This is an argument not for vast open-plan ballrooms — office workers need territory, too — but for windows opening on to the busy tribal encampment as well as on to the unchanging, uneventful world. This is the way that the village spinster behind her net curtains amasses a huge amount of information in the course of the year without ever having to ask a direct question. This sort of information is essential for the internal self-regulation of a tribe, but most office blocks are at present designed to prohibit it.

The primitive, non-linguistic nature of our basic tribal communication system is something that every motorist knows from experience. A car has only the most limited communication equipment, greatly inferior to most animals, but any motorist who suddenly pulls out of his lane without warning, or drives at thirty miles an hour in the fast lane, or commits any of the offences which endanger or frustrate other members of the motoring community, soon finds that the communication system is sufficient to bring him into line. Flashing lights, sounding horns, driving too close behind, overtaking inside and cutting across — the vocabulary of the car is primitive and restricted even by chimpanzee standards, but it serves its purpose. It also has its clear status display with fine gradations of age and cost, speed and luxury, which are well understood throughout the community. The new motorist may study the law and the Highway Code, but only when he joins the community of the road does he really begin to learn the communication system and become a part of it.

At a higher level, the communication network serves to transmit a vast body of information and experience throughout the tribe. Any tribesman who encounters an important fact or signal knows at once whom to pass it on to. This makes it as powerful an instrument for fending off disaster as the informal organization. It means that as soon as the commissionaire sees the factory inspector's car, he rings Bill to tell him to put the safety hood over the chain drive in number 3 shop. It means that when the chief accountant has finally got through the traffic hold-up he warns the transport manager to send the day's consignment down the A40 instead of the M4. It means the incoming stores clerk warns the turning foreman that the two-inch mild steel bar still hasn't arrived, instead of letting him find out for himself when he needs it next week. It means that people know everyone else's jobs and needs as well as their own, and are collectively using the communication network to facilitate the whole operation.

Over the years, this constant circulating of information, experience and judgment adds up to a body of shared knowledge and assumptions which gives a speed and precision to communication within the tribe that is not possible outside it. 'Communication' and 'community' are derived from the same root because they are expressions of the same reality, and those who talk about failures of communication would do well to reflect that communication can happen only in communities. I certainly found that as film producer on *Tonight* I could brief a *Tonight* director or reporter on the treatment of a film story in a few minutes, whereas with an equally skilled professional who had never worked with us it would have taken an hour's discussion and been far less clear at the end. The reason was that within the community of *Tonight* we had argued out the right and wrong ways in hours of doctrinal discussions based on hundreds of films and so we all knew the pitfalls too well to have to talk about them. With someone outside the community, I would have to point every single one out in advance—and I could never foresee them all.

The network is invaluable, too, in adapting to innovation. A new machine, or procedure, or manager, or product, is busily discussed by the network, ways of coping are passed on, judgments are ventured, circulated and revised, improvements are suggested and a complete body of practice and opinion is built up and shared by all those affected. Since the network also transmits the status-ranking, it knows whose opinion counts for much and whose for little, who knows what he is talking about and who keeps changing his mind, and adds or discounts significance accordingly. However ingenious the innovation, it is in the tribes and through the tribes that it succeeds or fails: and it is the communication network that makes sure that the best pooled experience and ideas and judgments are brought to bear on it to give it the best chance. The formal committee meetings and operational discussions are of course a part of this communication system—but only a small part.

Finally, there is the tribal memory and folk-lore. All sorts of events and experiences and stories from the past are handed down,

often as jokes. I remember a tribal joke in the B.B.C. about an interviewer in the early days of television questioning the Prime Minister,
and asking, 'The Tory party has sometimes been called a war-
mongering party: Mr Eden, is there one jot of truth in this allega-
tion?' I don't know why we thought it so funny: perhaps it was the
contrast between the aggressive independence of the first half and
the rapid degeneration to abject sycophancy in the second. But it
was quite clear what its folk-lore significance was: it enshrined in
ridicule the sort of toadying to senior members of the government
that would destroy the political independence of the B.B.C. Sometimes the stories are heroic narratives – 'The time of the electricity
strike when we had to quadruple our production of torches in three
days and nobody got more than two hours' sleep at a stretch,' and
so on. Few of them retain much factual accuracy, but accuracy is
not the point: like the apocryphal wartime stories about Churchill,
they express an admiration of actions and qualities that are valued
by the tribe, or (like the Hitler jokes) a derision and contempt of
those that are not, and their purpose is to communicate and share
common values and standards of behaviour.

These, then, are the chief elements which grow up in the corporate
tribe and, given time, are passed on as part of its informal tradition.
They are what remained in my school after the people and buildings
had all changed: they are the elements which, at every level from the
board to the shop floor, constitute a good little firm or a good company, or a good corporation; and they are also the elements which
constitute a bad one. Their mere existence does not guarantee
success, but their absence is a guarantee of failure. However, with a
tribe of the right size they are bound to grow up as the months and
years go by, and they outlast individuals; whether they adapt to
change or fossilize, whether they make for harmony or discord,
whether they further the corporation's aims or frustrate them, is the
measure by which the management of the corporation is judged.
There is no way of reflecting them on the balance sheet, but there
is a perfectly sound way of putting a valuation on them; they are the
difference between the book value of a company's assets, and the
value the stock market puts on the company. In the case of Marks
& Spencer, the book value of the equity (as at June 30th, 1971) is
about £130 million, but the market capitalization is £920 million:
a difference of nearly £800 million. In the case of Woolworth's (as

at the same date), the book value is £165 million and the market capitalization is £285 million, a difference of £120 million. In other words Marks & Spencer's tribal structure and tradition is worth £670 million more than Woolworth's. Perhaps when the chairman says in his annual report, 'Our staff are our greatest asset,' he is, in some corporations, speaking the literal truth.

15 Boom and Slump: the Expendable Generation

THE hunting band, the camp and the tribe. I have already suggested that these are the only units of organization apart from the family which we have brought with us out of our prehistory, the only groups we form by instinct. But ever since we stopped hunting and began farming we have been stumbling towards the formation and preservation of larger units: from the town to the city, and then to the nation; from the cohort to the legion, and then the army; from the small firm to the company and the corporation. I say 'stumbling' because there is nothing natural or instinctive about units of this size; the understanding of them and the devices for regulating them are part of a cultural tradition and continuity which we have built up and passed down during a mere ten thousand years.

But if the history of these larger groupings is short, this is only because they were, presumably, not a practical possibility for a hunting species which had to keep on the move. There was no question of building stable and permanent organizations; the tribe had lived in constant danger of extinction: not only from predators, disease and starvation, but also from annihilation by marauding tribes whose own source of food had disappeared. Perhaps if the food supply had remained stable and our method of controlling our numbers had worked adequately, we should all still be happily hunting the antelopes on the African grasslands: but we know it did not. Until we discovered farming, we had no answer. We had to live with insecurity—though insecurity is a retrospective value-judgment which would have been meaningless to the tribes that had never known security. But with farming (or just before it, as Jane Jacobs has argued so persuasively),[1] it became possible for us to organize and control and regulate, to take thought for the morrow, to build towns and cities, nations and civilizations, to believe in our own permanence and act on that belief. You do not devote energy and resources to planting olive trees or building great temples and harbours if you expect to have to up sticks and be off tomorrow, or next month, or next year. Nor do you set up a long-range planning department and invest millions of pounds for a return in ten or fifteen years' time; a corporation, like a civilization, rests on the assumption of continuing for as long as anyone can foresee. What makes Corporation Man such a novelty, even though Industrial Man has been with us for two hundred years, is that only recently have corporations come to believe in their own permanence, and to organize for it.

However, the fact that we did not evolve these larger groupings does not mean that we lacked any mechanism for dealing with boom and slump, or dearth and plenty, in our hunting days. Stability is not one of the laws of nature, and all species have to find a way of adapting to a changing environment if they are to survive. I believe we can trace some part of that mechanism, or at least discover intriguing parallels, in the behaviour of Corporation Man today; and so before we move on to the larger units of industry, let us think back once again to the hunting tribe and how it adapted to a changing environment.

It is inevitably the times of hunger that come to mind first. The effect of food shortage must have been to tighten the group structure and group discipline, and to increase the fighting as groups and tribes hunted into each other's territory. In times of severe hunger, selection pressures operate more rapidly in favour of the best adapted groups, and the best adaptation for us was group discipline, with the prize going to the strongest, fiercest and swiftest group. For gene-pool reasons, as well as fighting strength, we can assume that selection also favoured those who maintained tribal unity as well, who fought as a whole tribe and wiped out those tribes whose hunting bands stayed separate and fought alone. Corporation Man shows the same instincts in a business recession; all the individuals and groups who have been talking about breaking away and starting up on their own quickly forget the attractions of independence and stay close to the tribe, while all the corporate disciplines become stricter. Equally, the competitive struggle between corporations becomes fiercer and nastier when defeat means not just a blow to the pride and the pocket but the threat of extinction.

No one in the corporation welcomes a recession, but nevertheless it serves a salutary purpose today, just as it did millions of years ago, and still does for animal populations. Times of prosperity are times of danger, to species and to corporations. For a species, it can mean the preservation of genetically deformed or inferior individuals who would not have survived normal conditions, but who in times of exceptional ease can breed and so dilute the gene pool, which replicates the whole population. A drop in food supply sorts them out very quickly and leaves only the genetically superior to fill up the gaps and carry on the species. Of course we have not yet experienced a business boom that has continued long enough to have any genetic effect on Corporation Man, but it certainly affects his behaviour. When money becomes more plentiful, it is all too easy to use it to take the pressure off the tribes and ten-groups; create extra posts, put difficult work out to small firms instead of doing it yourself, lessen the demands and ease up on the penalties, and enjoy the fruits of prosperity in lunches and dinners and country-house seminars and golfing conferences and all the other instruments of enlightened managerial welfare. If this goes on long enough, the corporation can weigh itself down with people (especially around headquarters) who become unfit for a genuinely competitive industrial life. I hesitate to draw too close a parallel, but I encountered a paragraph on a quite different subject that applies so beautifully to this kind of sheltered Corporation Man that I have to quote it. It comes from Dobzhansky's *Mankind Evolving*:

> Norway rats (*Rattus norvegicus*) have been kept in laboratories since sometime between 1840 and 1850. The modern laboratory rat belongs to a well-defined variety that differs from its wild progenitor in many ways. The laboratory rat is entirely dependent on the protected state of the laboratory where food, water, mates and shelter are provided, and the struggle for survival no longer exists. Among other differences, laboratory rats have smaller adrenal glands and less resistance to stress, fatigue, and disease than wild rats. Thyroid glands have also become less active in laboratory rats, while, on the contrary, sex glands develop earlier and permit a greater fertility. They have smaller brains and are tamer and more tractable than the active and aggressive wild rats. The genetic changes which occurred in the laboratory rat would, undeniably, make them unable to compete successfully with wild rats in the environment in which the latter normally live.

A corporation that lets the human equivalent of *Rattus norvegicus* establish itself in the years of prosperity will find itself in trouble when the depression sets in. Joseph's way was the wise one: work as hard as ever during the fat years, and store all the surplus corn in the granary for the lean years that are to come; then the population will not have relaxed and expanded and softened, and there will be food to tide over until the fat years return. This was precisely the policy of Britain's top financial manager, Jim Slater, during the stock-market boom of the mid-1960s. After the first few fat years he started piling up cash until the granaries of Slater Walker were as liquid as Pharaoh's; consequently he was able to survive the long downward slide that caused such agony to his less provident rivals.

Some people outside industry assume that it is pure greed which makes corporations compete aggressively for higher and higher profits and growth, but greed hardly comes into it at all. Status, of course, is an important incentive, but so is the fear of hard times ahead, and consequently the need to preserve the integrity of the stock, to set difficult targets and keep all the ten-groups busily at work, so that when the lean years come they will be hard, muscular and disciplined enough to survive in the wild rat race.

There is, however, another danger in prosperity, and it concerns a special group in the tribe and the corporation: the newly matured young males who have not yet acquired families or territory. In many primate species—and, I suggest, quite clearly in our own—they are recognized as a distinct sub-community. The fact that they are only just entering maturity makes them particularly competitive for status amongst themselves. As we have seen, status-striving and status battles are always the product of an unsureness about your own status-ranking. Once you know it, and know that everyone else knows it, you do not have to assert or prove anything, but at the onset of maturity it has yet to be established, or rather it has to be established in a new way. It is the time when the simple animal dominance of the playground first starts to be modified by proficiency at adult, hunting skills; modified, but not replaced—physical animal dominance remains significant, but it is no longer the only or ultimate measurement of status. In a few years the new status-ranking will have been established and tacitly accepted by everyone, and the pressure is taken off the struggle: in a stable tribe the rankings change very little after the first shake-down, but the shake-down can be clamorous and convulsive, and since there is always an adolescent generation coming along it is a permanent feature of tribal life.

The absence of territory and family has another effect on this group: it means that they are not tied to the camp with so tight a bond as the rest. They are no longer so young as to need it for protection, nor so established as to be an important part of its social structure and hierarchy, nor do they have children to look after and defend and teach. They are more free now than at any other time in their lives to wander and explore, which has historically served a useful function: it prevents excessive genetic isolation. By wandering from camp to camp in the tribe and choosing a wife from any one of them, they prevent excessive in-breeding: and the ones who occasionally venture into the camps of other tribes promote a cross-flow between separate gene pools which is an additional survival factor. I do not suggest that this happens in any literal way in the corporation (nor do I suggest that it does not), but the fact that this period of maximum exploration and minimum group loyalty has had evolutionary value suggests that we must still expect to encounter it among the young men of the corporation.

There is, however, another consequence which has a great deal of practical application; the young men are an instrument of social unity between the ten-groups. Since intermarriage between all the camps in the tribe is a genetic necessity, it means that the hunters will have brothers and sisters, sons and daughters, in-laws and cousins, scattered throughout the tribe. Moreover tribal unity and identity are greatly strengthened when the males during this period of their lives form ten-groups of their own which cut across the territorial boundaries between the hunting bands. It means that when they grow up and take their place in the hunt and the camp, they have memories of former ten-group comradeship with other hunters in other bands, and this too must inhibit damaging conflict between mature ten-groups within the tribe, as well as helping to foster a sense of tribal solidarity and weld the single genetic group into a single fighting group when necessary.

I myself had an exceptionally interesting experience of this principle in 1958. A survey of television had criticized the B.B.C. for neglecting the adolescent audience, and the B.B.C. committee

which was discussing this discovered that it was perhaps not ideally
constituted to pass judgment, since no one round the table was ever
going to see forty again. So they set up a sub-committee of people
in their twenties; there were ten of us, from documentaries, current
affairs, drama, light entertainment, design, and the regions. Since
we were not taken off our normal jobs we worked fairly hard for a
month or so, going out in the evenings to talk to teenagers about
their viewing habits and opinions and attitudes, and meeting once
a week during the lunch hour to pool our findings and discuss our
next area of inquiry and research. After six weeks we produced a
fairly comprehensive report (it had become clear that except for pop
music there was no such thing as a separate adolescent audience —
they liked good programmes and disliked bad ones, like everyone
else), and that was that. But the value to all of us, we agreed, was
enormous. It gave us an insight which none of us could have
achieved otherwise into the standards and beliefs and doctrine of
all the other departments represented, it gave us a much clearer
sense of what the B.B.C. as a whole stood for, as opposed to our
own departments, and it left us with an informal network of friends
in other departments whom we could ring up for advice and information and recommendations whenever we had to go beyond
our own specialist expertise. It is clear to me now, as I look back on
it, that these side effects were at least as valuable to the B.B.C. as
the report itself, and I suspect that in any corporate tribe with rather
watertight internal partitions it would be worth while giving a lot of
thought to devising research-and-recommendation projects of this
nature simply in order to bring young ten-groups of this type together and construct informal, lateral-communication networks for
the future.

The danger that prosperity brings is that this group of young
males can become too large. Excessive numbers in a group that is
young, healthy, energetic and highly status-competitive, and also
at its lifetime's lowest level of tribal loyalty, can build up a dangerous
head of aggression. What happens? I believe we can find the answer
to this question in the phenomenon of mass hysteria. Mass hysteria
has never been satisfactorily explained, although it has often been
observed and described: I have done more than observe it — I have
experienced it myself.

It was a strange episode, and a trivial one in many ways, but it is still printed sharply on my memory. It happened one day in the spring of 1939 in my school playground. The current craze was for playing soldiers, and various groups of us were drilling and marching and firing imaginary rifles. Then somehow these isolated groups started to coalesce and first march, and then run, round and round the playground. Someone started to chant a slogan from a current recruiting poster in a crude, basic rhythm, and we all picked it up: 'Join the modern army, join the modern army!' More and more people joined us and joined the chant, until the entire school was charging round and round roaring the same mindless, meaningless chant in a rhythm — tum-ti tum-ti tum-tum, tum-ti tum-ti tum-tum — which I can still hear in my mind more than thirty years later. The bell rang for the end of break, but we were past taking any notice of it. I remember a part of my mind wondering if I would get into trouble — I was a circumspect and conformist child — but I realized that amongst so many I would probably not be recognized and certainly not singled out: if I was punished, the whole school would be punished, in which case the only humiliation would be to be one of the tiny handful of goody-goodies. For a few ecstatic minutes I experienced the exhilarating liberation that accompanies loss of identity, and then somehow — I still do not know how — the Gadarene rush was halted, the exhilaration died away, and we trooped off sheepishly into our classrooms.

We have witnessed this sort of mindless mass-behaviour many times: football crowds and student demonstrations and political rallies, the Hitler Youth movement and the Mosleyites and the storming of the Bastille. No one doubts that it is a single phenomenon common to the whole of our species, and it seems to be totally destructive: and yet if it is a continuing part of human nature then it must have had some survival value. My belief is that it is one of the means by which we used to limit the size of tribal populations.

The normal method of regulation in a fairly static state would perhaps have been for small parties to go off and start new hunting bands, or even new tribes: to find an unoccupied area with a supply of game, and establish a sort of colonial settlement. But in time of continuing population growth when all the land that could support life was annexed as tribal territory, simple colonization was impossible. The numbers of the new generation would start to build up inside all the tribes, beyond five hundred and even beyond a thousand; the risk of overcropping the herds would become acute, and the entire population would be in danger of extinction. I suggest that in this situation there were tribal gatherings at which mass hysteria started to operate, the young men began chanting, and finally they all hurtled off to annihilate a neighbouring tribe and occupy their hunting territory. Perhaps they would succeed, and solve their problem. Perhaps they would be defeated, and solve the other tribe's problem. Either way, nature would win; the population would stabilize again, and overcropping would be averted.

There is nothing in this argument to suggest that this involved only, or principally, the newly-matured young without territory or family, but in all cultures today they seem to be the group which is most prone to outbursts of collective hysteria. They are, moreover, the most expendable group in many animal communities: the famous mass emigration of the lemmings has the same function of relieving population pressure, and it is entirely composed of the young of the year – the males, and those females who are not pregnant; and there are many other species whose young adult males (and sometimes young adult females too) are driven out to make room for the next generation and reduce the number of mouths to feed. Moreover, it is through the swelling number of young adults that a tribe first realizes it is getting too large. Smaller children are vulnerable to disease and predators in a hundred ways, but the mature young males and females are clearly here to stay. Certainly it seems to have been the young males of our species who have always gone off to the wars. Even when I was in the army the marriage allowance was kept uncomfortably low for officers and soldiers in their teens and early twenties: the explanation for this official discouragement of matrimony was that this was the time when the army wanted men to give undivided dedication to the service and be free to travel the world or stay away late without causing domestic dissension and disruption, but it is hard not to suspect that at the back of it lay a desire to minimize the number of widows and orphans left by this vulnerable and expendable group. Any company that takes on large concentrations of these young males in times when there is plenty of work is obviously laying down a powder-keg for the trouble-makers to ignite when the recession comes. It is difficult not to suspect that the universities, too, are suffering from concentrations of these young people, in groups that are beyond acceptable tribal size, and without adequate tribal structure. I would have thought that—on the principle of the foreman and the subaltern—a university would need one young member of staff, almost full time, to look after every forty or fifty undergraduates, and that there should be self-contained college or faculty units of not more than five hundred each, however large the total university, to give even a reasonable chance of avoiding aggressive outbreaks. But even when there are no aggressive and volatile concentrations, there is still a problem for a corporation which recruits a lot of young men during the fat years and is then left with too many on its hands when the lean years come. My observations suggest that the corporations who do best are the ones which stay lean and muscular even in the fat years, and use the young men to start up new hunting bands and new tribes around new products and services, rather than have them stay around in the established tribes to make life easier for everyone else. Some of them will want to leave and go to other corporations, some will want to start up on their own: this is what the young males are for, and it is a misunderstanding of their role to apply the standards of territoried older males and call them restless and unstable. It also means that when the climate gets colder and the recession settles in, the established tribes will not have grown too large; and if some of the new enterprises fail and leave the young males out in the cold, at least they can fend for themselves and not have the problem of supporting wives and families. But whatever the circumstances, they do have an abundance of energy and dedication, and a great desire to establish the highest possible status in the shortest possible time—a desire which, as they grow older, gradually turns to the defence of existing status. This, and their exploring instinct, together with their minimal attachment to an established tribal group, makes any ten-group of young men a very powerful force for developing new products, processes, services, and markets; in new growth areas, experience and judgment matter less—they can even be a disadvantage—and energy and enterprise matter more. In the old areas the clash of the two can cause friction, heat and explosion.

There is another interesting parallel here with the animal world. Wynne-Edwards points out that in harsh and unstable climates there is frequent emigration, and rapid interchange and new formation of populations, which means that populations throughout the whole area show a remarkable genetic uniformity, whereas in stable and serene conditions there is much less cross-flow and far greater distinctiveness and genetic variation between populations.[2] I have noticed this in the corporations: the older-established and stable industries preserve a great deal of individuality, but the new unstable ones—television, advertising, publishing, journalism, films—have so much interchange that the separate competing companies might almost be branches of a single firm, since so many beliefs and assumptions and practices are the same right across the board.

In general, however, the effect of instability on the corporation is to produce a sort of long-term pulsating effect. Boom is centrifugal, slump is centripetal. During the fat years people, especially the young males, want to move out and explore and do better for themselves faster than they can within the tribal system; they chafe at delay and deliberation, and they see the old men missing all the opportunities because they are out of touch. In a slump, everything changes: it is cold outside, the tribal solidarity is secure and attractive, the old men may come up with a job if treated with the proper respect, and obedient conformity is a small price to pay for the security of belonging. Several people have noticed how the argument between centralization and decentralization, though it never ends, goes in phases: that there is no correct state to be achieved, even for a single corporation, let alone as an absolute rule for everyone. There is simply a central mark, and the needle moves from one side to the other. My guess is that the needle follows the movement from boom to slump and back. In the fat years all the central restrictions are questioned, the disciplines and rules all seem like curbs on the initiative and enterprise that are getting competitors ahead faster, the ambitious young men are setting up on their own and making a fortune, and all the talk is of removing central controls and giving everyone more independent authority. Then the lean years come, and the danger is suddenly not of missing the boat but of running it on to the rocks. Proposals are carefully checked, budgets are rigidly enforced, everyone makes sure no one under him is wasting money or taking unacceptable risks, and the central control that was the millstone round everyone's neck now looks much more like a lifebelt.

12

16   The Gathering of the Tribes

FOR millions of years the tribe was the largest unit we knew and, as I have suggested, it found a way of adapting to the cycle of scarcity and plenty, and of controlling surplus population. It was not, however, a particularly comfortable or agreeable way, and no one could be blamed for trying to find a more satisfactory arrangement. That arrangement, as we know, was found some ten thousand years ago with the development of farming, when it became possible to increase the supply of food by agriculture, instead of reducing the demand for it by warfare. Of course the system did not suddenly click into operation, and it does not require a long or deep study of our history to observe that we have continued to operate the two systems in parallel; but for the first time we have devised an alternative system, and (at least on its results so far) I regard it as a notable improvement.

The new system, however, brought with it a problem. For a number of reasons, the chief of which may have been the need to defend the agricultural settlement against marauding tribesmen, the single tribe was too small a unit. It became necessary to bring a number of tribes together for collective security, and—on the principle that if the enemy has a battleship then you have to have one too—there were competitive advantages in bringing together the largest congregation of tribes in the district. Moreover, once a number of tribes congregated into a township, they began to discover all the ways in which specialization and division of labour can increase the supply of food and improve the quality of life: a town can have a doctor, but a village cannot have a quarter of a doctor. The problem, however, is that we had and have no innate instinct for the formation of these larger groupings: we have had to work it out for ourselves or take it over as a working system from our parents and grandparents, or else do a bit of both. To trace the story of our trials and errors in this task throughout the course of recorded history would be beyond the scope of this book—and fortunately so, since it would also be beyond the capacity of its author—but it is not necessary. Since the process has to be passed on or discovered anew, it still happens all the time: in every expanding corporation the mistakes are still being made and the answers are still being discovered every day. Many corporate executives are at this moment perpetrating errors of human organization which would be seen as elementary howlers by the chiefs of what they would call 'primitive' African tribes.

The most obvious and most common mistake, which has already been touched on, is to try and control the larger grouping within the framework of a single tribe. This is the most likely mistake if the increase in size is the result of organic growth rather than alliance or acquisition, because there is no particular point when subdivision has to occur; consequently the pressure rises gradually as numbers go up in twos and threes, and it is easier to explain difficulties away by blaming people or circumstances than by looking at the system of organization that has lasted so well for so long. Instructions are not transmitted, or are misunderstood, salesmen offer impossible delivery dates because they did not see the revised schedule, a machining error goes on unchecked for three weeks, deliveries go to the wrong customers, parts are not ordered, there are delays with men idle followed by bursts of frenzied overtime, the accounts get in a mess because there is no time to do anything about it, and the boss who ought to be around more than ever is in fact seen less and less because he is sorting out rows between departments, soothing ruffled customers, sweating through the books with the accountants or trying to reach an agreement with the unions. It does not occur to him that all this springs from the fairly quick growth from five hundred to sixteen hundred: he sees it as new young lads who don't give a damn about anything except the pay packet, or as the loss of pride in work, or as a general decay of national moral fibre afflicting everyone except himself.

When a firm reaches this stage, it suffers from just about every corporate disease in microcosm, and everyone can produce his own diagnosis: lack of proper financial control, unclear lines of authority, insufficient personnel motivation, inadequate stock and production control techniques, failure to make a long-range plan, no management development programme, or just a 'breakdown in communications'. There is hardly a single management technique that cannot be prescribed with some justification, though there is none that will solve the problem. Once a tribe outgrows its natural maximum size it creates all the problems in the book, and usually simultaneously. The term 'breakdown in communications' is the currently fashionable way of avoiding saying what is wrong; but it is worth repeating that communication happens only in communities, and if the community has broken down there is no way of preserving communication.

The irony is that communication could not possibly break down if it were not for communication techniques. It is only the availability of documentation, drawings, lists, schedules, memos, notices, instructions, and of course the telephone, that gives people the illusion that they can control more than a thousand people as a single unit; without these, sheer practicalities would force a subdivision into separate tribes long before. All these devices and techniques are, of course, invaluable; but not as a substitute for talking to people. I sometimes believe that a manufacturing plant where no one could read or write would have a much better than average chance of profitability. If that meant that the designer had to explain in person to the setter and operator how to machine each new part, it would not necessarily be a great loss. The loss would be in the area of recording, and certainly it would do no harm to go through every piece of paper circulating in a company to see if it is an extension of memory (good) or a substitute for dialogue (bad). When Simon Marks instituted his famous 'Good Housekeeping' revolution at Marks & Spencer, it began simply as a blitz on unnecessary paperwork, and since they saved 120 tons a year (the equivalent of 26 million forms) and £250,000 on printing in the first year, it may be said to have succeeded. But in fact it revealed something even more profound. People throughout the organization were using paper as a poor substitute for personal contact. Merchandisers would endlessly discuss the figures revealed by sales charts – why was this cardigan selling so much faster than that? – when any girl on the woollens counter could have told them it was the neckline that all the customers went for. After the Marksist revolution, when every headquarters manager and executive and director visited at least one store a week to talk to the staff in the front line, they encountered the reality of the business, instead of seeing it through a chart darkly.

The other most common fault occurs at the opposite end of the scale, and is the result not of unstructured organic growth but of an inadequately integrated merger or takeover or acquisition. (I am not talking here of conglomerate-building or asset-stripping operations, but of genuine attempts at full integration.) There is presumably a convincing initial reason for entering into this kind of alliance, even if it bears little relation to the ultimate reality, and my guess would be that the underlying motive is not often, if ever, the simple desire for growth and profits. Nearly always it is a sense of danger, an apprehension that bigger and fiercer competitors will mop us up unless we become bigger ourselves. But whatever the reason, there is an assumption that the coming together can create a whole that is greater than the sum of its parts, and this is where the trouble begins. Whatever the commercial or industrial or financial advantages ('savings on duplicated research ... rationalizing marketing operations ... comprehensive service to customers ... export drive ... '), the genuine integration of two independent tribes into a larger unit means a shattering convulsion of their separate cultural systems. The single overgrown tribe may have plenty of difficulties in splitting up into two or three separate tribes, but at least it is spared this one: it can preserve its territories and status system and doctrine and leadership style and the rest of its cultural tradition more or less intact. But two tribes that have developed separately, however great their respect for each other, have to put all these in the melting-pot if they are to emerge as a strong single unit. Indeed mutual respect may be a barrier: a tribe that feels it is just as good as the other will find it harder to see reasons for change; a clear sense of who is the master is essential for any real integration. But integration is very easy to block: each tribe simply continues as it was. It finds itself unable to divert any people or resources to joint ventures, explains that this is the wrong time to institute the common accounting procedures, insists on taking decisions on its own authority as it did before, never seems to have got the facts and figures out yet, and reduces the game to stalemate around the table of the policy co-ordination committee. None of the advantages are gained, time and effort are wasted, initiative is inhibited, everyone plays politics, and the last state is worse than the first.

How do you overcome the resistance, and integrate two self-contained tribes? I would suggest that, whatever announcements may be made for the sake of appearances, you do not even attempt the operation unless both parties are clear that one of them is leader, and the other is becoming a part of an existing organization. This is often the hardest condition to accept, but unless it is accepted there is very little else that can be done: two separate status systems and command structures cannot exist side by side and be described as integrated, nor is it sensible or possible to destroy them both and start building a new structure on the rubble of two shattered businesses. One must be preserved and strengthened, and the other must be assimilated into it.

This, of course, is all very fine in theory, but a great deal harder in practice, and one of the things that makes it so poorly understood is the shortage of people with a long record of success at achieving it. There has, however, been one quite outstanding example in recent years: between 1958 and 1969 Joe Hyman carried out a spectacular series of acquisitions which took him from the proprietorship of a £180,000 warp knitting company in East Anglia to the chairmanship of the Viyella International Federation, comprising ninety companies, and with a stock exchange valuation of close on £50 million. In a depressed textile industry it stood out as the one shining beacon of consistent growth and profitability until the famous 1969 palace revolution when Hyman was voted out of the chairmanship and the company joined the I.C.I. empire. The highly successful combination of some twenty or more acquisitions (some of the companies were acquired as groups) suggests that his methods are worth recording.

Hyman's first principle was never to make a hostile takeover: every one was with the agreement of the taken-over company. The next was to move into the company himself: he did not believe that integration by proxy was possible, so he took a house or flat in the district and lived with the business. In the initial stages this might take several days a week, shading off as time went by. He reckoned that it had to be a part of his own job for the first year, then be watched closely by him for the next two, and then be monitored for two more: after five years it could stand on its own. The third principle was to find the leader: one of his rules for every division and subsidiary in Viyella was that every chief executive must name his successor on the day that he took up his appointment; consequently he would not start integrating the company unless he had the man who was going to run it sitting next to him. To find the leader he held seminars of anything from a dozen to twenty top executives, and before long he would identify the man he wanted, and they would start work.

Very few directors survived — there were four hundred fewer when he finished — and most of the casualties were members of the families that used to own the business, but in principle he worked with the existing executives, though some of those fell by the wayside too. Another principle was never to leave a man in the job he had held before. By turning narrow, functional managers (sales, production, etc.) into genuine boards of directors thinking about the future of the whole business, he was able to make them start looking at the merger as an expansion of horizons instead of as a defeat. At the same time, the change of job wiped the slate clean; a manager in the same job is defensive about his way of doing it — re-education is a form of personal criticism.

The first reaction was always suspicion and fear, but there were a number of factors on his side. The businesses were mostly family businesses, and once the family directors had gone the executives were not implicated in the wrong decisions, or lack of decisions, in the past: they could change direction without losing face. Then, Hyman kept the central faith intact: they believed in high quality, up-market textiles and so did he. He was not asking them to change over to the cheap and tatty end of the business. And as the seminars went on, all sorts of privately held information about the company became public as the executives pooled their knowledge of the business. Also — another principle — Hyman always lunched with the executives, and if there was no dining-room he had one installed. Gradually a ten-group started to emerge and grow together, socially as well as operationally: hostility turned to reluctant admiration and then, in a surprising number of cases, to hero-worship. It was clear that Hyman understood the business and its finances better than any of them, and a lot of what he was saying was confirmation and extension of what the younger managers had been muttering to each other over their coffee for years. Now they were offered a glorious vision of a new, thrusting, successful textile industry, with all the latest capital equipment, carrying out all the operations — spinning, weaving, dyeing, finishing — on all the fibres — nylon, Terylene, cotton, cotton-and-wool — to replace the out-of-date, fragmented little family businesses employing too little capital and too much labour on a single fibre and a single process.

This vision, however, could be realized only through Viyella, and Viyella was Joe Hyman. He was never in any doubt that allegiance to Viyella had to begin, and continue for some years, as allegiance to him. Nor was he satisfied until the members of a new firm had a sense of belonging, until being a part of Viyella was an aspect of their personal identity. 'I have to become a myth,' he used to say. 'People must believe I'm here even when I'm not.' He was acutely conscious of the need to foster and encourage this myth. He used to work in his house next door to the factory through the night, alongside the night shift, and stroll round now and then to stretch his legs—and also to show the shift workers that he was there too. During one of these strolls he was locked out by the night-watchman. He had to summon help to break into his own house at four in the morning. This, to him, was an invaluable addition to the myth, a story that would go on being told and referred to down the ages.

It is unfashionable management theory, but nevertheless I can think of few cases of successful and lasting integration in industry or history that did not have a hero and a task, a great leader and a promised land. Usually, too, the starting point was a fear of extinction, a need for an ally to face the danger alongside you. Given these prerequisites, the task is then to achieve cultural integration through doctrinal alignment. The central faith must be shown to be the same, but the means of preserving it have to be changed. Hyman's commercial and industrial logic entailed a big doctrinal shake-up—carrying far fewer lines in far greater bulk, not supplying customers who ordered less than a certain volume a year, shift-working, giving big management jobs to men in their twenties and so forth—but this in fact was the key to unity: when so many techniques and procedures were in the melting-pot, it was fairly easy to put certain aspects of the old culture—command system, status-ranking standards of judgment—into the pot with them. The new ideas were part of a total package, and the package had Viyella on the label and Joe Hyman inside.

Successful integration, at least in my experience, is harder and rarer than the subdivision of an overgrown tribe: there is nothing natural about the welding together of two culturally distinct units, whereas subdivision of a large tribe is quite natural and, as we have seen, still happens among the Australian hunting tribes. But which-

ever way the larger grouping is now formed, if it is to be held together as a single unity, then something has to do the holding, and,
as I have suggested, we are still discovering what that something is;
we do not have an innate or instinctive knowledge of it. But if we
are not to live all our lives with the constant anxieties and insecurities
of tribal life, then the tribes must be combined into a more powerful
unit, and that means taking the first step towards the foundation of a
kingdom. And the kingdom is the unit with which we are now
concerned.

Kingdom is perhaps an exaggeration: two or three tribes linked
together might be more aptly described as a barony, and even ten
or a dozen are closer to a duchy, or at most a principality; and of
course all these can exist either independently or within corporate
empires. But they all have this in common: there is a central group
whose job is to direct, control and regulate the tribes who do the
work, and this is the point at which government, management and
politics all begin. To be a good tribal chieftain is a big job, and the
tribal chiefs are the backbone of the corporation: but they are not
the brain. They need an unusual combination of qualities and
qualifications—authority, experience, judgment, the respect of the
tribe, knowledge of the business, sense of priorities—but familiarity
with sophisticated management techniques is not one of them.
Once a central group is formed, however, direct personal contact
with everyone becomes impossible, and you cannot run the business
by the seat of your pants any more. The instinctive has to become
explicit.

Yet some things cannot be changed, and among them are the basic
building-blocks: the ten-group, the camp and the tribe. Consequently the central organization itself has to develop around the
king's ten-group, the council of state. Experience suggests that the
council of elders which guides the whole kingdom is at its best when
it is fairly small, perhaps numbering only four or five including the
king and the prime minister, the chairman and the managing director. But in every large corporate state it is necessary to form a
number of ten-groups to look after certain aspects of the king's
job—a financial ten-group, a legal ten-group, an administrative
ten-group—and it is not difficult for the headquarters operation to
grow into a tribe in its own right, or even to become several tribes.
It is in fact all too easy, and for a reason well known to anyone

who has worked in a large organization. Once you have a head-quarters tribe, or even sub-tribe, it is almost impossible to avoid having a permanent residence; and the permanent residence, the headquarters, the central office (call it what you like), becomes the palace. And throughout history, and around every corporation and state, the palace has exerted an almost irresistible attraction on the ambitious and the status-hungry. It looks like a quick route to the top, a place where a bright young man can be noticed early and promoted rapidly, or an older one can demonstrate his fitness for high office. The fact that in every kingdom and corporation there unquestionably has to be some kind of court leads to pressures to increase its size, and it can quickly become a monster which con-sumes the wealth of the state. Perhaps the king needs only one financial adviser to start with: soon the adviser needs a group round him—an internal accounts specialist, a tax specialist, an investment specialist—and in time each of them needs a group, and a sub-tribe is formed. The same is happening to the legal department, the central buying department, the personnel department and all the rest of them; all of them have unanswerable arguments for having their offices in the palace. Everything that annoys or worries the king or his prime minister can be solved by a new man or a new group in someone's department, to see that it doesn't happen again. The Northern regional manager failed to depreciate his equipment fast enough? We will create a post in the finance department for a man to keep a permanent check on depreciation rates in all the regions—he will save five times his salary in profits tax. All regional managers will submit their depreciation proposals to him six months before the end of the accounting year. Sales executives are changing their cars too quickly? A man in central purchasing will keep an inventory of all company cars with their cost and mileage, and permanently refer it to the second-hand rates and instruct each executive when to trade his vehicle in. He will save five times his salary in transportation costs. And so it goes on. Parkinson put for-ward the theory that the day a firm moves into its own new building is the day it starts to die—St Peter's, Rome, was completed as the years of papal power ended, and the completion of Versailles coincided with the decline of Louis XIV.[1] Like most of his breath-taking exaggerations, there is a disturbing truth at the root of it. The new building gives permanence to the size of the court it can contain, and since a desire for external status prompts kings and chairmen to have the largest possible building, they are saddled with a huge permanent court as well. If the corporate headquarters can be divided up into self-contained tribes of not more than five hundred or so, with a clear role, an evolved leader and an objective measurement of success and failure, the corporation may still survive and prosper: but if it tries to operate a headquarters of five thousand as a single unit, then the malignant cells will be almost impossible to check.

It is also desperately easy for the people around the court to become the focus of the king's attention, so that he spends nearly all his time running his palace instead of his kingdom. They are, after all, the people he sees every day, and it is easy for him to accept his role as leader of the palace tribe and look to the palace as the instrument through which he and the prime minister achieve their aims. This of course means delegating to the priests and courtiers little corners of authority over the outlying dukes and barons and tribal chieftains—it is so much easier if you can put something right or get something done by sending for someone in the same building, and what is more it is natural tribal behaviour. But as the palace becomes more and more of a self-contained tribe, so it drifts away from the rest of the kingdom, and the outlying dukes and barons and chieftains see in its carpeted warmth, its bars and cinemas and squash courts and swimming-pool, its vast army of parasites and sycophants not the heart and brain and nerve centre of their kingdom but an alien institution which soon becomes their prime aggression focus.

The palace tribe is the central problem for any leader who wants to run a kingdom. It is no answer to fix a limit—the operations may absolutely demand a large number of people at the centre. Marks & Spencer, with its highly centralized purchasing and marketing organization, finds it needs close on 2,000 people at headquarters, and since it has virtually no regional organization, just the 250 stores, many people wonder how it can manage with so few. On the other hand Viyella, with Hyman's belief in decentralized operations, ran the same number of people—about 30,000—with a headquarters staff of 40, including secretaries and switchboard operators and the commissionaires; there is no universal rule that can be numerically expressed. Nor is the evolutionary nature of our species any help:

on the contrary, our nature inclines us to split up into totally self-contained tribes, and it is our nature that leads us towards a palace tribe that loses touch with the kingdom. Nevertheless there is a way of holding together a group which is larger than the tribe, and our history is (among other things) a record of how this unity is forged, sustained and dissolved. We are now discovering and adapting the techniques of the Roman and Islamic empires, the British Raj and the Catholic Church to the needs of I.B.M., Unilever and General Motors. With all the vast differences that divide them, they are united by certain enduring features which, if we can isolate them, will give us a most valuable insight into the nature of Corporation Man.

17 The Dispersed Tribe and the Unity of the Kingdom

A CORPORATION, as we understand it today, is a far more recent notion than a manufacturing business; it is also very different. Manufacturing businesses, of the sort that began to dominate our lives about two centuries ago, were defined by their product: if it was yarn they were spinning businesses, if it was cloth they were weaving businesses, if it was steel they were in the steel-making business, and that was that. Few employees were asked to do much more than learn a process and then keep on applying it. If demand rose, more machines and people carried out the same process: and while everybody hoped the business would grow and prosper, it nevertheless had a slightly temporary feeling about it. The business existed for as long as people wanted the product, but if they stopped wanting it then presumably the business would cease to exist. If you invested in it, you were basically investing in the product, as if it were an extension of the commodity market, and your chief concern was the same as with any other commodity—how strong was the demand and how great was the supply? A manufacturing business of that sort required very little in the way of management: it chiefly depended on capital, entrepreneurial flair, a pool of cheap labour, a source of power, strict industrial and financial disciplines, access to raw materials and access to markets.

The corporation did not begin until a new idea started to grow: the idea of permanence and, even more important, confidence in, and commitment to, permanence. This is not to say that some Victorian mill-owners did not believe their business would go on and on, without any foreseeable end to the worldwide demand for Lancashire cotton; but that is simply blind optimism. The commitment to permanence says, in effect, that whatever may happen to the market, the technology, the raw materials, the processes or any other variable, we shall still be in business; our aim is not to produce a particular product, or carry out a particular process, or provide a particular service; our aim is corporate survival, whatever internal changes or convulsions it may entail. The investor is invited to invest not in the corporation's product, but in its ability to survive and grow. Donald Schon pointed out in the 1970 Reith Lectures that it is no longer any good simply thinking of 'the laundry business': housewives buy their own washing-machines, chemists come up with drip-dry cotton and permanent-crease Terylene, manufacturers develop throwaway paper clothes, retailers open launderettes and start nappy services, and what has happened to your laundry business after all that? The only constant is that people like to wear clean clothes, and if you are committed to permanence you have to be in the forefront of as many of these developments as you can. If you are exclusively committed to a steam laundry, you are committed to obsolescence.[1] It is clear that this process is accelerating, not so much because there are no longer any simple processes that have to be carried out year after year, but because it is now economic to build machines to carry out those processes; and now that the computer is taking over the simple clerical processes in the same way that automated equipment and transfer machines are taking over the mechanical ones, more and more people are spending more and more time creating, or adapting to, change and innovation. And what is a corporation then?

Of course, it still manufactures goods; but the emphasis has been shifting steadily away from what the corporation *does*, and on to what it *is*. A few years ago there was a bright future for a firm that published school textbooks: in a few years' time it will only have a future as a part of an integrated corporation producing complete science and arts courses on slides, transparencies, cassette films, discs, tape, wall charts, and teaching machines, with a comprehensive system of liaison with schools and universities to keep the content up to date and to keep improving the techniques; instead of the solitary author there will be production teams comprising film directors, writers, professors, schoolteachers, photographers, animators, graphic artists and learning programmers. They will be supplying every age group from three to twenty-five and on into adult education and industrial training, and covering every branch of every subject that enough people want to learn. It will be no use trying to judge that corporation by a single product: its success will depend on the continuing value of a whole range of instructional devices and packages which are constantly being revised and improved and extended. From being a single entrepreneurial act, like weaving bales of cloth or publishing a textbook, the corporation has evolved into a place of continuing entrepreneurial activity.

It is this, of course, that creates the central problem of organizing the corporate kingdom. So long as all the employees are only following simple instructions and carrying out routine procedures, there is no great problem in organizing a large number of people: it is not hard to tell a mill to produce 10 per cent more of one quality cloth next month and 10 per cent less of another, and to give them correct details for dispatching new orders. But even in the oldest and simplest businesses, more and more change and complexity have crept in over the years: in the newer ones they have been there from the start. And the problem is this: how do you incorporate such a wealth of innovation, creativity and enterprise, with all the attendant administrative complications, within a single corporate kingdom? How do you free people from the shackles of bureaucracy without losing all power to deploy the resources of your kingdom as a single unit? In military terms, how do you avoid such a vast and inflexible concentration of troops that you can never adapt in time to shifts in the battle, or such a loose assembly of independent units that you never know where they are, what their strength is, or what they think they are doing?

If we wanted to strangle our learning systems corporation at birth with red tape, we now know how to do it. We bring all twelve thousand employees into a single building, and set up departments by function: separate departments of writers, of film directors, of graphic artists, of photographers, of learning programmers, of film cameramen, of sound recordists; separate technical departments for slide projectors, for tape recorders, for film cassettes, for printing, for film editing, for programmed learning machines; an advertising department, a sales department, a market research department; a department for schools liaison, and another for universities liaison; and interwoven with these would be an accounts department, a personnel department, a stationery department, an accommodation department. We would then appoint an editor without authority over any of them to produce a geography course, and make sure the medical department had a bed ready for him.

If, however, we want to survive and grow, we create ten-groups: we bring together the sort of team I outlined earlier — film director, school teacher, writer, artist, professor, etc. — and ask them to design and produce a first-year physics course. We then build them into a tribe; perhaps the tribe is called 'first-year courses' and has ten-groups for each first-year subject, but it is much more likely to be called 'physics' and take the subject right through from the first beginnings up to degree standard. We have other tribes for all the other subjects. We have technical tribes responsible for all the different types of equipment, but they have to sell their services on their merits, as do our printing tribes and film developing tribes. Every tribe, of course, is treated financially as an independent firm, with its own budget and accounts and profits target, and it has its own separate building.

A tribal organization like this should prevent the bureaucratic stagnation and paralysis that results from size without structure. It does not, however, solve the problem of deploying the resources of the kingdom as a single unit. The separate tribes can be so separate that they might just as well be independent firms: they derive no benefit from their association since they do not fit into a master plan, nor do they have access to a wider network of information, and can call on no wider human or financial resources for equipment purchase, advertising, research, etc., than if they were in business on their own account. They have to make the same mistakes all over again instead of learning from the others, they have to pioneer new markets and products and techniques themselves instead of sharing the experience of their fellow tribes, and they can only offer their customers the solution to a small part of their problem instead of being a part of the total solution which the corporation supplies. Somehow they have to keep their tribal independence and yet be welded into the corporate kingdom.

You can make the problem sound insoluble, but in fact a number of our great corporations have found a way of uniting these apparently conflicting requirements. They would all explain it in different ways — in terms of organization structures or liaison committees or information procedures or some other management device — but behind them all there is the same instrument of unity; the king's tribe. In almost every way this operates like other corporate tribes, but it has one great difference: it is a dispersed tribe. The members do not leave their own tribes to join it — they remain in them, scattered throughout different buildings, or different cities, or different parts of the world, and what holds them together is not charts or memos or procedures, but tribal membership and tribal unity. No one appoints them or tells them they have joined, and there is no formal membership: even the existence of the king's tribe is seldom consciously realized or acknowledged; but in every large corporation it is very much of a reality, and it is the force which enables all the other tribes to operate independently and yet work together.

In Chapter 4 I touched on the question of dispersal when describing how a member of a ten-group can spend months away from the group and still be a part of it. The Rothschild family provided one of the classic examples of ten-group dispersal in business, when the five sons of the founder settled in London, Paris, Vienna, Naples and Frankfurt, and by their total mutual trust and understanding founded Europe's greatest private banking dynasty which is still flourishing 160 years later. A dispersed tribe is too large to have quite the same tight unity of a dispersed ten-group, but the Jesuits, for instance, have been able to disperse round the world and still remain very much a part of their order after many years on the other side of the globe. The king's dispersed tribe comprises the five hundred to a thousand members of the corporation who know that the king, the chairman, knows them: almost all of them are the people he would invite if in an hour of corporate crisis he had to address the top executives and managers in a hall that would only hold five hundred or so. They may not see him very often, but they expect him to know them and acknowledge them; whereas other tribesmen are pleased if the king recognizes them, they are bitterly hurt if he fails to.

In a small corporate kingdom of ten or a dozen tribes, something under ten thousand people altogether, the king's dispersed tribe will presumably include everyone of seniority: the tribal chieftains, as the leading ten-group of warriors, will be among the most significant members of it, next to the king's council of elders, but there is a place in it for even the most junior manager. As the kingdom grows larger, however, the composition of the king's tribe starts to become critically significant, and for an obvious reason: the strength and unity of the kingdom depend on the degree to which the tribal chieftains feel identified with it. So long as the chieftain knows the old man, so long as the chairman says, 'Morning, Jack, how's Betty keeping?' on the one or two occasions in the year when they meet, the tribe is welded to the kingdom. If, however, the chieftain's name is Albert and his wife was called Mabel and left him twelve years ago, that weld becomes very insecure. It is personal loyalty that unites a tribe, and if it is missing no amount of organizational procedures and financial controls can replace it: but every loyal tribal chieftain is a guarantee that five hundred or so tribesmen can be in personal contact with a loyal member of the kingdom, and that the whole tribe's operation will be directed in a spirit of loyalty. But of course the difficulty of maintaining this personal loyalty and identity rises with the number of tribes: when there are two or three hundred of them—especially if they are geographically dispersed—it becomes critical. Of course it is possible for a cluster of them to remain loyal to a baron or duke, but then their loyalty to the kingdom is in his gift and if he becomes disaffected or recalcitrant he is dangerously powerful. It is for this reason that ambitious corporate barons and dukes are often anxious to keep their subordinate chieftains out of the king's tribe. Equally, as the kingdom grows, it becomes more and more important for the king to make a conscious and deliberate effort to ensure enough contact with the tribal chieftains to weld them all into his tribe.

It would be fascinating to analyse the constitution of the king's dispersed tribe in a number of our great corporations, but extremely hard to get at the real truth since several thousand would claim membership and the chairman would publicly acknowledge them all: only in the deepest private confidence would he admit his inability to put names to faces or faces to names. But I suspect that if the truth could be established, we would find three main ways in which the king's tribe goes wrong; all three results in the alienation of tribal chieftains and other important but distant executives, but the reasons are different.

The first is most common in times of adversity: it is the dominance of the palace tribe which we have already touched on. The king spends far too much time with comparatively unimportant palace officials, usually because he prefers their suave reassurances to the harsh truths that come from tribal chieftains. The second is the stagnant tribe, when very few new people join each year. This often goes in parallel with powerful dukes and barons, who block the membership of new candidates, and a king who spends too much of his time away from the kingdom so that the new people he meets are not members of the corporation. The third is the sectarian tribe. Most corporate kings have risen up through their success in one branch of the kingdom, one region or product or division in which they had conspicuous success, and it is natural for them to give senior posts to members of their earlier ten-group whom they know they can trust; but as time goes on, unless they make the effort, it is very easy for more and more people from that single area to join the tribe and influence the climate in which the king moves in a way that builds up irritation and resentment among less favoured divisions.

All these forms of imbalance in the king's tribe are dangerous for the same reason: they create a short cut to the top. Membership of the king's tribe is an honour, and all the members of that tribe believe they have earned it through the objective value of their service to the kingdom. Once they see a whole lot of people whose service to the kingdom is small start to join the tribe, they feel that the value of their own membership is debased. So long as continued success and high corporate status are the criteria, the kingdom is healthy: when subjective favour replaces objective achievement as the quali-fication for membership, this is the start of tribal alienation and loss of central control. And although these unhealthy tribal formations have separate causes, they have a central fault in common: the king is not meeting enough of his subjects. 'Queen Elizabeth slept here' is one of the indicators of a good monarch who knew her duty in times of national division when unity was of prime importance: 'England' was a difficult concept for people to be loyal to, but a real live queen who waved from her carriage and stopped in your town and talked to the mayor and the squire and the rector and spent the night up at the manor house, that was another matter. She, of course, had the great advantage that the telephone and telex had not been invented, that written communication was laborious and slow, and that there were no planes or cars or trains to let her feel she could always get there in a few hours if there were a crisis: she knew she had to go in person, and plan the visit well in advance and irrespec-tive of any operational requirement. Technical progress has not altered that necessity; it has merely provided a variety of excuses and delusions for chairmen who start to feel uncomfortable north of Watford. The royal progress is just as necessary for the corporate chairman as for the Tudor monarch if the king's tribe is to be a healthy, living community: it is also a more productive activity than sitting behind a desk at the top of a London tower-block setting up committees to investigate the breakdown in communications.

The chief purpose of this royal progress, or chairman's visit, is to keep the tribes welded into the kingdom, and to update the king's dispersed tribe by ensuring that the rising young men come to his notice; but it does have certain more immediately visible practical advantages as well. One of them is cross-fertilization: by going round every part of the business at the highest level, the chairman can often give one tribe some surprisingly useful information about what another tribe is working on or thinking about — new techniques, new potential customers, new sources of supply, new activities that qualify for government grants or tax rebates, opportunities to economize by working together, or stimulus to beat the other to it by competing. There is really no one in the corporation except the chairman who has access to so much high-level and perhaps confidential information about every aspect of the business combined with the opportunity to circulate and discuss it amongst the top people in every outpost. The prime minister, the managing director, is too closely focused on immediate operational needs to have much time for this sort of visit or to exchange this sort of almost accidental information; it is a part of the chairman's job that no one else can discharge so effectively.

The chairman's progress is also one of the fastest ways of getting things done. No amount of memos and directives from palace officials can achieve as much as quickly as a personal word of reproof or commendation from the king. There are many Marks & Spencer stories about Simon Marks's royal visits (on one of them, to Scotland, he could visit the Paisley store only after it had closed for the day, and the whole staff asked if they could be allowed to stay on in order to see him), and many of them illustrate this principle. Once, on a West Country progress, he visited the Exeter store and gave the manager a rocket for displaying some folding bags by stuffing them out with newspaper. By the time he got to the Torquay store after lunch, all folding bags were displayed flat and empty. Such was the force of his command (and the speed of the dispersed tribe's communication network) that probably every bag in every store in the land would have been flat and empty by tea-time.

However, on this occasion he sent for the manager and asked why the bags were not padded out. The manager mumbled something in total confusion about understanding that Sir Simon preferred them flat, at which Marks (with a twinkle in his eye according to some accounts) replied, 'Listen, lad, just because I like them flat in Exeter, it doesn't mean I like them flat in Torquay.' This illustrates an almost equally important point: any number of corporate practices become enshrined in unchangeable ritual because 'the old man likes it that way' or 'the old man can't bear it', when the only authority is a chance remark in a special context. If the old man actually travels around he can loosen up some of the rigidity by his presence and his questions. Rigidity is the product of insecurity; if people get a chance to see the king themselves, to talk to him and listen to him, much of that insecurity will disperse. Instead of having their actions and decisions constricted by a host of mysterious injunctions and prohibitions from some unknown but terrible figure hundreds or thousands of miles away, they will be much happier to use their own judgment and initiative so long as they feel they could creditably explain the reason for their action to the man they have actually met. The image of the boss stands behind every executive's shoulder; by coming round in person, he makes that image much more distinct and accurate, and greatly increases the chances that the executive will act as the boss would wish, that he will follow the spirit of the corporation and not just obey the letter of the law.

There is one other reason why the chairman has to keep in personal contact with his tribe, and it is perhaps the most important of all. Long-term survival demands that the right man or group shall be in the right job. In an ideal stable situation leaders evolve through their ten-groups and tribes and there is not often a problem, but where there is rapid change and growth the correct selection and placing of leaders assumes overriding importance. In nearly all corporations this is one of those cases where the present is the enemy of the future: if a man is making a great success of his job, it is all too tempting to let him go on doing it year after year. If a new company has to be started, it is all too tempting to find someone who can be spared. The managing director has to think of this year's results and next year's forecasts; the chairman must think of who ought to be at the head of the corporation's affairs in ten or fifteen years' time, and what experience they ought to be gaining now.

There is no personnel inventory or management development programme that can make this sort of judgment for him; it may be drawn from a chance remark which shows that a good executive has begun to start thinking like a director; or from a couple of minutes' conversation which reveals that a man who was stimulated and extended by his job a year or two ago is now starting to outgrow it and be bored by it; or by a feeling that another man who would have rejected an offer of an early retirement last year would accept it gratefully this year. These feelings cannot be measured or tabulated, nor can any less senior official make these judgments; only the chairman has the necessary knowledge of where men are needed, what qualities they require, and who within his kingdom is the best man for the job. Putting the right man and the right task together can be a creative act, just as putting the wrong ones together can be a destructive one. Only by personally welding his dispersed tribe into a unity of all the best men in the kingdom, only by progressing around often enough to keep making the adjustments in this constantly changing equation of men and tasks, can he be in a position to go on making his unique creative contribution to corporate renewal.

18 Evolution and the Committee

THERE is a story that Alekhine, when he was world chess champion during the 1930s, stopped for a drink in a Paris boulevard café and an old man shuffled up to him with a chessboard and asked if he would like a game. Alekhine said he would, and the old man—who clearly had not the slightest idea who his opponent was—began to lay out the pieces. When the board was set, Alekhine removed his king's rook. 'But Monsieur,' protested the old man, 'why do you believe you can afford to give me a rook? You do not even know me.' 'Monsieur,' replied Alekhine, 'if I could not afford to give you a rook, I *would* know you.' The story is a good illustration of one of the principles of a dispersed tribe (in this case the tribe of international chess players); that if it is functioning properly, you can know negatives. You trust the network so completely that you can be sure something is not so, or has not happened, because you just know you would have been told if it had.

A corporation gains enormous strength if the king's dispersed tribe constitutes a network of this nature, but it cannot be achieved by royal progresses alone: their great contribution is in binding the periphery to the centre, whereas this network is built like a spider's web, with lateral as well as radial links. It cannot function unless people with no direct operational relationship are in the habit of ringing each other up whenever they come across a piece of information, or meet a person, or hear of a development, or have an idea, which is of no use to them but might be of value to the other chap: the sort of nervous-system communication that happens in a good factory tribe—the example of the commissionaire warning the operator to put the hood on the chain drive, given in Chapter 14, illustrates this kind of lateral link. It may sound easy and obvious, but it is not. To start with, you have to know enough about the other chap's job to realize that it might be of use to him: and that means not just knowing the post he occupies, but also knowing what he is trying to do and how he is trying to do it and what are his main hopes and fears. Then you need to be sure that he respects your judgment and accuracy and reliability, so that he will give proper weight to the information or recommendation. Finally, you need the incentive to take the trouble over something which does not help your job or get you any credit. For all these reasons, this vital lateral communication hardly ever happens between people who do not know each other, or have met only occasionally and socially, and it happens best between people who have at some time been part of the same ten-group, and if they have ever been in the same sub-tribe or tribe, that is a help.

The ideal network in a king's tribe would operate like the Midwich Cuckoos in John Wyndham's science fiction story: those strange children who seemed to share a collective brain, so that, however far apart they were, the moment one of them learnt something the others all knew it too. A village or a small, self-contained firm of tribal size can come very close to this, but of course it is the constant physical proximity that makes it possible. The dispersed tribes which work best have certain things in common, of which the most important is continuity: the members have grown up together in the corporation, and have moved around enough over the past fifteen or twenty or thirty years to have worked fairly closely with a large proportion of the dispersed tribe, so that when they graduate to it they already have quite a rich network within it. And then they make sure there is frequent contact across the formal operational boundaries within the king's tribe: in a compact operation this can be informal, but in more diffuse and decentralized businesses it has to be specially arranged, so that 3M for instance nicknames itself the Minnesota Manufacturing and Meeting Corporation. However it is achieved, the result is a regular bringing together of people who would not necessarily meet in the course of their immediate operational duties; but it is hard to see exactly what this achieves without looking more closely at the role of the meeting in the life of Corporation Man.

If you asked any given Corporation Man the purpose of the meeting he was just off to, he would usually be able to give an answer: to review next year's budget proposals, to plan the new product range, to discuss advertising policy, to brief sales managers on the new bonus scheme, or any of a thousand other objectives. I am writing this page at ten past ten on a Monday morning, and the effort to visualize how many meetings are taking place at this moment stretches the imagination beyond its breaking point. And yet the sheer volume itself is significant: this activity could not go on in such volume with such frequency if it were unnatural. In fact, so far from being unnatural, meetings serve an underlying need of our species; they are an integral part of every human community, civilized or uncivilized, modern or primitive, of which we have knowledge or record. This does not mean that we are wrong to describe them, as Corporation Man describes them, by their operational purpose: but it does mean that we would be foolish to ignore their underlying compulsion. Foolish, because if we accept only the operational purpose we are in danger of assuming that the meeting will result in the furthering of corporation objectives, whereas those who habitually attend meetings are well aware that in practice no such consequence can be assumed. This will not, however, leave all those who were there frustrated at the waste of time, nor will it stop the same meeting from taking place at ten o'clock next Monday morning, and the Monday after, and the Monday after that.

The reason is that the species we belong to, and from which we have descended, survived by keeping together, and irrespective of the demands of the job, Corporation Man needs to come together regularly with other members of the species—operational objectives can always be found to justify this deeper need. I suspect that meetings are most frequent and most enjoyed by men whose work keeps them solitary or in very small groups for most of the week, and who do not serve on any committee in their neighbourhood either, just as they are most resented by members of tightly knit ten-groups. There is a need to feel the security of the group around you, even if you do not belong to a real or effective one. In addition, there is status satisfaction in being able to summon people to your presence and look round the office at the group which acknowledges your leadership. For both these reasons, and particularly in large office blocks full of small offices, it is all too easy for meetings which start with sound operational objectives to fossilize into ritual assemblies whose only value is to treat cases of social deprivation by regular group therapy.

In practice, even the most apparently futile of meetings usually serves some wider corporate purpose as well as preserving the mental health of those who attend: it builds and maintains the communication network, it gives a feeling of security, it helps to sort out status and quasi-territory, and it reaffirms identity and the sense of belonging. No corporation could survive or be described as a corporation if every member travelled in from his private house by his private car to his private office, met no one during the day, and travelled back in the evening. Any Corporation Man who found himself in that position for a few weeks would start to wonder how long it would be before he got the sack. A certain amount of factory work is in fact very like this, since the noise or the demands of the operation make each man into an island: it is hardly surprising that if the corporation does not bring its members together for regular meetings, they seek assembly and association through the unions. But at the higher and more comfortable levels, most corporations have found ways of channelling this need for association into useful and productive purposes, and in fact the more visibly effective and valuable the meeting the more it fulfils all the social and therapeutic needs as well.

These purposes are of course tremendously varied: but the kinds of meeting are much fewer, and a look at them may enlarge our understanding of corporate communication. There are in practice only three kinds, although there are subdivisions: the small meeting, or committee, of ten-group size; the larger meeting of something around fifty or sixty; and the large assembly of several hundred. All the intermediate sizes are of course possible, and there is no firm boundary at which the meeting is declared to be in a different category; nevertheless the three kinds are distinct in operational and social function and have to be treated quite separately.

The meeting of ten or so is the most common. The one feature which distinguishes it from the larger meetings is that everyone present can contribute to every part of the discussion. Once this becomes impossible the meeting stops serving its purpose, or becomes a small version of the next size. It can, however, stagger along if some people never open their mouths and become in effect spectators, or if some people contribute only on some points and some only on others, so that the meeting is in practice several different meetings held consecutively. In a sense this meeting is impossible to generalize about: the actual committee meetings that take place in corporations vary in size from two or three people to twenty or thirty, the agenda can have anything from one to over a hundred items, they may be high or low level, hostile or friendly, and they can change their entire nature halfway through with a new item on the agenda. And yet, from all the seemingly endless variants of this meeting, it is possible to isolate four or five essential ones which keep recurring in every tribal community. They all involve about ten people, and they may well go back many thousands of years into our prehistory.

The obvious one is the planning meeting of the hunting band, the ten-group. It can of course be the meeting of a permanent ten-group, like our morning meetings to plan the day's programme on *Tonight*, but it does not have to be. Any gathering of ten-group size with a joint task in which the members succeed or fail together, even if they only meet each other once a month, comes under this heading. Out of this meeting comes a decision, a report, a recommendation, a plan of action, which is usually (though not necessarily) put into effect by that same group. The decision is taken by the leader, and the purpose of the meeting is to bring everyone's special knowledge, experience and ideas together to enable him to come to the best decision. It may also include the allocation of duties amongst the group when the plan has been decided on. At the end of it every member knows his task, and everyone else's, and how they all fit into the overall objective, and they go off to carry out what they have determined.

The other necessary meeting of the ten-group takes place at the end of the hunt: in practice this may be the beginning of the next planning meeting, but in any case it is the first occasion when the hunting band reconvenes. This is where they talk over the events of the hunt and see if there are any lessons to be drawn. It is the first stage in the corporate digestive process referred to in Chapter 14; they chew over the raw experience and information to see if there is anything nourishing to be extracted from it. Later on, when it has been digested, it can be circulated through the body of the corporation by other ten-groups, and at the meetings of forty or fifty and the large assemblies of over two hundred which we will meet in Chapter 19.

Then there is the meeting of the king and his council of elders. In a sense it is a ten-group meeting, but it differs from a hunting band in enough ways to be considered separately. Hunting bands decide amongst themselves how the job shall be done, but the king and his elders have to decide what the job is, and in which direction lies the best hope of survival and success for the whole community. Moreover, the king and his elders do not themselves execute what they decide at their meeting, nor is any one of them individually responsible for any specific success or failure in the past: they have nothing to defend or excuse, no hope of individual glory or fear of individual shame. This above all is where the modern corporate king goes wrong: instead of appointing a true council of elders—full-time directors without executive office—he fills his 'board' with divisional heads, the corporate princes and dukes from production and marketing, or product ranges, or geographical regions, and then finds he cannot really get impartial expert counsel. Each nobleman is grinding his own axe, and even when he is not, the king cannot be sure he is not. So he turns to his accountant and legal adviser and company secretary and head of public relations, and the court starts to dominate the nation.

A good council of elders normally seems to be small—about four or five including the king—though it also has frequent discussions, formal or informal, with all sorts of people from inside and outside who may contribute to their deliberations. Its basic concern is with the tribe in relation to the wider world, the world of prey and predators, scarcity and plenty, allies and enemies, the world outside its jurisdiction and beyond its control. For the corporate kingdom this means capital markets and government policies, investment and taxation, competition and acquisition, new technologies and new markets—everything which impinges on the external identity of the tribe and the kingdom, and may affect the direction in which it will have to move. The elders are also concerned with the internal health and fitness of the kingdom, with its strength, its freedom from internal strife, its ability to respond instantly and move rapidly when situations change. In earlier, political communities the result of the deliberations of the king and his council was called lawgiving when applied to these internal affairs as they affected the permanent identity of the kingdom: today it is called 'corporation policy' or 'the way we do things here', but the effect is the same.

When specific action has to be taken, this leads to a fourth kind of ten-size meeting, when one or more of the elders from the king's council discuss with one or more leading prince or duke the action that must be taken to achieve the objectives the king and his elders have fixed. For any corporate organization, this meeting is the crunch: it is where conclusions are turned into decisions. Sometimes it is an easy, happy meeting – but all too often it is not. When the policy of the elders is unwelcome there is a sequence of standard responses from the duke, the divisional head, all of which can cause friction and resentment. The first is to criticize the objective itself: 'Why the hell do we cut home expenditure anyway?' The elders can easily take offence at this, but in fact it is a useful opportunity to educate executives in the wider issues which may one day confront them. And if that question is answered, the next standard response is to criticize the application: 'Why don't you get South Region to cut back? They spend far more than I do.' This section may well produce, under powerful emotional pressure, a better solution than the elders had seen, and if so they would be foolish not to adopt it. This is easier for them if they have raised the matter as a discussion ('The least damaging way we can see is for you to cut your expenditure – but you may think of some other course'), rather than a briefing session ('This is what we have decided you must do'). If the executive sees he has to admit defeat in both these arguments, the third course is to prove that it is impossible. But the elders, by insisting that it must be done, can quickly force him into the position of saying it is impossible for him, leaving them free to suggest they should try and see if one of his subordinate barons could do it for him. Since he knows that his subordinates would all leap at the chance whether they could do it or not, his fourth and final response is to resort to salvage, to see what he can pick up to replace the loss ('Well, I shall need direct authority over the regional personnel officer, and six extra posts in overseas operations, and an increase in the European budget ... '); and it is only at this stage that the elders counter by making it clear that his personal status is unchanged and can be enhanced by a successful conclusion of the operation ('We hate having to do this to you of all people, because morale is so high in your division; on the other hand, we believe you can achieve it with as little damage to corporate morale as anyone we know').

This meeting happens in modified form all the way down the corporation, and it should not be rushed; it is an important instrument of vertical communication. Under the pressure of argument, the resentful junior learns, even if traumatically, a number of new and important facts about the wider environment in which he works and the higher considerations which affect his labours. He goes away realizing that to win the next argument by countering with better alternatives, he must think about them from his superior's point of view and not his own – a valuable preparation for succeeding to his senior's job. Equally, it educates the elders, or whichever other corporate superiors have to pass on the bad tidings: by having to meet every objection, they are forced to make sure that their decision is based on solid factual and logical grounds, while the contrary facts and the arguments brought forward give them valuable understanding of their subordinate's job and its problems. When this meeting is reduced to brief unexplained directives, or replaced by written instructions, one of the prime instruments of corporate communication is removed. In a corporation where everyone has grown up together it is much easier, because on the whole everyone knows how the others will react and takes account of the likely objections while formulating the decision, but in a newly formed or newly merged operation this meeting must take place if a proper community is to be created.

The fifth and last small meeting is the one referred to earlier in which the king and his elders meet all the divisional heads or departmental managers who make up the ten-groups of operational leaders. This is the meeting most often by-passed, since unlike the others there is rarely any immediate operational need for it; but in a dispersed tribe it is of great importance. Its prime function is to make the individual generals look at the whole war, and to give the cabinet of elders insight into the feelings of the whole army. In corporate terms, the executives go away with a better understanding of their place in the whole enterprise, and the board go away with a fuller and more accurate sense of the feeling of the whole body of the corporation. If all the executives together say the new system of forecasting does not work, it is more forceful than if each one mentions it separately. If half say it does and half say it doesn't, the snags can be argued out here. This is where the elders get the feedback from previous decisions in the most reliable form, and where they get the best guidance on how to achieve in practice the objectives they have determined on ('We need to expand our dollar income from synthetics — but should we increase our home production, or start up new plant in dollar areas, or acquire overseas companies, or what?'). This is where the best practical solutions are likely to appear — not the best view of what needs to be done, but the best view of how to do it.

In a changing situation, this meeting has another significant function — the revision of doctrine. It is the place to question practices resulting from decisions taken long ago when circumstances were different, but which have rigidified into unchanging ritual, the place where everyone should be encouraged to ask 'Why?' about any and every time-hallowed and unquestioned assumption and procedure. Often this will result in useful simplification and sometimes considerable money-saving; but even if the answer to the question 'Why?' produces a very good reason, the act of uncovering that reason is a valuable piece of education.

There is one other permanent need in every corporate community which this meeting serves: the regulating of boundaries between the separate areas of quasi-territory. A specific dispute between two neighbouring executives will normally be sorted out separately; it will only be discussed here if it starts to threaten the unity of the realm, but this is the place to establish and revise the relationship between the executives and the boss, and the principles which regulate the internal boundaries between executives. The less this has to happen, the healthier the state of the corporation. But to keep this sort of discussion infrequent the tribal structure has to be very good: tribes and tribal groupings must have clear objectives with little or no overlap, they must have all the necessary authority and resources to do their job on their own, and there must be no court officials with little enclaves of authority in their gift. When tribal structure is undefined, when functional authorities multiply and the palace grows larger and larger, these sources of uncertainty and dispute spread into every activity, and this meeting has time for little else. The consequence is that it delegates the less pressing topics to a lower level, and sets up that bane of corporate life and prime indicator of structural deficiency, the permanent committee: in other political institutions it is usually called a law-court.

The permanent committee is not inherently wrong; it could for instance be a good ten-group systematically scrutinizing all aspects of the business and reporting to the board. But nearly always it is a law-court, and often gives itself away by terms like 'liaison committee' and 'co-ordinating committee', indicating that everyone arrives in a spirit of competition and hostility, briefed to gain the maximum possible advantage for his tribe and to make the fewest possible concessions, and usually with considerable powers to delay or frustrate the reaching of any binding decision. From time to time a subject crops up which unites the whole committee, and a useful decision or recommendation is produced, but then of course the committee is no longer acting as a law-court: it has become a working ten-group. The more cumbersome and detribalized a corporate organization becomes, the more these law-courts multiply and the busier they become. They have a fatal, seductive fascination for underemployed managers and officials: they offer a morning or afternoon of invigorating, competitive activity or pleasant, somnolent ease, according to choice and the agenda, and give the illusion of achievement without effort or risk. There is no product by which any committee member's performance can be measured, and no outcome for which the responsibility can be pinned on him. The permanent committees which exist for litigation and negotiation are malignant growths which endlessly consume managerial and executive time without nourishing the body of the corporation, and surgery is the only cure.

19 The Tribal Assembly

THE small meetings of ten-group size take place all the time, and, besides serving the needs of corporate digestion and communication, they are the instrument through which Corporation Man achieves his daily, monthly and yearly objectives. They are convened for an operational purpose, even if they do not serve it, whereas the two larger kinds are not. But in a dispersed tribe, the other two take on a special tribal significance which is almost entirely connected with digestion and communication. The problem they can solve is the problem of passing it on: however good the communication within ten-groups, the report the divisional executive brings back to his ten-group of regional heads is not an unblemished reflection of the real event, and by the time the regional heads talk to their area managers another selecting and distorting lens has been interposed. Even if the instruction of what the area managers have to do is faithfully preserved and accurately transmitted, the reason for doing it has probably taken a bashing on the way down, and the image of the chairman and the board which they piece together is bound to be a grotesque caricature of the reality. Even the most loyal, honest and devoted executives will — indeed must — carry back a violently distorted selection of events; the less loyal or honest can play havoc with them to their own advantage. And the same applies in reverse: at each level the members of the ten-group will tell their leader about the feeling in their tribes, and this too is bound to be selected, even if unconsciously, to help their own cases. It is this defect in the two-way repeater chain which is responsible for much of the failure of the corporate transmission system.

This defect can only be remedied by the king and his elders personally explaining the reasons for decisions to far more people than is practicable in ten-groups, and by that same large number of people being given the opportunity of asking the questions that are on their minds and of getting grievances off their chests. This need seems to be best served by a meeting that can comfortably reach a size of forty or fifty, and perhaps go up to a hundred. It is large

14

enough for everyone to realize that it cannot be conducted as a general discussion, but not so large as to inhibit questions from anyone who wants to ask. Once numbers rise above a hundred or so, people feel it is assertive to claim the privilege of asking one of the few questions there is time for, so nobody asks any, or only the top people do; there are deep inhibitions about asking questions when you feel that your status in the group is low. For this reason the status spread should not be too great either. And finally, but most important, it is vital to the success of this meeting that there should be a fair amount of dialogue, so once the numbers reach the point where anyone has to raise his voice above normal conversational level, the success of the meeting is threatened. As I have said, experience suggests forty or fifty as the size which most satisfactorily meets all these requirements, with a hundred as the upper limit; there is of course no lower limit until the point where the meeting changes to a ten-group discussion.

If these meetings are held regularly, they do not need to be held frequently, and the royal progress is usually a good occasion for them; every member of the king's dispersed tribe should take part in at least one of these sessions a year with the king. The effect, of course, is to correct the distortion. If you can match the executive's account of his meeting with the king against your memory of the man you listened to and questioned and even argued with, you are much more likely to deduce the reason behind the decision even if it is inaccurately relayed to you; equally, if you felt any warmth towards the king (and I believe there is built into us an instinct to do so if we possibly can), you will be inclined to choose the more charitable of two possible explanations. And of course the simple act of saying what you wanted to say to the man you wanted to say it to can relieve pent-up frustrations wonderfully.

There is a further value to these meetings if the king is wise and reasonably secure. Two of the major disqualifications for a leader are to be deaf to the warning signals from the pack and to fail to learn from past experience. At these meetings the king can remove fears that he may suffer from either. Candid admission of past errors usually works marvellously in these gatherings ('Yes, the 450 model was a ghastly failure, wasn't it? I'll tell you what we did wrong ... '). The audience is not worried by the failure one tenth as much as by the fear that the board might still be pretending to themselves that it was a success. And the king should take all reasonable suggestions and criticisms seriously by really arguing them out ('I think you're right about the demand, but how would we produce them that cheaply?'), rather than crushing them with authority ('Sorry, it wouldn't work—Next?'), or patronizing by too easy acceptance ('Good idea, we'll certainly discuss it'). If the purpose of one of these meetings is to give early advice of new plans or products or procedures, it is a good occasion for the king to get guidance on specific applications and practical difficulties which may be seen more clearly by people closer to the tribesmen who will have to put them into effect: for that reason they should be presented before the final details are fixed beyond revision.

As well as at least one meeting each year with the king, everyone in the king's dispersed tribe may need to attend several others where the king is not present, either within their own tribe or with people doing similar work in other tribes: the fifty-group meeting of area sales managers, of production engineers, of works accountants, of research managers. The larger the corporation, the more often these meetings need to be held. It is all too easy for valuable ideas, information and experience to be locked up in a lot of isolated ten-groups dotted around the corporation. The larger meetings can turn these little pools of valuable folk-wisdom from a scattering of stagnant ponds into a chain of linked reservoirs. It is no good hoping to do it by circulars and memoranda—it must be done by personal contact. This is because—to revert to an earlier parallel—the fifty-group meeting is another chain in the digestive process. Anything brought to this meeting will have already been chewed over by a ten-group, but it needs a further stage of argument and discussion and collective rumination before it can be circulated right through the corporation.

Obviously the small tribal firm hardly needs to arrange this sort of meeting: if its members are all in the same geographical location, exchanges of this kind will take place informally without pre-arrangement. But in larger companies and corporations it is all too easy for outlying tribes to become narrow and isolated. They are cut off from the process of learning and adapting which is constant at the centre, and they make mistakes and miss opportunities in a way which seems incredible to anyone who has kept up to date. It is the lateral links which prevent this kind of isolation. And of course it is an invaluable meeting for bringing together members of the dispersed tribe.

The last of the three kinds of meeting is the assembly of the whole tribe, the gathering together of five hundred to a thousand people. There is no possibility of dialogue and not much point in inviting questions; the assembly is an audience. And whereas anybody can chip in to a ten-group discussion, and most executives can handle a group of fifty to a hundred of their subordinates, a full assembly is daunting to those who have never addressed one before. To do so requires experience, confidence, and a certain amount of technique: ordinary conversational voice levels and ordinary small movements of the facial muscles and hands and body will not carry beyond the twelfth row, and if a microphone is used as a substitute for technique it only makes a flat and dull performance audible at the back. Perhaps this is why the full assembly is the most disastrously under-used management instrument in the modern corporation: firms with large numbers of salesmen or agents usually realize the value of it, but the corporate need is not restricted to salesmen.

In any discussion of what happens to a group of individuals when they become an audience, the first question to ask is, 'When is an audience not an audience?' In theory the question is unanswerable: the number can be quite small if they all know each other and the speaker, and if they are closely packed in a tight space in the dark. If they are all total strangers and have never seen the speaker before and are scattered thinly around a huge, high, light auditorium, then twenty times the first number may still fail to become an audience. But in practice, for the purposes of studio television programmes, from which I have gained my most direct experience of audiences, we set a minimum of 200–250 people, though we preferred more. The crucial measuring instrument is laughter; the point at which a joke gets an immediate solid laugh instead of a scattering of smiles and sniggers and titters is the point at which a group of single individuals has become an audience. Once that point has been reached, you are in communication not with a wide range of diverse intellects, but with a single collective entity; after a while you do not hope a joke will get a laugh, you know it will, and that knowledge itself is a guarantee that you will deliver it with such confidence that it does get the laugh.

Laughter is central to the understanding of audience behaviour. The French philosopher Henri Bergson explains it as an act of collective aggression, on the grounds that it is rare for individuals to laugh when they are on their own and that the baring of the teeth and shortening of the breath are physical expressions of aggression.[1] At first sight this is ridiculous: laughter is warm and friendly, not aggressive at all. On reflection, however, it is less ridiculous: the warmth and friendliness are within the laughing group. If you are the only person not laughing in a roomful of laughing people, and even more if they are all laughing at you and against you, the friendliness vanishes and you realize the exclusion and aggression the laughter implies. The comedian who makes us laugh is identifying an aggression focus, a kind of behaviour or attitude or person we reject or exclude, often (according to Bergson) for ancient survival reasons; it is behaviour which can lead the hunting band or the tribe into danger. (Compare the hooting of cars at the motorist whose road behaviour endangers everyone's survival.) Even the man who treads on a banana skin represents this in a basic way: he is too inflated with his own importance to notice small danger signals, he is the high-dominance low-intelligence leader who spells extinction for the group. Most broad humour depends on someone's unawareness of what the rest of us know. This is too complex a theory to pursue any further here, but the important point is clear: laughter is a collective activity which affirms and defines group membership and identity and standards by what it excludes and whom it includes.

Queen Victoria's diaries revealed to me a significant aspect of laughter. I had dipped into them once or twice in the library, and smiled quietly at the naive charm of the early entries. Then I went to a performance of *The Hollow Crown*, an anthology of the literary efforts of British monarchs, and in a crowded theatre I listened to Peggy Ashcroft reading some of the same extracts. The whole audience fell about with almost painful laughter, and I was doubled up with as much ecstatic anguish as anyone. Why? What had happened?

What had happened was that when I read the diaries in the library they generated a small private amusement, but spoken with Peggy Ashcroft's art in a packed theatre they generated a collective discovery for all of us in the audience, a discovery of unity and identity precipitated by our sudden collective realization that Queen Victoria was not one of us; and by this discovery we were welded into a single group. The same can happen in reverse: film sequences which made me sob with laughter in a crowded cinema raise no more than a slight smile when re-run on television a few years later. Often the discovery is a simple reaffirmation of a uniting emotion, but sometimes it can have national importance; we shall never know how many people were privately amused before 1961 by Macmillan and the rest of the British politicians, but *Beyond The Fringe* and *That Was The Week* transformed private amusement into a collective realization that they were funny, and the British national attitude towards politics has never returned to the solemn respectfulness of the 1950s.

Laughter is the key to understanding the nature of audiences, but they have other ways of expressing a collective response: applause, cheers, booing, restless movement and withdrawal of attention, extreme stillness and silence—all these, even if they start with one person, can quickly generalize into a group reaction. And together they add up to a language: it is a very primitive and limited language, closer to the baying of hounds or the howling of wolves than to human speech, but it is sufficient for its purpose: and the purpose is a collective tribal communication with the speaker. It is not only 'community' and 'communication' that come from the same root; 'communion' does too. If the speaker is in communion with the community, they communicate, and the audience's expressions of collective response tell him at each stage how the community is accepting him. Lloyd George, who understood audiences as well as most people, used to go to large public meetings with half a dozen topics in his head which would each have done for a speech. He would start on one of them, and if it aroused no response he would move on to the next, and so on until he felt more reaction to his subject. Then he would develop the topic that provoked it, and at each stage thereafter the audience's reaction would guide him towards the areas in which he could best express the emotions, the aspirations and the aggressions in which they found their strongest unity. He was sometimes accused of inventing government policy while he was speaking: perhaps there are worse times to invent it. I have seen something similar myself. In the autumn of 1965 a Labour M.P. on *The Frost Programme* defended the government's record on the grounds that it was still coping with the results of thirteen years of Tory misrule. This had been said by many M.P.s on many television programmes for the past eighteen months: but *The Frost Programme* had a studio audience of two hundred, and they broke into a spontaneous groan. For the first time, the community had a chance to communicate its views on that line of defence, and it was never heard again.

For the corporate tribe, and above all for the dispersed tribe, the full assembly is a unique and irreplaceable instrument of communication. It enables the leader, king or elder, duke or courtier or tribal chieftain, to sense the true collective feeling with a certainty that is beyond flattery or politeness or misrepresentation. It enables the whole tribe to decide if the leader is leading them in the right way, and to warn or encourage him collectively without risking personal careers or reputations. Above all it enables the tribe to make a collective discovery of its identity, what it stands for and what it stands against, what it believes in and is proud of, what it rejects and despises. There is a deep need to know this tribal feeling: with the decline of large political meetings, which told us very well, has come the rise of the opinion poll: the decline of other large gatherings has generated the top ten lists for records and books, film and television programmes; all of these attempt to remedy the loss of this ancient method of reflecting the collective tribal reaction, but none of them provides the sensitive, living interaction between all the assembled individuals which gives such power and truth to the instantaneous response of an audience.

I am sure this need to congregate in groups of five hundred or so is a primitive one: how primitive is another matter. It might be a part of the mechanism for regulating the population of the tribe, the coming together to see how many of us there are this year, and to update our ability to recognize the separate individuals from other camps and hunting bands; and as I suggested earlier, if there was a dangerous surplus of young people it might be at this gathering that emotions rose beyond the normal to the hysterical, with violent consequences. But this gathering also has a powerful unifying function; and one of the chief and most primitive instruments for binding the tribe together is song.

There is still some strange irrational compulsion for a tightly-knit group to have its song: schools, regiments, football teams, religious groups, political parties, revolutionary movements — it expresses and affirms unity at a depth that is beyond words. It is a primitive ritual chant which could have grown out of a group before the development of language, or at least alongside it. The singing of its song by a group can draw out collective emotion and express solidarity in a way that nothing else can, though the time and place and mood must be right. When they are wrong, it sticks in your throat: how shall we sing the Lord's song in a strange land?

I do not know of any systematic research into the songs of the modern corporations, but I know they have them—or had them. I.B.M. in its earlier days had a book of I.B.M. songs which they sang to familiar tunes, though if you confront the suave and sophisticated modern I.B.M. executives with their memories of it you encounter the slightly sheepish evasions of emotion recollected in embarrassment. N.C.R. had a song, and so did (does?) Hoover, and I am sure there are many others. I would dearly like to know when the songs started, when they stopped, and how the dates related to the growth and profitability of the company and the number of staff employed. The great place for corporation songs today is Japan ('Grow, industry, grow, grow, grow! Harmony and sincerity! Matsushita Electric!'), and in some companies the corporation song is sung before work every day, almost as if it were part of the morning service.

I do not suggest that the route to corporate success lies in teaching all staff a song and making them sing it together in groups of five hundred: song expresses a unity that already exists, it does not create it when it is not there. I do, however, suggest that everyone in the corporation needs to attend at least one meeting of five hundred people, one tribal assembly, each year, and that if the meeting bursts into community singing at the end of it, the sense of belonging to the corporation will, to say the least, not be damaged. But it is the coming together that matters, even in the prosperous, centrifugal, fat years—though it is in the centripetal, lean years when the cold winds blow that Corporation Man most needs to affirm his membership of the tribe and have the tribe confirm it. In times of danger, insecurity and threat to collective survival—powerful enemies at hand, the loss of a trusted leader, profound and disturbing changes, terrible disasters which threaten livelihood—the need becomes so strong that the assembly is likely to take place anyway, even if it is held by the union leader outside the factory gates. The question then becomes not 'Shall we hold a meeting?' but, 'Who is the real leader of the tribe?'

I suspect that even in the most primitive times, the tribal assembly was the occasion where the tribal leader proved his leadership by public acclamation. It does not have to be a formal gathering—an annual dinner or cocktail party with a speech from the king or chieftain may be enough for some tribes, whereas others, if they are more geographically isolated and dispersed during the year, may want to take over a theatre or cinema and devote a day or more to the occasion and build other small or medium size meetings into it as well.

The leader's speech is the climax, and he can use it not only to confirm his own leadership but also as the occasion for a collective affirmation of unity by the whole tribe. In fact the tribal assembly serves so many deep instinctive needs that, although we have already looked at some of them separately, it is worth listing them here to illustrate how close this assembly lies to the root of tribal identity.

(a) It permits the tribe to see itself as a group and discover basic facts about itself ('We're mostly over fifty'; 'We're a young bunch'; 'There's only two women among the lot of us'; 'A lot of people look less prosperous than last year'; and so on). These basic facts about the group may be important when deciding how much weight to give to various group reactions.

(b) As mentioned earlier, it allows the group to make statements and discoveries about its collective identity by its reactions to speeches by the leader and others.

(c) It gives the leader an opportunity to demonstrate his fitness to lead the tribe by showing that he is in touch with their feelings, that he is hearing the signals from within ('I guess we've all had our bellyful of economy drives that start out as fundamental reappraisals of policy and end up as thinner carbon paper and thicker toilet paper; though I suppose the toilet paper is fundamental in its way').

(d) In the same way it lets the leader show he is aware of the tribe's environment, the competition and the customers and all the marketing considerations ('We have to face the fact that the days when we could blind our customers with science are over').

(e) It is a proving ground for new aspirants to high office. Speeches by elders, dukes and courtiers give the tribe a chance to make collective judgments about leaders other than the king, which may, among other things, sort out the succession.

(f) It is an opportunity to keep status in line with achievement, and bestow status on those who have earned it through acting in the ways that best serve the survival needs of the group ('A special mention for appliances division, who in a tough situation brought out four new models and have moved up from fifth to second place in market share; the 480 model only took seven months from the go-ahead to the launch').

(*g*) It is the place to confirm old aggression focuses and identify new ones ('There's a firm around — I'm not mentioning any names — who don't seem to care very much about the safety of the consumer; in fact I hear that with their latest dishwasher they're throwing in an offer of free funeral expenses').

(*h*) The standards of group behaviour can be confirmed and clarified by judicious apportioning of praise and blame (' ... been too prissy and uptight with the press. But we're improving. I saw a statement from Harry Ferguson, the South-West regional manager, last month. A couple of years ago, the manager would have said, "No comment", but Harry said, "If any customer's unhappy, you can take it from me that the corporation's unhappy." That's what we have to aim for ... ').

(*i*) In a changing situation, this is the best time for the king to make sense out of recent experience, to show the pattern it fits into and indicate what general collective lessons should be drawn from the experience, what doctrinal points must be reviewed or changed, what new doctrines are being developed.

(*j*) Following on (*i*), this is a unique opportunity to point new directions, to start moving away from established practices and long-standing assumptions, to prepare the tribe for a change in its internal arrangements or external identity.

(*k*) Whatever else happens, this is a time to reaffirm the faith (' ... quality of our products, and our service to the community by enabling our fellow citizens to lead an easier and richer life ... '), and show that it remains unchanged and unchangeable.

In a self-contained tribal community, a village, a little one-man firm of a few hundred, all these objectives will be achieved by the informal network that grows up over the years among people who spend all their working lives together, who grow up and grow old side by side. They will gather together from time to time when they need to, but this sort of informal assembly can happen spontaneously and without arrangement.

An informal network, however, cannot exist naturally in a dispersed tribe; it has to be built up, and the three kinds of meeting described in these two chapters are the frame it is built on. In a corporation that has grown organically and not too rapidly there is likely to be a fairly good informal network anyway, and probably enough of these meetings will take place for operational purposes to keep it working. But in a new corporation, or one that has grown rapidly, or one that has acquired, or merged with, others, indeed wherever the natural organic community does not exist but has to be manufactured, these meetings become more and more important whether operations demand them or not. Under heat and pressure and with the exhilaration of success a ten-group can be formed in a few weeks: intensity of experience is a fair substitute for simple duration in the forming of human communities, though the links formed so quickly need to be constantly maintained to hold the group together, in a way that is not necessary in a community with deeper roots. But the larger meetings do not happen with the natural spontaneity of the hunting band; they have to be convened as a deliberate act of policy.

If a corporation is to adapt to change, to be flexible in its operations, then a flourishing, healthy community with frequent contact in every kind of grouping and cross-grouping is the only real means; so long as everyone in the dispersed tribe understands what the whole job is, where the tribe is going, where he fits into it and what everyone else is up to, so long as there is a rich informal network with people thinking with or ahead of each other and trusting each other's loyalty, then there are insurances and safety nets at every point. Without this sort of community you have to fall back on authority; operations have to be controlled by detailed and explicit instructions, by regulations, memos, edicts, rulings, standing orders and ritual observances, and the driving power is supplied by sticks and carrots. Then the instructions are misunderstood, the rulings are wrongly worded and half the people do not hear about the alterations, the memos are countermanded, the edicts are not sent to European Operations because someone was off with flu, the ritual observances are continued long after they stop serving a useful purpose, the sticks do not hurt and nobody likes the taste of the carrots, and we say we have a breakdown in communications. That breakdown is the result of trying to extend the old system of functionaries carrying out unchanging procedures on standard products, into a world where no procedures are unchanging and no products are standard and the only functionaries are machines. The answer, as we all know, is to decentralize operations: but decentralized operations are chaos and anarchy unless all the people responsible for them are strongly centralized in their minds and their hearts, so that however scattered they are, they all belong to a true community, a strong and united king's tribe.

20 Authority, Doctrine and Ritual

So FAR we have discussed the three ancient human institutions—the hunting band, the camp, and the tribe—and have seen how Corporation Man has adapted them to his needs. We have also seen how a dispersed tribe can be formed to hold a large group of tribes together in a corporate kingdom. However, that kingdom cannot be controlled by the same instinctive self-regulation which, as we saw in Chapter 14, constantly monitors and adjusts the collective behaviour of a single, territorial tribe. If a kingdom is to have the unity and strength and clear identity of a tribe, the instinctive has to be made explicit. Principles have to be established, and standards of conduct have to be accepted, throughout the kingdom. The king's tribe is of course the instrument; and an essential part of its task is to construct and maintain this apparatus of unity and permanence.

This permanent identity of the corporation has only recently become important. In the simpler days of Industrial Man, when the product defined the company, it was the efficiency of management that mattered, and that usually boiled down to a single ten-group, the board, or at most a single tribe. The rest were functional production units with little need to feel part of a wider and more nebulous idea like a corporation. They were not asked to show creativeness or entrepreneurial flair, only skill, efficiency, honesty and compliance with instructions. But over the last fifty years or more there has been a wider and wider extension of the function of the creative entrepreneur throughout the corporation. Today's tribal chieftain is no longer measured simply by the efficiency with which his tribe executes orders and carries out prescribed functions, but more and more by his flexible and independent response to changes in the technology and the market. Tomorrow's prizes are reserved for the corporations that are made up of networks of enterprising and profitable small companies, tribal in size, and almost self-contained, left as far as possible to their own devices.

But how far is 'as far as possible'? Or to put the question another way, where do we stop on the road from bureaucracy to anarchy?

Bureaucracy is the first response to complexity: a doomed attempt to hold an ever-growing organization together in a single tribal structure long after it has grown beyond the limits of tribal size. It tries to do everything at the centre: co-ordinate at the centre, have specialist departments at the centre, refer queries and anomalies to the centre, issue instructions from the centre, hold information at the centre, keep power at the centre. As we have seen, the end of this process has been delayed by the apparatus of typewriters, duplicators and copiers, telex and telephone, which have given the centre the illusion of control long after the reality has departed. But the bureaucratic approach to the running of the corporate kingdom has been losing ground for some years, and in its place we see a much more natural subdivision into genuine corporate tribes. This is the development of the multiplicity of 'profit centres', the clustering of a larger and larger number of these virtually separate tribal businesses within a single corporate kingdom. The greatest and hardest change to make is an emotional one, the change from controlling people to trusting them; the change from giving them functions and procedures and checking that they have performed the functions and carried out the procedures, to giving them power, resources and a target and letting them use the first two to hit the third by whatever functions and procedures they choose; in short, releasing them from the shackles of middle management and allowing them to be chieftains.

It is of course a much better system in survival terms. A number of discrete cells are in less danger than a single vast cell. The succession is far better secured if there are many heads of businesses to choose from than if all senior men except the chairman and managing director are specialists in production or research or sales or accountancy, with no experience of priority balancing for overall profitability. It is also a much more satisfying system in human terms—far more people are given the chance to grow and expand to the limit of their ability, to use with greater freedom their instincts to explore and compete and create. But as this process accelerates it raises in the most acute form the question, 'What is the corporation?' How far can you go on and on decentralizing operations and delegating authority and still remain in effect, rather than just in name, the unit to which all the others belong? What are the basic elements of sovereignty which must be kept at the centre, in an

African kingdom or a medieval state, in the Roman Empire or the British Navy or General Motors, however much independent power is allowed to the men whose provinces or territories or baronies or operating divisions combine to form the corporate kingdom? What has to be lost before the unity is broken, the centre loses control, and the kingdom degenerates from a living reality into an empty name?

To answer these questions with specific reference to the modern corporation, we have to ignore the tremendous diversity of operations which make up all the different tasks of the hunting bands, and examine the part that does not change, the apparatus of permanence which has been growing up inside corporations under pressure of necessity, as it grows up in all large human organizations that intend to endure. And when we look closer, we see that this permanent identity is composed of four elements, and that they are responses to the four ways in which the corporation can be destroyed: conquest by outside enemies; tearing apart by internal strife; loss of strength and skill and vigour until it fossilizes, or decays and wastes away; and loss of cohesion until the grouping falls apart into single tribes. These four dangers are ever-present: all but the last threatened even the primitive hunting tribe, but they are a much more powerful threat to a less natural, larger grouping like a state or a corporation. The larger grouping is a response to the first danger, the threat from outside, but it makes the next two much more acute, and creates the fourth. Together these four elements determine the role of the king, the corporate chairman, since they are all central to the survival of the kingdom; but as corporations decentralize, every duke and baron (or profit-responsible executive), indeed every member of the king's tribe, needs to be permanently aware of them, since it is through them and them alone that the control and the cohesion operate. They are the line between the king and his kingdom.

The response to the danger of conquest by outside enemies is strength. To be strong in defence and dangerous in attack, the king needs a powerful army and the chairman needs large profits. They are much closer to each other than they appear at first sight. An early agricultural community living off poor soil may have to keep everyone at work all the time to scrape a subsistence; there will be no one to spare, eating the food produced by the others, for training and weapon manufacture and manoeuvres, since everyone is flat out producing enough for themselves. But as the community finds new crops and learns better farming methods, it has some produce to spare, some surplus over running costs, in fact some profits. It can use these to feed its own young men while they build defences or train for the army, or to pay mercenaries. In the public corporation it works in a surprisingly similar way: the best defence against takeover is a share price high above the asset value, and this is achieved by a long and strong profit record or a high expectation of future profit. There is little point in paying £500 million for a company whose net worth is only £100 million, unless they will go on working as willingly and successfully for you as for the previous owner: you either rule them with their consent and approval, or risk losing a fortune. On the other hand, a company with a disastrous profit record, valued by the market at £70 million and whose assets can be sold off for £100 million, is asking for a hostile takeover. And of course it works in attack as well as defence—a highly valued company can buy up others with its own shares at a far lower real cost than the cash equivalent.

For this reason the chairman more than anyone else in the corporation is pressing for profits to distribute, and he often has to press against considerable resistance. The tribal chieftains look upon them as taxes: they would much rather have all the money back again for next year's budget, to build up their tribe's power and status, and their own status within the tribe, by putting the profit to new buildings and plant, more staff and higher salaries, or perhaps a higher standard of tribal hospitality. If a chairman has a proper organization of profit-responsible tribes, there will for this reason be tremendous pressure from the chieftains to close down loss-making areas of the business when they see their hard-won profits being poured away into them. It is painful enough to see profit distributed: to see it dissipated is unbearable. Just like taxes, profits can always be a source of tension between the king and his chieftains, and the tension is increased or relaxed depending on their judgment of how wisely the profits are being employed; but the discipline of profit is at the root of corporate existence. When Durant was running General Motors, the separate divisions had their own bank accounts and the chairman had to go round almost with a begging-bowl to get the money for central operations. With such an arrangement it is questionable whether General Motors could have been properly called a corporation at all. I suspect that even in a communist state, the low-cost high-efficiency industry is very strong and much harder to meddle with than the weaker ones: the state has too much need of it to take risks.

Strength, in attack and defence, is the first absolute requirement of any corporation or state or tribe, but not the only one. As the competing kingdoms establish their external identity, as each carves out his niche, there are many differences which can be resolved without war. For states, this heralds the growth of diplomacy; for the corporation, it means the growth of new or greatly enlarged departments at the court of the corporate king. To protect the strength and external identity of the corporation may mean protracted lawsuits, sensitive negotiations with the government, ingenious arrangements with overseas capital markets, major rearrangements for taxation purposes, swift action on vehicle safety or pollution control; there may be licensing or joint trading agreements with other corporations, new companies may have to be taken over and incorporated. To enable the best decisions to be taken, masses of facts will have to be compiled about what is happening in the world outside. No important decisions of this nature can be delegated, because only the king combines in one person the understanding of the corporation, the understanding of the world beyond it, the responsibility for its future identity, and the power to make things happen: but a large number of people can be employed to collect and digest the information on which his decision will be based.

There is one further significant point about the corporation's external identity. If the corporation is a large and important one, that identity will be a factor in many outside people's attitudes and decisions: how foreign governments, Members of Parliament, civil servants, graduates and local government bodies make up their minds about the corporation, and what decision they come to, may significantly affect that corporation's future. Is it a tough, money-grabbing, polluting, hire-and-fire industrial juggernaut with nothing but contempt for the community, or is it a creative, enlightened, public-spirited group of intelligent and civilized human beings dedicated to improving the quality of life? One reputation or the other may have a profound effect on permissions, concessions, recruitments, and government legislation, and it usually depends not so much on facts learnt from experience as on impressions picked up from television, newspapers, advertisements and hearsay. Moreover this reputation is at hazard whenever even the most junior official talks to the press. An assistant manager of a small and remote up-country factory of a vast corporation has only to say to a reporter, 'Frankly, our company's policy is to maximize profits and let the community sweep up the mess', to have the chairman bursting blood-vessels. It is often this sensitive and passionate concern with reputation (or 'image') that gives a chairman a name for interfering with detail: but that sort of detail is no detail. Any branch executive of Coca-Cola may perhaps choose his own advertising agency without referring the decision higher: but if the ad is a couple of half-naked hippies sipping Cokes on an anti-Vietnam protest march, he is damaging the image of the good, clean, fresh, healthy, patriotic American beverage in a way that is very much the chairman's concern. Consequently more new departments of state grow up round the chairman, in his capacity as custodian of the corporate image: press relations, public relations, prestige advertising, pamphlets, films, lecture services, community relations, and even a college of heralds (now called design consultants) to devise heraldic badges, crests, symbols, colours and livery suggesting 'modern technology' or 'friendly and intimate' or 'reliable', which will be blazoned on products, containers, vans and aeroplanes and carried to the furthest corners of the globe.

It is, however, not sufficient to preserve the corporation from its enemies and strengthen its bonds with its friends if rebellion and civil war are destroying the corporation from within. To prevent this, every kingdom has had to evolve the second element in the apparatus of permanence, the response to the danger of tearing apart by internal strife. For this the essential instrument is the king's authority. Just how far that authority extends in practice is something every kingdom and corporation must work out for itself; what some executives would think an intolerable intrusion into their division's operations would be unquestioningly accepted as normal practice by their counterparts in another firm. In the best corporations the informal understanding within the king's dispersed tribe usually ensures that the question never has to be raised. But even in the loosest and most utterly decentralized organization, three absolutes remain. The first is the acceptance of the king's authority. However much freedom of operation is allowed to executive dukes and managerial chieftains, there are times when the wider interests of collective survival demand actions which, from the point of view of their dukedom or tribe alone, look misguided or damaging. The history tribe of our learning systems kingdom may think it crazy to postpone the modern history course, with its wealth of film and photographic material and a strong interest expressed by California and Texas, in favour of the less promising medieval history series: but if the corporation is closing a deal with the governments of New Zealand and Australia for a complete secondary course in all subjects for every school in the land, then if they want medieval history they must have it. If the history chieftain tells the king he must wait till the modern course is complete and so loses the deal, most of the point of belonging to the kingdom is destroyed—it has degenerated into a sales agency. If the king cannot enforce obedience in such a case, he has no kingdom.

But even when the tribe complies with all his instructions, the king may still have to exercise his authority over its internal affairs. If a frontier province is so incompetently governed that the enemy can easily overrun it, then the whole kingdom is in danger. If the science division has such a bad reputation for the quality of its scholarship that we keep losing contracts to provide entire courses for whole schools in all subjects, then our corporate survival is threatened. In both cases the king has no alternative: the frontier or the division must be strengthened even if it means removing the responsible governor or executive; and of course the corollary of this is the king's authority to remove any man from his office if the safety of the kingdom requires it.

In addition to the king's authority, there is his jurisdiction—his right to pronounce the verdict in disputes between rival tribes. Internal disputes are inevitable in any tribe or kingdom, especially when areas of quasi-territory overlap. Who should authorize advertisements in the national press—marketing or public relations? When marketing take the responsibility, public relations say the ads put their image in Washington back to where it was ten years ago. When public relations take over, marketing say they lose fifty thousand dollars' worth of business with every shot. Only the king can resolve this dispute, and once he has given his ruling there can be no further argument. If he says P.R. must have the final say, and the chief marketing executive then puts in an ad without submitting it, then he must be banished. If he is not, most of the corporation's energy will soon be consumed in civil war.

As well as acceptance of the king's authority and jurisdiction, the preservation of the unity of the kingdom requires absolute allegiance from every subject. Kings may vary in the tolerance they show to vices like incompetence or laziness, but there can be no tolerance of treason. Giving damaging information to the press or betraying plans to a rival are the actions of an enemy, and anyone who does so declares himself an enemy of the king; these are unpardonable offences. Probably the most acute moral discomfort that the modern manager or executive suffers in his relationship with the corporation is when he applies for a job with its rival: even approaching a friend in another part of the corporation to suggest a transfer to his division can provoke furtive and guilty behaviour.

These are the two prime duties of any king or chieftain or chairman, any man who embodies the unity of a number of groups who band together for collective survival: he must secure the external identity of the state against destruction from without, whether by enemies or the forces of nature or circumstance; and he must preserve its internal unity from destruction from within, whether by treason, rebellion or civil war. If he fails in either of these tasks, the failure is immediately visible and the consequences are likely to be sudden and dramatic. But the fact that the kingdom or corporation exists at all as an independent unit is proof that those tasks are being discharged, even if only precariously and with minimal efficiency. But when we move on to the other two requirements of collective survival, this is not so; failure in these can go on for a long time with no sudden surge of alarm or resentment and no sense of crisis.

The first concerns corporate health and vitality and muscularity, fitness in the sense of 'survival of the fittest'. In the simplest terms of a primitive hunting tribe, if the game keeps getting away from the hunting bands then the tribe is on the road to extinction. The failure of a single hunt may be a mistake in the planning or carrying out of tasks; in corporate terms, a disappointing result for the year may be traced to a misjudgment of market or production capacity. If so, it is the fault of the managing director, and the kingdom may still be sound. But the hunt may fail because the hunters are getting fat and slow, there is confusion about roles, no one trusts the man in charge, the only hunter who could read the signs was off visiting another tribe, or someone forgot to mention about the lions who were hunting in the same area the night before. If the corporate parallels of that kind of failure keep happening, it is beyond the power of any chief executive to put things right: like physical fitness, corporate fitness takes time to build and it requires constant effort and attention to maintain it. It is a part of the total corporate identity, and since the king's job is to ensure the long-term survival of his kingdom whatever changes and challenges it meets in the world outside, its fitness to meet those challenges in the long-term is his constant responsibility.

The seat of a corporation's fitness is its doctrine, its store of tribal wisdom. Doctrine, as we have seen, is a body of principles and general lessons argued out by a group of people on the basis of their experience, and every corporate activity — product design, pricing policy, advertising methods, process planning, bonus schemes, the lot — is a product of doctrine; policy made or action taken on the basis of shared and rationalized experience. But the king is the fountainhead, and his doctrine concerns the survival of the whole corporate kingdom.

If the corporation is to survive, it must keep this doctrine renewed, keep it circulating, and constantly test it against new information, ideas and experience. The communication network, above all within the king's tribe, is vital to this, and consequently the corporate king has a special responsibility for keeping the communication system alive, for making sure that different groups from his dispersed tribe keep meeting each other, as well as making personal visits to as many tribes as possible.

But even if information does circulate, there is another danger: that instead of passing into the living body of corporate doctrine, the information will bounce off solid rock. It is all too easy to accept doctrine as final once it has been formulated, to let it become hard and rigid so that it cannot adapt to a changing world. Even the doctrine of a small ten-group can grow rigid, but the higher up the corporation the rigidity sets in, the more it threatens corporate survival. If the king and elders let their doctrine fossilize, the whole enterprise is in peril, because their doctrine expresses the identity of the whole corporation; all other doctrine is founded on it. For this reason it is the king more than anyone else who has the responsibility for keeping doctrine from becoming fossilized. Once a point of king's doctrine has been established, most people are happy to accept it for ever, and the longer it is established the more blasphemous it will seem to question it. But if the king himself brings the question out into the open, everyone can discuss it freely—indeed some of them may have discussed it privately already, but been afraid to risk their reputations by raising it publicly. It is natural to imagine that there must be a good reason for anything a lot of people have assumed for a long time, and it sounds like criticism of one's superiors to suggest they have been acting for years on a false assumption. The king has no superiors to affront: he can establish as doctrine that all questioning of doctrine is good— but only he, as king, can establish it.

Fossilized ritual is almost as dangerous an enemy to corporate fitness as fossilized doctrine. Whole departments can grow round unnecessary ritual. There was one corporation which developed a sizeable department to deal with the purchase and distribution of stationery and office equipment. The purchasing side held endless discussions and negotiations with suppliers, they had a large storage warehouse with a vast inventory and catalogue to be up-dated, a reordering system, annual stocktaking and expensive fire insurance, every secretary in the corporation had a copy of the catalogue with stock numbers, and a variety of order forms, and even so they were always running out or unable to get what they wanted. I am not sure of the amount they saved the day they told every manager to let his secretary go out and buy what she wanted from the local stationer out of petty cash, though it was a startling sum. But the purchasing and indenting ritual had been going on for years without a thought. All ritual should be deemed useless unless it is proved useful; but it cannot be stamped out unless this attitude to corporate rituals is made explicit by the chairman himself, unless he is regularly discovering and pillorying useless pieces of ritual, and unless he publicly commends everyone else who finds and destroys a choice example. There is of course far too much for the chairman to eradicate on his own, but it is his concern more than anyone else's. His first survival preoccupation is to keep adapting the corporation to the changes in the world outside, and fossilized ritual combined with fossilized doctrine (and doctrine is only ritualized thought) is the great obstacle to corporate adaptation.

There is one other aspect of fitness which is uniquely the king's preoccupation: the danger that the tribesmen may grow soft and flabby, and that the young men may not learn the disciplines and skills to turn them into good hunters in the years to come. As we have seen, it is in the fat years that the chairman has to worry most, to make sure that the disciplines of cost and quality and time are maintained: it is not just that they are hard to recover when the lean years come—if new people learn the softer ways they may find it physically impossible to tighten up later. We found this with television film editors: we needed high speed at all costs, and the young lads straight from school never knew any other way of cutting; when they graduated to assistant editors they were very fast even if not very good. Later they became good and stayed fast. But the older editors who had come over from the film industry had learnt the trade at a far more careful and stately tempo, and they could not go faster without ruining their work. Some had nervous breakdowns. Like so many other disciplines, it had to be learnt young or not at all. If the chairman sees signs of this kind of deterioration, he must step in, however satisfied the managing director may be with the results.

But even if the young men do not grow up in the easier and softer ways, they may still be trained to chase the wrong kind of game—the kind that is abundant now but rapidly dying out. This is why the chairman-king has special interest in the recruitment and training of the year's new intake. The managers can only see them as a deadweight to be turned into useful pairs of hands as fast as possible: the king's mind is on the situation fifteen years ahead, when the graduates in their early twenties will be pushing forty. Will the corporation be bursting with research engineers when it needs an army of technical salesmen who speak fluent Japanese? Should every potential tribal chieftain have six months in the tax accountant's department and six months in community relations? Is the whole training programme a waste of time—should they learn the job on the job? Will they grow up remote from the men who do the work — is there a horizontal gap being built into the corporation? In the same way he may form a ten-group to study and prepare for a new market or a new technology long before it becomes operationally justifiable simply because he sees that the corporation will have to move in that direction in the years to come. Long-term survival means regeneration and renewal, but they often encounter resistance, since they are a tax on the time and effort of people with enough to do to secure this year's survival. It is a tax that only the king has the authority to impose.

It is also the king who has to watch for the dangerous rise in tribal numbers when times are easy. Everyone can make a good case for recruitment, and if the money is there it is an attractive way to spend it. If the result is new ten-groups all hunting hard, growth of numbers may be no bad thing, so long as new territories are being opened up. The danger arises when the purpose of recruitment is to take some of the load off the existing ten-groups: it may be easy to feed them all in the days of summer sunshine, but the consequence may be the most clamorous and convulsive strife when winter comes. To survive the cycle of dearth and plenty the whole body of the corporation, not just the bodies of its individuals, must remain lean and muscular.

21   The Instruments of Corporate Identity

THE fourth ingredient in corporate survival is the most personal of all. External strength, internal order, the general fitness and flexibility of the corporation—these are primarily the concern of the king's tribe and the various levels of management. But cohesion, the sense of belonging to the whole corporation, of being a citizen of no mean city, this is something that grows (or fails to grow) inside every single employee. On his first day at work a man is conscious of little more than just doing a job, and he encounters only the foreman and a few other men and women; after a while he may be accepted on probation as part of a ten-group; later still he may be a full member of the ten-group and begin to feel part of the whole tribe; but even if he becomes a foreman or a manager there is no need for him ever to go further. Tribal membership is enough for any tribesman. It is not, however, enough for the corporation; if it is composed of tribes like that, it is on the edge of anarchy, of falling back into its component parts, of being utterly at the mercy of its tribal chieftains, of totally losing control over its external identity. If it wants to operate as a single corporate unit and not a holding company, it has to find ways of making every individual feel he belongs not only to his local tribe but to the corporation as well. And of course it succeeds: it is undeniable that two men who have spent their working lives in the same corporation, but have never previously met, experience a kind of fellowship at their first encounter which they would never feel towards any other kind of stranger. But how does the individual encounter and begin to feel part of the wider corporation beyond his ten-group and his tribe? What is 'the corporation' to the employee, over and above the place where he earns a living and the few people he meets there, and distinct from the external identity by which the general public recognize it? To answer this question we will have to look again at some of the elements we examined in the context of a simple territorial tribe, and see how they have to be consciously

233

and deliberately extended and formalized if they are to be spread through the whole corporate kingdom.

The first necessity is a good communication system, which as we have seen is not dependent on paper or wires. 'The Corporation' has a certain number of physical expressions, but at root it is an idea, a complex and many-sided idea, which is the entire cultural tradition of the king's tribe. The more clearly and fully the individual members of the king's tribe perceive and share in that cultural tradition by frequent contact and discussion, and the more fully the managers and foremen of the tribe are taken into the confidence of their tribal chieftain who belongs to the king's tribe, the more the idea of 'the corporation' will get through to the individual members. The occasional larger meetings, especially an assembly of the whole tribe, greatly increase the speed and certainty with which the idea takes root. (Even if the meetings are union meetings, those too will transmit a view of the corporation, though it may not be the one the corporation would choose.) And almost equally important is continuity: the longer the members of the working tribe have been in the corporation, the more folk-wisdom they will have to pass on, and the more they will come to embody in their attitudes, behaviour, judgments and assumptions the corporation's cultural values.

Most corporations now take direct action as well. They issue house magazines and newspapers to all employees, they pin bulletins and news sheets to notice-boards (some even mail their employees at home to make sure the wife sees the good news too) and they show films made for internal consumption. In addition a great deal of prestige corporate advertising is drafted with the employee very much in mind. It is easy to dismiss it all as paternalistic brain-washing propaganda, and certainly the corporation's motives are not altruistic: but in practice it seems to be most effective where there is already a strong sense of community, and to work not as a substitute for non-existent communication but as an enhancement of a system that is already there.

The communication system, however, is only the means by which the picture is transmitted; what are the elements of which that picture is composed? The first, I suppose, is the simple addition to one's identity: 'You're in the army now', as I and several million others were endlessly told in our first few weeks after conscription.

The army was in a hurry to turn us into soldiers, and could not let us wait to discover its identity gradually: within a few hours we were all in full uniform, blazoning to the world that we belonged to the British Army and the Royal Signals, however deep the doubts and misgivings inside the tunics. All the same, it was proof that the army accepted and acknowledged us—the army, not just the lance-corporal in the stores who issued the battle-dress. No one outside the army was allowed to wear it. In fact, some visible display of corporate membership is a symbol of much greater potency than most corporate executives realize: their refined and sophisticated gradations of status of the sort we looked at in Chapter 14 make simple membership a trivial thing to parade. But some badge or tie can be a powerful magic—as it is for all of us if it represents a level of status we would be proud to reach. If the badge is not issued until the end of a probationary period—even if only a fortnight—it takes on even greater power. It is the first step on the status ladder, and the higher you climb the more carefully you think before you jump off. It also makes you look out for the other badges of the honours system, and thereby grow further in understanding of, and identity with, the corporation.

Most corporations extend this offer of identity through member-ship of sub-groups, the many social and sporting clubs which offer further group membership and opportunities to climb other status ladders. The league and knock-out matches they play against other tribes create valuable lateral links at the lowest level. And by getting into the football team or organizing the Easter outing, the employee gains further points of distinctive identity within his tribe, besides being entitled to wear the club tie as another badge of status and membership.

I recently encountered surprising evidence of the power that badges of conformity can exert. A friend of mine was with I.B.M. in the days when everyone from the lowest management or salesman level up had to wear a white shirt. It was never a written instruction, but everybody obeyed it nevertheless. Then, in their liberalizing era, it was made clear that the instruction no longer applied, and no one's promotion would be affected by the colour of shirt he wore. But it was no good: everybody went on wearing white. A few tried to break the habit, but it was too strongly embedded in the tribal culture. They felt they were rebelling, or at least that everyone would think they were rebelling. My friend left I.B.M. seven years ago, and is not very fond of white shirts, but he still wears one to work every day: the compulsion is too deeply ingrained to resist. In the same way there was an I.B.M. taboo on pipes, and—at least in the presence of the board—he and the other pipe-smokers never smoked them; it was held that pipe-smokers were complacent. He smokes his pipe freely now, but still feels, though he knows it is irrational nonsense, that all other pipe-smokers are complacent.

If the corporation does have any badges or other outward signs to show that it has bestowed its identity on an employee and accepted him into the community, that is the first strand in the cord that binds him to it. It takes a little longer to find out the second: the way the corporation treats individuals, the way it exercises its authority, its system of personal justice. Does it give days off for compassionate reasons? Willingly or reluctantly? Does it trust your word, or keep checking up on you? Does it always want proof of every penny you pay out for it? Are people interested if you put up an idea? If you're off work, do they go on paying you? How long for? If a man is injured, does someone visit his wife? Will they help you out in a tight spot? How much holiday do you get? Do they give you a say in things, or just tell you to shut up and get on with it? If business turns down, do they just hand you your cards, or are they sympathetic and reluctant to lay off? If you retire after forty years, do you get a party and a gold watch and a speech from the boss, or do they just put your cards in with your last pay packet? When you've retired, do they still invite you on outings and to Christmas parties? Is the consensus of tribal opinion 'They look after you', or 'They just chuck you on the scrap heap'?

There are hundreds of events in the tribal year which give the employee answers to these questions; some he finds by his own experience, many more by the experiences of his friends and through the tribal communication network. Together they add up to the most powerful single factor in determining whether the corporate employees are integrated into the corporation or alienated from it. If the consensus is that they just chuck you on the scrap heap, the victims of the system will turn to the union in much the same way, and for much the same reason, as their forefathers turned from the parson and the Established Church to the preacher and the Nonconformist chapel in the eighteenth and nineteenth centuries. And once that has happened, once the battle lines have been drawn, it is appallingly difficult to make peace and create unity ever again. Once the cultural tradition of the tribe includes the assumption that all managers are enemies, that they don't give a damn about you, that they're all looking after number one and lining the shareholders' pockets, and the only way to survive is to grab every penny you can while you can, then virtually every action of management can be shown to confirm it. And because of the enduring nature of this cultural tradition, the assumption becomes self-proving and self-perpetuating: by far the easiest way to lead is to fill the mould created by your predecessor, and if that mould is shaped like a battle-axe, if the tribe is shaped to accept and deal with a battle-axe, the easiest thing is to turn yourself into one. Everyone will understand, they will all know what to do, and it will all go on as before. Lord Robens, when he was chairman of the National Coal Board from 1960 to 1971, said you could still tell from the attitude of the men at any pit whether the original owner had been a good employer or a bad one. One lot would look at an offer in a fair and reasonable spirit, the other lot would be full of truculence, suspicion and mistrust. (I sometimes wonder how far Stalin and his successors imposed a new tyrannical system on a suffering nation, and how far they simply fell into a mould left vacant by Nicholas II and formed long before by Peter the Great, Ivan the Terrible and Genghis Khan.)

If, however, the tribal verdict is 'They look after you', the chances are that the congregation will not desert to the chapels but remain with the state religion. In corporate terms, the state religion enshrines the beliefs of the board and management: it springs from the central faith, and (if it is accepted by the people) it ties the individual behaviour and moral standards of every member of the corporation to its external identity and its long-term objectives. But if the mass of corporation members turn to the Nonconformist chapels, the trades unions, they reject the corporation's standards and replace them with their own ideals, such as job-protection and worker-solidarity. For example, if the central faith of the corporation is tied to high quality craftsmanship, a man whose shoddy work fails inspection will, in a Nonconformist tribe, just be thought unlucky to have been caught out: in a tribe of the established faith he will be held to have let the tribe down. Since the central faith is so close to corporate survival, the link between it and the personal morality of every employee is of inestimable value; but it has to be earned. If it is there, in the cultural tradition of every tribe, then not even the king can change it: if he deviates from it he will be harshly judged, and the moral standard will remain unaltered. This sort of moral condemnation rises in exact proportion to the degree in which it threatens survival: for instance a head of a university science faculty who in a scientific paper omitted some inconvenient facts and embellished some more promising ones would be finished; the reputation of the university would be gravely damaged. But exactly the same treatment of facts in a paper listing the hours worked by his staff, to show the grants committee that he needed two more lecturers, would be viewed somewhat more indulgently.

There is one special constraint on the corporate religion: it cannot be in conflict with the standards of the wider community in which the employees live, and the more it appears to be in harmony with it the better. Sometimes the corporation makes this connection in tribal assemblies, sometimes by word of mouth. I have even seen it done during sales training, on a Metropolitan Life Insurance film strip on how to close a sale. After going through the various forms of resistance and the ways of overcoming them, it finished by reminding the salesman that it was a grave disservice to a fellow American to let him risk leaving his wife and children penniless: overcoming his ignorant and irrational resistance was an act of kindness and virtue.

The new corporate employee will have far less to do with the corporate doctrine and rituals than with the religion. There will be, as we have seen, any amount of tribal doctrine and ritual, and some of it may be general to the corporation: but by their nature they are detailed, specific and local. Much more significant in showing him the approved standards of behaviour are the systems of payment, promotion, seniority and special reward. These show in fine gradation the kinds of people, qualities and behaviour which the corporation is looking for; does it go for ability at all costs? Seniority at all costs? Does it reward the loyal and patient, or the pushers? Are you promoted for performance or sycophancy? There is plenty of evidence generated by a year or two in a corporate tribe, and it is much more significant and trustworthy than information culled from the house magazine. This understanding of the corporation is broadened when great men from outside the employee's own tribe come and visit. Are they treated with genial informality or respectful deference? Are they large bearded men with shaggy jackets or small and spruce with rimless spectacles? No single piece of evidence is worth much on its own, but as the pieces accumulate the common elements begin to stand out and the picture of the corporation, as distinct from the employee's own local tribe, becomes clearer.

Then there is the corporate folk-lore. I talked about the tribal folk-lore in Chapter 14, the word-of-mouth tradition of stories and legends and anecdotes from the history of the tribe; in a tightly-knit corporation the employee will encounter not just his own tribe's folk-lore, but the corporation's. There is a deep and ancient need in us to make sense out of important events, and to record the words and deeds of great men, as a part of the process of survival. This goes right back to our tribal hunting past; the story helps us to identify friends and enemies, safety and danger, courage and cowardice. It gives us a wider understanding of the world about us than we can gain from personal experience. It shows through its heroes the behaviour we should aspire to. The Homeric legends were just such stores; the strict verse-metre is a help to memory—it is harder to get the wrong word when you have a strict metre or rhyme scheme. They were sung by minstrels going from tribe to tribe in the days before the written word, and they gave sense and shape and morality to what was probably no more than a squalid little conflict over trading rights in the north-east Mediterranean. The arrival of print has not diminished the demand for this kind of verbal narrative, nor the supply of it. The corporation is full of stories about great triumphs, great disasters and great men. Especially disasters; since great efforts are made to keep the truth out of print (the Ford Edsel was a rare exception) the stories circulate with rich embroidery; the Rolls-Royce crash produced a flood of apocryphal anecdotes. Almost everyone has a version of how and why any great disaster happened and who was to blame—you only have to look at the newspapers after a flood or fire or crash or any other great catastrophe to see the process in operation at a national level. We desperately need to know the answers so as to stop it happening again, and if we can discover it was one person's fault we can secure our future safety by removing him. It is through this anecdotal folk-lore that a large part of the more nebulous idea of the corporation comes through to every corporate citizen; names of great heroes with their oddities of behaviour or appearance, a vague idea of the corporate geography of divisions and regions and headquarters, a smattering of its history, a picture of its main rivals, and the beginnings of insight into its standards and central purpose and its survival needs. Many of the stories are told over and over again — it only needs the excuse that someone has not heard it before, and the rest of the listening group enjoy it just as much every time.

The corporate folk-lore provides a part of the bond by which people from different parts of the kingdom, even if they have never met, can recognize each other as fellow citizens. If this bond is strong it is a sure indication of the strength of corporate unity. But folk-lore is only one of the strands; the central faith is another, and so are doctrine, rituals, and shared awareness of the quasi-territorial geography and the delicate gradations of the status system. There is even a sort of shared corporation patois: the pronunciation of the word 'shibboleth' was enough to tell Jephthah who were his own Gileadites and who were Ephraimite outsiders, and in the same way to refer to 'the B.B.C.' amongst B.B.C. men (instead of 'the Corporation') or 'our Marble Arch store' in Marks & Spencer (instead of 'the Arch') would be a complete giveaway: like pretending to be a devout Irish Catholic, and then saying 'the Pope' instead of 'the Holy Father'. All strong, united corporations have these small but significant variants of usage and pronunciation, though most of them are totally unconscious of it. I was quite unaware, until a journalist pointed it out to me, that you can tell television people by the fact that they never say 'TV' and stress only the first syllable of 'television'; once it was pointed out, I realized that I always sub-consciously noted the stressing of the third syllable as a mark of someone outside the business.

And finally there is the king himself, the boss, the old man, the father figure, the subject of a hundred apocryphal stories, the focus of all unity and loyalty. The family business is an unfashionable idea at the moment — too many families traded for too long on family loyalty as an alternative to efficiency, competitiveness and fair wages — and we live in the age of management science and de-personalized, interchangeable chairmen and chief executives. But if you ever happen on a corporation with a king who is prepared to risk abusive terms like 'charisma' and 'paternalism', who consciously and deliberately puts himself across to all his employees as the human personality at the head of the business, you can be in no real doubt of the holding power, the magnetic attraction, of personal monarchy. I remember General Sir John Hackett saying, 'If you reach the rank of general without any personal oddities or idiosyncrasies, you'd better go out and get some damned quick.' I suspect that none of us in our hearts really believe in organizations that do not have a single, personal leader at the head. All our experience of successful ten-groups and tribes teaches us that in the end it comes down to one man. Of course he must have counsellors, he must delegate authority, and there must be constraints on his power; but he must be there, and he must be one man, a single clear-cut personality. And as with any leader, we have a great need to know that we can trust him, that he is strong and brave and wise and will protect us, so he starts at an advantage: charisma is not manufactured by kings, but by their subjects. If he is good at the job of monarchy (and it is a skilled trade) he will have a vast card-index memory. And, un-fashionable though it may be, his family is a part of it: people can identify with a family, and feel even more secure if there is a family up there at the top, even if it drives in a Rolls-Royce and has a yacht on the Costa Smeralda. Walter Bagehot was in no doubt about the appeal of a family: 'A royal family sweetens politics by the seasonable addition of nice and pretty events. It introduces irrelevant facts into the business of government, but they are facts which speak to "men's bosoms" and employ their thoughts.' (*The English Constitution*.) That passage came irresistibly to my mind when the Viyella switch-board operator described to me the excitement of the day Mr Hyman's son was born and how she got through to all the other corporation switchboards around the country to tell the news. Life is earnest and business is business, but if there is a man with a wife and children at the head of it we can tell ourselves that, poor relations though we may be, we are still part of the family.

In these last two chapters we have put together the component parts of the corporate kingdom, the elements without which no corporation can survive: the means to defend itself against destruc-tion from without, the means to preserve internal order, the means to ensure continuing health and vigour and skill, and the means of giving cohesion and unity despite geographical dispersal. Without these means no human political institution can continue for long: not the primitive hunting tribe, nor the Catholic Church, nor I.C.I. And of them all, it is the last — this shared sense of all belonging

16

together, the shared understanding and recognition of what it is we belong to — which is the hardest to build and the hardest to destroy: it can survive defeat and subjection, and yet be reborn. Poland was obliterated as a political unit, but the sense of cultural unity survived and was reincarnated. The Jaguar and Rover car companies were absorbed into the British Motor Corporation, but they are still there and could re-emerge tomorrow. We may discuss ailing corporations in terms of communication problems or poor personnel motivation, lack of corporate enterprise or growing too large: the corporate sickness has many symptoms and takes many forms. But there is only one form of corporate health: the continuity of a vigorous, successful and united community. And that community finds its focal point, the expression of its collective identity, in the person of the king, and preserves and renews it through the loyalty and unity of the king's tribe.

22   The Empire

IT IS the king's tribe that binds the kingdom together. So long as every tribal chieftain belongs to the king's tribe, then however many layers of hierarchy the organization chart may show, no one need in practice be more than one remove from the king; the king knows every chieftain, and the chieftain knows every tribesman. If the king's tribe is 1000, and each member is chieftain of 1000, this should give a theoretical maximum of a million: in practice, the maximum size for a kingdom is far lower. In the first place, the tribal maximum may be 1000, but the optimum is 500, which reduces the figure to 250,000. In the second place, many of the king's tribe are elders and courtiers with nothing like a full tribe under them, and others are dukes and earls, with their own smaller courts, commanding the allegiance of several tribal baronies. In the third place, it is normal (and healthy) for more than just one member of each tribe to belong to the king's tribe. These three considerations combine to reduce the actual size of an effective and practicable kingdom to a much lower figure. How much lower? In a sense it is pointless to try and fix the size of a corporate kingdom: there are too many variables. Moreover, unlike the tribe the kingdom is not a self-contained biological unit — it is an interlocking arrangement of tribes around a central tribe, which each corporation has to work out for itself. There is no reason why a firm of 5000 should not call itself a kingdom if it wants to.

Having said all that, I still find the 30,000 size running round in my head. It is only a feeling based on experience, but, for instance, the four most efficient and successful chain stores in Britain's high streets — Boots (43,000), Sainsbury's (32,000), Tesco (25,000) and Marks & Spencer (34,000) — are not too far from that figure, and two of America's most successful and united corporations, 3M and Coca-Cola, are in the same range. As a size for a town, it has the right sort of feel to it: it can have a single town centre and an administrative and social coherence that cannot be sustained at 70,000 or 80,000. Indeed there were very few towns much larger than 40,000, except for the great national centres, until the industrial revolution.

243

And in military terms it keeps cropping up throughout history as the largest self-contained and integrated formation that can be controlled on the field. It is about the size of the modern division: with any larger number, you are commanding a number of divisions. But illustration is not proof, and even these illustrations offer a fairly wide latitude. Nevertheless, even if the figure can range between 20,000 and 60,000, we still have to accept that corporations of 100,000, like Unilever, Dunlop and G.K.N., or 200,000 like I.C.I., British Leyland and G.E.C., not to mention the even vaster corporate giants right up to General Motors' 700,000 and A.T. & T.'s million, must be regarded as being in a quite different category from the simple corporate kingdom. At that level we are not dealing with kingdoms any more; we are dealing with empires.

Since 'empire' is an even more imprecise term than 'kingdom', it is even harder to state the point at which a small empire might start, but it is less hard to list an empire's identification marks. First of course is size: when numbers are so large that it is impossible for every tribal chieftain to belong to the king's tribe, it becomes difficult to run an integrated corporate kingdom. When it contains a large number of provinces the size of kingdoms, geographically separated and perhaps speaking different languages, when its asset value and market price are so high that a takeover is a practical impossibility, then it is unmistakably of imperial proportions. But to deserve the name of empire it must have something else: the same cultural unity, the same shared body of doctrine, the same central faith and folk-lore, collectively held and renewed, as a corporate kingdom; the only difference is that the dispersed tribe which holds it and passes it out to the provinces and on to the new generation is the emperor's tribe. And as with the kingdom, if it lacks that unity it may be a single unit legally and financially, but it can fall apart as quickly as it was put together. This of course has been the trouble of the conglomerates: it is easy enough to become a star growth stock by buying up under-valued companies and maximizing their assets, but what do you do then? To become a true united corporate empire with such diverse tribes is a mammoth task that has proved too much for any conglomerate so far: most of them end up as an uneasy amalgam of company doctors, management consultants, holding companies and investment banks. The separate companies lack that central community of experience and standards and cultural tradition that make up a true corporate identity; it is this identity that distinguishes both kingdoms and empires from looser and more temporary political federations.

For this reason, virtually everything that has been said so far about the corporate kingdom is true of the corporate empire: it is just a group of kingdoms united as provinces under the emperor in the same ways that the dukedoms and baronies are united under the king. The sheer size and diversity, however, make the government of an empire into a different kind of operation in a number of important ways.

The first and most obvious consequence of size, as we have seen, is that conquest by an enemy is virtually out of the question. A kingdom can never lose sight of the possibility of a hostile attack by a dangerous competitor, which in a year or two could so reduce its sales, lower its profits and bring down its share price that a takeover bid might be welcomed by the shareholders. The narrower the kingdom's range of products and the more limited its market, the more acute this danger becomes. But an empire is too large to be toppled by a sudden twist of fate or turn of the market, and it has the additional protection of diversity. The best illustration I can think of is the peppered moth. It flourished in the Midlands, and two hundred years ago it used to be nearly white in colour: it rested on the bark of plane trees, where it was almost invisible to the birds who lived off it. There was however a darker gene in the gene pool, and so darker moths cropped up from time to time and were quickly seen and devoured. But with the grime of the industrial revolution the plane trees went nearly black, and the white moths stood out a mile. Had there not been the diversity, that population would have been extinguished like a one-product kingdom. But the darker variety now had the camouflage; they filled up the population gap, and survived. The product pool and market pool of a corporate empire are likewise so varied that it can survive, and perhaps even profit from, the sort of calamity that can destroy a kingdom.

This same variety makes it possible for the empire to smooth the decline of a product or market without the convulsions that a kingdom might have to endure. The traumatic decline of the British cotton industry and the long agony of Lancashire went in parallel with the boom in synthetic fibres and the desperate hunger for trained management. An empire of all the fibres could have

smoothed the transition—as Viyella and Courtaulds later tried to—
so that cotton could have peacefully and happily contracted as
synthetics expanded. And when this is possible, there is a rich
harvest to be reaped. Although one of the greatest obstacles to
corporate unity is the need to lay men off, a kingdom is often so
much at the mercy of outside forces that it simply cannot guarantee
its own survival if it has to pay all its labour force even when there
is no work for them. Of course even an empire may have to close
factories at times—it is only a group of kingdoms; but by its
diversity and wealth it can sustain a lower profit or a loss in one of
them for longer than any kingdom which stands alone. This makes
it possible to offer citizenship to everyone in the empire, at least
once they have come of age by a certain length of continuous
service: citizenship in the case of the corporation—sometimes
called 'staff status'—is a public declaration that you cannot be laid
off, and an implicit undertaking that the corporation's affairs will
be conducted with the maintenance of full employment as a part
of all policy. When this happens, it is usually the end of strikes:
there may still be union activity, but the whole climate changes.
I have already suggested that a part of the strong sense of belonging
in Japanese corporations stems from their refusal to lay off: I.B.M.,
which follows the same policy, has no unions at all in its United
States factories. It is the same principle as universal suffrage: to
give all citizens the chance to vote you out is to undertake to bear
their welfare in mind while you govern, which means accepting the
same sort of constraints as guaranteeing to see there is always work
for them.

Size and diversity do not of course mean that the corporate
empire can stop worrying about survival: only that as it grows the
emphasis at the top shifts more and more from the short-term
operation to the long-term realities, from the government to the
state, from the hunting bands to the camp. Indeed the government
of a corporate empire is almost totally concerned with the
Empire's continuing identity. If it is concerned with operational
errors in the kingdoms, it is not for the errors in themselves, but as
symptoms of a disease. I have noticed this in television: most bad
programmes are reasonable ideas that for some reason or other did
not come off. You can see what the producers were trying to do,
and having failed at it yourself from time to time you sympathize.

But just occasionally there is a programme that was doomed from the start, that could not possibly have succeeded: then you start to worry about the health of the whole body, because if anyone can reach the seniority needed to approve such a programme without acquiring enough experience to know it is a non-starter, then the whole system is suspect. It means that some central point of doctrine has not been passed down. One of the few inexorable destroyers of empires is this creeping decay from within. Almost always it is a consequence of poor communications (and therefore poor community maintenance): it means that the lifeblood of the organization, the shared corporate culture, is not being pumped out to the extremities any more. When he realizes this is happening, the corporate emperor is liable to fall for anyone who seems to offer a remedy—management consultant, computer expert, behavioural psychologist, astrologer or practitioner in internal public relations. But if the community is healthy, if the doctrine and the rest of the culture are being properly transmitted and renewed, if the collective survival kit is in good working order, then the corporate emperor is free to look outwards.

He does not, however, look at the world with the eyes of a corporate king. A corporate kingdom has to adapt itself to its environment—to competitors, suppliers, governments, technologies—but an empire is so large and powerful it can begin to adapt the environment to itself. It can never do so completely, and it can often try and fail: but for an emperor, some control of the environment becomes a real possibility. His provinces will have to go on playing the game as hard as ever, but he can try and arrange for them to play downhill with the wind behind them the whole time.

In corporate terms, any company under the size of a kingdom is a fighting unit. It is usually one among many within its industry. Some warlike small duchies are expanding and have to be vigorously resisted, some established principalities are encroaching on the sales and product territory of neighbours, some have their backs to the wall and are fighting with the fury of desperation, and with the disregard for conventions that accompanies fear of extinction. A kingdom has a little more breathing-space, but it is constantly under pressure from rival kingdoms and aggressive smaller units: Marks & Spencer are surrounded by British Home Stores, Littlewoods, and Woolworth's, and in special parts of their business by Sainsbury's, Mothercare, Burton, Richard Shops and many others, all of them waiting to snap up any customers they lose. Everyone knows that their field of operations is a battlefield.

Empires, however, are another matter. They are so large and well established that a fight to the death is out of the question. It is not merely that it would be a long, costly and vicious battle: it is that the rival empires need each other. The great empires of oil or heavy electricity, automobiles or steel do not want to conquer all their enemies – the dangers and worries of total monopoly would be a bitter reward for a devastating conflict, and the conflict would be very nasty. A frightened empire is an ugly enemy, as Ralph Nader discovered. The result is, of course, an exact parallel to Professor Wynne-Edwards's discovery referred to in Chapter 10: conventional competition. A price war in the oil or automobile industries would mean ever-diminishing revenues for ever-increasing effort, as would a competitive auction of oil royalty offers to the Middle Eastern sheikhdoms: the classic over-fishing situation. So the competition is conventionalized. Professor Niko Tinbergen has filmed herring gulls doing exactly the same thing – when defending the frontiers of their nesting territory they confront each other with fury, beaks wide open. But they do not attack each other – they furiously pull up clumps of grass. It is called 'displacement activity' and is a form of ritualized aggression.[1] There is much ritualized aggression between empires – in packaging, styling, quality of service, free offers, press and television advertising – and the tribesmen on the frontiers are kept on their toes: but a fight to the death would upset the delicate ecology of the industry, and it never happens.

Some observers have taken this to mean that the corporate empires can completely manipulate the consumer. This of course is not so; in the automobile industry, for example, the consumer still has a great deal of choice – conventional competition can still be vigorous within the conventions. And there are always the energetic and enterprising kingdoms and duchies threatening the frontier provinces of the empire; Gillette on its own might never have offered the consumer a stainless steel blade, but a tiny English barony, Wilkinson's, put one on the market with such enormous success that they had to compete or risk the permanent loss of a province. Nevertheless, an empire's survival is never seriously threatened by its rivals, though the other diseases of kingdoms may prove fatal to it. The slow decay from within, the fossilization of doctrine and the relaxation of corporate fitness — these three are the real imperial enemies.

It is not only the competitive environment that the corporate emperor can hope to manipulate in ways not open to a single kingdom. He can influence the economic climate as well. If a king is thinking of exporting to a small developing country, he has to study the economic projections and calculate the amount it will be able to spend on his product and the market share he might capture. An emperor can actually influence the level of spending power by his investment decisions. This is not arbitrary and unfettered power: there will have to be sound financial reasons for the investment, and other empires will be investing too: but his decision will still influence events as well as respond to them. And not only in developing countries: Ford (and I expect most other empires as well) have an expert whose job is to give the corporation early warning of likely devaluation in countries where it has movable investments. If a number of corporate empires get the same early warning and all of them suddenly change to a stronger currency, the likely devaluation becomes the inevitable devaluation.

This sort of consideration, too, has led to a misunderstanding; because the corporate emperor is so far removed from the product and the customer, because he is looking towards and participating in the economic development of different countries in ten, fifteen or twenty years' time, it is easy to think that any good banker-economist can run a corporate empire. It is certainly true that running a corporate empire demands all his skills, and that the activities at the very top are closer to those of an investment bank than a factory or a refinery: but an equally important ingredient in all decisions is a deep understanding of the business, born of long experience and endless reviewing and revising of doctrine, a long recollection of successes and failures and the lessons drawn from them all. And even more important, the emperor is an emperor, the top of the status ladder, the focus of admiration and unity, the chief of his dispersed tribe and the central figure of the entire corporate community. That great office cannot be filled with distinction and conviction by some economics expert who has just come over from a merchant bank.

The power to influence, and in part control, both the economic climate and its competitors' behaviour gives a corporate empire a freedom, a stability and a certainty of permanence beyond the dreams of kings. But the more those two variables come under control, or at least into the realm of confident prediction, the more sharply the third feature of the environmental landscape stands out, the last unpredictable obstacle on the road to imperial security: the government. And the story of how Corporation Man is overcoming that obstacle is one of the most absorbing of the untold stories of our time.

I hasten to say that I cannot tell the story: the facts are hard to come by and harder to verify. The occasional instance slips out. There was the case of Australia's balance of payments problem with Japan, which could have been solved by exporting cars to Japan, but was not so solved because General Motors had told their Australian company to export all their output to the United States. There was the American company which was forbidden by the U.S. Department of Defense to export a paper mill to Rumania, so their British subsidiary exported it for them. But reports like these are rare, and neither the corporations nor the governments have any desire to add to them; both have an interest in preserving the fiction of the sovereign state. Nevertheless, although the story cannot be told, the general pattern is becoming clear.

Until 1945, war was the dominant political issue in advanced industrial countries, and consequently national defence and foreign policy were the first concern of government. In this climate a nation's industry was as important a resource as its army—the great national companies like Krupp and Skoda, Boeing and Vickers, were virtually arms of government. But ever since 1945, world war has been receding as a political issue: this does not mean that we do not retain a lurking dread that some lunatic may blow us all to pieces, but it does mean that it is no longer the overriding political preoccupation. Its place at the top of the electoral charts has been taken by unemployment and national prosperity: the 'thirties, not the 'forties, are the spectre that haunts today's political leaders. But the 'thirties saw more than the slump: they also saw the birth of Keynesian economics, and of the idea that the elected government has the power and the duty to ensure the full employment and rising prosperity of the electorate.

The problem for post-1945 governments was that they could not command corporations in the way they could command fleets and armies. They could manipulate the knobs on the Keynesian dial, but these were insensitive and unspecific: the point of balance between 'inflation and balance of payments crisis' and 'squeeze and unemployment crisis' was dangerously elusive. Nor did the instruments have a control for relieving local unemployment in electorally important areas, or for raising the level of productivity and increasing the total wealth of the country. Government's province is the distribution of wealth, not its creation. For these and many other reasons politicians needed some power over the actions of corporate kingdoms and empires if they were to be re-elected.

They were, in fact, rather slow to realize how well equipped they were with the instruments of persuasion. It was not only that the corporate kings and emperors had to seek government permission for many activities, especially at the highest level of exchange controls, capital movements and the like; they also increasingly needed government support in their dealings with foreign countries. And most of all, the purchasing power of the government as a customer with its massive taxation revenues gave it tremendous leverage when suggesting, for example, that a corporation would have more chance of a contract if the tender specified that a new plant would be opened in a depressed area to execute it. To say that the corporations resented this power might be an overstatement; they were glad of the business. But the gain in security of work was a loss of freedom of action. Government contracts are an addictive drug (as they are also sometimes narcotic and even hallucinogenic) and prolonged dependence can damage the corporation while being almost impossible to break: and—to change the metaphor—many firms like Rolls-Royce and Lockheed who grabbed the rope the government had thrown them because they thought it was a lifeline discovered too late that it was a noose. The corporation's interests may overlap with the government's at many points, but they are never identical: for example, the re-election of the present government for a further term rates a good deal higher on the government's list of priorities than on the corporation's. Political logic and industrial logic rest on different premises and lead to different conclusions.

But as the governments began to realize their power, so Corporation Man found his defence: it was called 'internationalism'. Many corporations were already manufacturing and selling overseas for straightforward industrial and commercial reasons, but the new political reasons gave these activities a tremendous impetus. The logic is obvious: all governments need the corporate empire's investment, especially if it means more jobs and more exports. Once the corporations are truly international, with half or more of their profit coming from overseas activity, they are no longer at the mercy of their national governments. They do not have to invest the money at home at all—many foreign countries will welcome them. If an American corporation had to run down its home operation to a holding company, the imperial capital could shift to London or Paris, as Constantine transferred the geographical location of his empire from Rome to Byzantium. And of course their leverage on other governments is enormous—Ford of America is Britain's third largest exporting corporation, bringing her £200 million of foreign exchange a year. The international empires also have tremendous scope to exploit the differing national tax laws, exchange controls and customs regulations for maximum corporate benefit. Furthermore they can manufacture where labour is cheapest and sell where profits are greatest. The logic of internationalism is inescapable.

All this of course is not so easy as it sounds: it means extending the corporate culture, and spreading its religion and doctrine, to many nations outside the national culture in which the corporation was born, most of whom speak different languages. But it can be done, and I speak from experience—brief experience, but significant. In 1967 I was one of a ten-group that mounted the first world-wide live television programme—a two-hour hook-up from fourteen countries. The ten-group, all senior television producers, included a Canadian, an American, a Frenchman, a Russian, a Japanese, an Italian and three Englishmen; we all spoke English. The difficulties and pressures were considerable, but the project excited us all, and as the meetings went on the true ten-group spirit grew up as everyone's loyalty and professional skill and commitment to the group objective were progressively tested and proved true. The consequence was a warmth of fellow feeling and respect which still endures and has proved, at least to me, that in those terms an international community is a perfectly practicable possibility: and what I have discovered in a ten-group is equally possible, given a little more time, within an emperor's tribe, and within the various provincial governors' tribes that compose the empire. Governments find great difficulty in forming international communities, but under the stimulus of industrial, financial and political advantage the corporate empires are building them all the time.

Many of the international corporations are now calling themselves 'multinational'. I suspect it is a public relations device to dissemble their national origins and deflect the charge of economic imperialism. 'No, we're not an American corporation, we're multinational. Just happens we're all from Poughkeepsie.' Up till now no great corporate empire has done a Constantine; the American international corporations are just that, and so are the Dutch and the French and the British and all the others. Nevertheless, as they encompass more and more foreign nationals within the emperor's tribe and the governors' tribes, so they come more and more to deserve the title if not of 'multinational', then of 'international' in the very fullest sense.

Corporation Man, therefore, is an international man. Not, of course, at the lower levels of tribal operations; it is only in the high courts of the empire that he enters an international community. This does not mean surrendering his national identity, but it does mean belonging to a dispersed tribal community of many nationalities. And what is more, he is an international man at the highest level: at the heart of the corporate empire, his dealings are with financiers and economists, with statesmen and top civil servants, with presidents and prime ministers, as the representative of an international power at least as formidable as most of the world's national states.

23 The Century of Corporation Man

Up TILL now we have been content simply to observe the behaviour of the Corporation Man and try to deduce his essential nature from the way he works and the organizations he builds. We have followed him from the hunting band into the camp, and from the camp into the tribe. We have seen the tribes coming together into kingdoms, united by the king's dispersed tribe, and now we have looked at the growth of the empire. But the question we have never asked about Corporation Man is whether we like him. Is he a friend or an enemy?

In a sense it is too late to ask; he is here to stay. It seems almost inevitable that well before the end of this century most of the wealth of the Western world will be controlled by three to six hundred giant international corporations; the only argument now is about the exact number. If this century is the century of the common man, the next will just as certainly be the century of Corporation Man. The small private corporate kingdom controlled by its proprietor will be as rare an anachronism in the future as the landed aristocrat is today. All the same, the few landed aristocrats I have met seem to bear the affliction of unorthodoxy with remarkable cheerfulness: they have survived the common man's century without beating him and without joining him. We cannot beat Corporation Man, but we do not have to join him if we discover that we do not like his face.

It is of course not very easy to discover anything at all. The corporations are experts at concealment, and employ further experts to burnish the corporate image, by selective disclosure of favourable information. Moreover, when we contrast their glowing self-portraits with their actual behaviour as we encounter it directly as customers, employees and members of the public, or vicariously through friends, hearsay or the occasional scandal, we become aware that the benign smile is painted on a mask. We only see occasional shadowy glimpses of the face behind, but we cannot help wondering why, if the face is friendly, it should bother with a mask at all.

Besides, we see enough to know how unfriendly the face can be. There are too many accounts of oppressive, unjust and despotic behaviour to employees for us to sustain the myth of universal benevolence. It is not an answer to say that people can always leave: they are encouraged to become part of the corporate culture and to commit themselves to the organization for life, and if they discover too late that the loyalty flowed in one direction only, their simplicity does not justify the corporation's duplicity. It is too easy for a corporate executive to talk about freedom and democracy at home while running a repressive autocracy at work. Many of the battles for the rights of man that have been won in the nation's political arena are lost daily in the executive offices and boardrooms of the corporation.

We also find out enough about the corporation as a neighbour to know that excessive trust in its neighbourly instincts would be misplaced. Its concern with our rivers and coasts and atmosphere, like its concern with safety and fair prices, is concern that it should not be found out. It may be shamed into neighbourly behaviour, but since the instincts are not there it needs our constant vigilance to stop it dumping its trash in our back yard. And when we try to influence its actions, we discover something else: it is ultimately answerable only to itself. It has to operate within the law, but beyond that it is free. The power of any government over it, as we have seen, is diminishing, and at best is only a bargaining power. The power of the community is only the power of restraint by shame, adverse publicity and the fear of restrictive legislation. The power of the shareholder, except after years of disastrous results, is so dispersed among hundreds of thousands of people as to be impossible to mobilize. The power of the emperor's ten-group and his tribe is the real force; it is a significant force in any community, and yet not accountable to the community's elected representatives. And in the absence of any information we are bound to suspect that the private agreements and understandings between the 'rival' corporate empires operate for their benefit and not for ours.

For all these reasons we remain deeply unimpressed by the corporate apologists who assure us that the corporation is the abject slave of its shareholders or an extension of the community welfare service. The true face of the corporation is the face of self-interest, a face (if we are honest) not widely different from our own. So if we want to know if corporate man is friend or foe, we have to ask how far his self-interest coincides or conflicts with ours.

Very simply, his interest is in the creation and distribution of wealth for his own advantage. Not necessarily for his own profit: he will certainly try and arrange for himself a comfortable present and a secure future, but profits as such are a local convention. Many of the vast Japanese corporations show a tiny return on assets; it is their growth rate and sales volume that are impressive. Corporation Man, once survival is assured, seeks challenging hunting activity and the tribal honour and status that reward his success. If success is measured in profits he will seek profits: if the convention is growth, or production volume, or capital formation, he will compete for those. But whatever the convention, the corporation offers millions of people rewarding work, the chance of status, vigorous tribal activity, a channel for aggressive instincts, and an identity, while all the time increasing the wealth of the world. What other institution can say the same?

The only one that has tried to do so has been the national state. If it does so by industry, it merely creates more corporations — the ownership, as we have seen, has very little effect on corporate behaviour. The only other way it has found, as a state, has been by armies and war. War certainly provides employment, in the services and in armaments factories, it gives identity and status and competitive activity, and it channels aggression. As world population rises, war, as we have seen, offers the solution by decreasing demand just as the corporation offers it by increasing supply.

We are all aware that national wars brought us to the edge of extinction a quarter of a century ago. When the national state was the only organization with real independent power, the final arbiter of status among nations was war. With the international corporation, we have evolved a displacement activity. We now look to the national state to order our communities, to protect our property, to maintain a just, free, stable and prosperous society; but not to express our competitive aspirations and channel our aggressive impulses. The World Cup and the Olympic Games and the Space Race are the appropriate arena for national pride: for the more serious tribal contests, the international corporation, with all its faults, offers a far better hope of survival for the species. As Dr Johnson said, there are few ways in which a man can be more innocently employed than in getting money.

The corporation is in business for a long time, and it needs peace and stability more than anything. The corporate emperor has to see further ahead than any presidents or prime ministers serving four- or five-year terms. Long-term investment demands prediction, and war is the great unpredictable: it may generate short-term business profits, but the long-term self-interest of more and more international corporations is on the side of peace as it is on the side of wealth. Moreover the growing internationalism of the corporation makes national wars less and less of a practical possibility: how do you turn your nation's industry over to war production as its operations become more and more entwined with other countries who do not share your intentions, or who even oppose them? Could the government of an advanced industrial nation resist the combined pressures of all the corporate emperors and international bankers, and prepare to go it alone? Could it guarantee its food and fuel and aircraft supplies against their wishes? It has to choose between the suicide pact of a nuclear strike, or peace. There is still the great divide of the Iron Curtain, but already the logic of prosperity is leading to closer and closer commercial and industrial connections; Corporation Man does not put ideology before profitability.

But almost more important than the dispersed operations of the international corporation is the dispersed tribe. The comradeship of international corporate tribes is a valuable counterweight to the chauvinism of national governments. It is this more than anything else that gives me hope. Of course the hope is qualified: the menace of industrial pollution and resource exhaustion is now obvious, and the corporations are the chief offenders: but all the same a mass of small companies is much harder to control than a few vast ones. Corporate emperors need status and acceptance too, and the condemnation of the wider national community in which they compete for honour and respect is a powerful deterrent. The dangers are still real enough to make confidence in our future a premature emotion, but for me at least the internationalism of Corporation Man outweighs them. Kenneth Clark observed in *Civilization* that nearly all the steps upward in civilization have been made in periods of internationalism. The international corporations are forces for internationalism, and the nation states and national

17

governments are forces against it. If the balance is now tilting away from nationalism, we have much to be grateful for.

I know that it is foolhardy to look at history in three-hundred-year cycles, and yet the past nine hundred years have seen three great periods of internationalism, all of them three hundred years apart. There was the great twelfth-century renaissance, the age of the Gothic cathedrals, which ended with the dynastic nationalism of the thirteenth century. Three centuries later there was another great period of civilized internationalism, the fifteenth century, the age of the Italian Renaissance, the age of Erasmus; and that ended with the religious nationalism of the sixteenth century. Another three hundred years, and there comes the enlightenment of the eighteenth century, Gibbon and Voltaire, before the political nationalism of the nineteenth century put an end to it. It is tempting to think that we are once more emerging from nationalist darkness, and that the twenty-first century, the century of Corporation Man, will continue the three-hundred-year cycle with another period of internationalism and another step upwards for civilization. Certainly I find it hard to imagine what harm the international corporations can do to the human race in the twenty-first century that would be comparable with the harm done by the national states in the twentieth.

Source References

CHAPTER I. THE EVOLUTION OF CORPORATION MAN

1 J. M. Samuels and D. J. Smythe, 'Profits, Variability of Profits and Firm Size', *Economica*, vol. 25, no. 138 (May 1968).
2 Konrad Lorenz: *King Solomon's Ring* (London: Methuen, 1952); *On Aggression* (London: Methuen, 1966).
3 Desmond Morris: *The Naked Ape* (London: Cape, 1967); *The Human Zoo* (London: Cape, 1969).
4 Robert Ardrey: *African Genesis* (London: Collins, 1961); *The Territorial Imperative* (London: Collins, 1967); *The Social Contract* (London: Collins, 1970).

CHAPTER 3. THE HUNTING BAND

1 Antony Jay, *Management and Machiavelli* (London: Hodder & Stoughton, 1967).
2 Lionel Tiger, *Men in Groups* (New York: Random House, 1969).
3 Carveth Read, *The Origin of Man* (Cambridge: Cambridge University Press, 1925).
4 Eugène Marais, *My Friends the Baboons* (London: Methuen, 1939).
5 'Atticus', *Sunday Times*, February 23rd, 1964.
6 C. Northcote Parkinson, *Parkinson's Law* (London: Murray, 1958).
7 Robert Spillman, 'How to Raise Productivity, *Management To-Day*, September 1969.

CHAPTER 4. THE BOND

1 Quoted by Rensis Likert, *New Patterns of Management* (New York: McGraw-Hill, 1961).

CHAPTER 5. THE INSTRUMENTAL FALLACY

1 Douglas McGregor, *The Human Side of Enterprise* (New York: McGraw-Hill, 1960).

2 Rex Winsbury, 'The Managers of Japan', in *Modern Japanese Management* (London: British Institute of Management, 1970).

CHAPTER 6. THE LEADER

1 Tiger, *Men in Groups*.
2 Quoted by Tiger in *Men in Groups*.

CHAPTER 8. LEADERSHIP AND LISTENING

1 V. C. Wynne-Edwards, *Animal Dispersion in Relation to Social Behaviour* (London: Oliver & Boyd, 1962).

CHAPTER 9. THE HUNT AND THE CAMP

1 Lucy Mair, *Primitive Government* (Harmondsworth: Penguin, 1962).

CHAPTER 10. THE CORPORATION TRIBE

1 Wynne-Edwards, *Animal Dispersion*.
2 Theodosius Dobzhansky: *Mankind Evolving* (Yale University Press, 1962); *A Century of Darwin*, ed. S. A. Barnett (London: Heinemann, 1958).
3 E. T. Hall, *The Hidden Dimensions* (New York: Doubleday, 1966).
4 J. B. Birdell, *Man the Hunter*, ed. R. B. Lee and I. de Vere (Chicago: Aldine, 1968).
5 J. B. Calhoun, 'Social Aspects of Population Dynamics,' *Journal of Mammalology*, no. 33, 1952.

CHAPTER 11. THE TRIBAL CHIEFTAIN

1 Alexis de Tocqueville, *Democracy in America* (London: Oxford University Press, 1946).

CHAPTER 12. TRIBAL UNITY: REBELLION AND CIVIL WAR

1 Alfred P. Sloan, *My Years with General Motors* (New York: Doubleday, 1963).

2 P. F. Drucker, *The Concept of the Corporation* (New York: John Day, 1946).
3 Quoted by Ardrey in *African Genesis*.

CHAPTER 15. BOOM AND SLUMP: THE EXPENDABLE GENERATION

1 Jane Jacobs, *The Economy of Cities* (London: Cape, 1970).
2 Wynne-Edwards, *Animal Dispersion*.

CHAPTER 16. THE GATHERING OF THE TRIBES

1 Parkinson, *Parkinson's Law*.

CHAPTER 17. THE DISPERSED TRIBE AND THE UNITY OF THE KINGDOM

1 See Donald Schon, *Beyond the Stable State* (London: Temple Smith, 1971), a book based on his 1970 Reith Lectures.

CHAPTER 19. THE TRIBAL ASSEMBLY

1 Henri Bergson, *Le Rire* (Paris, 1900).

CHAPTER 22. THE EMPIRE

1 Niko Tinbergen, *Signals for Survival* (B.B.C. Television). See also his book, *The Herring Gull's World* (London: Collins, 1953).

Index

Index

Computers, 190
Constantine, emperor, 252, 253
Control procedures, 15
Corporate: authority, 81; citizenship, 246; culture, 247, 252; doctrine, 238, 252; duplicity, 255; emperor, 246, 247, 249, 257; empire, 243-53; fitness, 229; health, 228, 242; identity, 229, 233-42, 245; king, *see* King; kingdom, 241, 243, 244, 245; religion, 238, 252; rituals, 230; songs, 216; status, 139-50; survival, 36, 233; unity, 246
Corporations, 9, 10, 11, 13, 15, 41, 49, 73, 74, 84, 85, 87, 93-4, 97, 98, 101-3, 104, 118, 189, 190, 195, 196, 203, 219, 222, 224, 228, 234, 239-40, 246, 251, 256; boundaries in, 132, 133, 134, 135, 142, 207; character of, 225; competition in, 135; elders of, 104-5; employees and, 236, 246, 255; expansion problems, 131, 176, 178, 225; groups in, 31, 93, 127, 128; international, 252; managers: selection of, 82, 222; meetings of, 129, 130, 200ff; mergers, 65, 179, 180, 192; policies, 97, 98, 204, 224; songs of, 216; status, 68, 139ff, 150; unity in, 126-38; *see also* Hunting band, Leader, Ten-groups, Tribe
Corporation Man, 19, 20, 28, 36, 38, 47, 54, 64, 72, 87, 132, 136, 137, 139, 142, 143, 145, 148, 169, 170, 188, 200, 201, 202, 209, 216, 221, 250, 251, 253, 254-8
Council of elders, role of, 203, 204, 205
Courtauld's, 246

Darwin, Charles, principle of, 18
Decentralization, 220, 222
Department of Economic Affairs, 134
de Tocqueville, Alexis, 116
Dialectical tribes, 113
Dobzhansky, Theodosius, 112, 170
Doctrine, 160-61, 229, 240, 244; fossilized, 230, 231, 249
Donnelly Mirrors, 57
Dual authority, 97, 98
Dual loyalty, 97
Dunlop, 244
Du Pont, 16

Economica, 16
Elders, 215
Elizabeth I, queen, 195

Emperor (corporate), 246, 247, 249, 257
Empire, 243-53
Engineering factory organization, 27, 44-5
English Constitution, The (Bagehot), 241
Este, H., 47
Executive: and foremen, 129, 130; and mergers, 183
Expansion, dangers of, 65
Expendable personnel, 168ff

Factory-floor consultation, 93
Farina, 159
Farming, 32, 168, 178
Fear, 36, 54, 59, 171
Ferragamo, 159
Ferrari, 159
Firms, size of, 106-7
Folk-lore, 165-7, 239, 240, 244
Ford Company, 16, 249, 252
Ford, Henry, downfall of, 94
Foreman (supervisor), 128, 129, 130
Freud, 17, 49
Frost, Robert, 135, 176
Frost Programme, The, 214, 215
Future Came Yesterday, The (film), 28

G.E.C., 244
General Motors, 16, 49, 122, 129, 133, 137, 159, 188, 223, 224, 225, 244, 250
Genetic isolates, 112, 113, 172
Gillette, 248
Ginzburg, Eli, 69
G.K.N., 244
Gods (classical), and central faith, 159
Government: authority of, 100; corporations and, 251, 252; power over industry of, 251, 255
Group: aggression, 59; behaviour, 218; meetings, 199-208, 210; objective, 45, 46, 80; organization, 31; recognition, 107, 108, 109, 114; system, 29; understanding, 35
Groups, 31, 32, 39, 43, 47, 49, 117, 127, 129, 137, 179, 180, 187; competition in, 135; formation of, 44, 45, 48; integration of, 181, 182, 183, 184; sizes of, 38, 39, 106, 107; *see also* Ten-groups

Hackett, General Sir John, 83, 241
Hall, Edward, 112
Harvard Business School, 16
Hitler, 65, 71